LOCATING SOFT POWER IN INDIA-BANGLADESH RELATIONS

Komal Kaushik Baral

KALPAZ

First Published, 2018

Published by

Kalpaz Publications
C-30, Satyawati Nagar,
Delhi – 110052
E-mail: kalpaz@hotmail.com
Ph.: 9212142040

Printed at: G. Print Process, Delhi

Cataloging in Publication Data—DK
Courtesy: D.K. Agencies (P) Ltd. <docinfo@dkagencies.com>

Baral, Komal Kaushik, author.
Locating soft power in India-Bangladesh relations / by Komal Kaushik Baral.
pages cm
"A thesis submitted to Sikkim University in partial fulfilment of the requirements for the degree of Doctor of Philosophy"
Includes bibliographical references.
ISBN 9789386397546 (HB)

1. India—Foreign relations—Bangladesh. 2. Bangladesh—Foreign relations—India. I. Title.

LCC DS450.B3B37 2018 | DDC 327.5405492 23

Dedicated to
Amma and Baba,
without you, none of these
would have been Possible

Contents

Foreword

The idea of soft power is not new. The term was first used by American scholar Joseph Nye, who used opinion polls to understand 'attractiveness' and 'charm' of a nation , and also to understand if this 'charm' can be translated to influence the foreign policy behaviors and outcomes vis-à-vis other states. Traditional international relations theories have defined power as an ability to influence others to get the desired outcomes. A country is powerful if it has a relatively large population, territory, natural resources, economic strength, military force, and social stability. There are several ways to affect the behavior of others. One can coerce others with threats, can induce them with payments or also can attract or co-opt them.

Commonly there are two types of power one is 'hard' power and the other is 'soft' power. In 'hard' power the theme is coercion, use of force, or inducements as a means of persuasion. It includes military intervention or protection, economic sanctions, or reduction of trade barriers. 'Soft' power is attracting and co-opting, indirectly convincing. It includes cultural, historical, and diplomatic influence. In today's world the soft power is very popular and also is demand of the present time. In assessing international power today, factors like culture, ideology, institutions, technology, and education are becoming more important, whereas geography, population, and raw materials are becoming less important.

If soft power is the ability to shape the preferences of others through appeal and attraction, then a defining feature of soft power is that it is non coercive. The currency of soft power are culture, political values, foreign policies, education, governance, values, ideas, and visions. It is also the ability to attract, and attraction often leads to acquiescence. Soft power uses a different type of currency—not force, not money—to create cooperation. It uses an attraction to shared values, and the justness and duty of contributing to the achievement of those values. Soft power itself is a changing complex, in which the formation and transition of power depends on the contradictory movement of its various components. Unlike nationality and ethics, a country's popular culture, quality of government, diplomatic tactics, educational attractiveness, and so on require a relatively shorter time to form and develop and hence are more changeable.

This book attempts to employ this concept of soft power to understand if it has by any means, contributed to the strengthening or betterment of India- Bangladesh relations. Contrarily, has India or Bangladesh employed their soft power tools to resolve their bilateral issues or better their relations? In this sense, this study differs from the earlier conventional works on India-Bangladesh relations which have been focusing only on binaries: extending from political, economic and strategic aspects. Essentially, this study tests India's power projections and employment of attendant tools in case of Bangladesh. And, has it resulted into a success in resolving contentious issues between the two. Admittedly, some of the contentious issues between India and Bangladesh date back to the 1947 partition era, that is when Bangladesh was East Pakistan or even before. The creation of Bangladesh, post partition from Pakistan, did not resolve them until recently. For instance, the land boundary treaty between India and Bangladesh was signed recently in 2014. The same is true with water –sharing agreement. Trade between the two seems to have been stabilized. Therefore, the question which the study seeks to answer is the following: has there been a role of soft power in the resolution of these disputes? This question becomes important because India's links with Bangladesh are civilizational, historical and cultural and there is lot to share between the two.

However, it should be remembered that the intangible nature of soft power makes measurement and comprehensive understanding or its implications a challenge for all. What policy outcome the soft power actually effected, and whether any soft power influenced the policy outcome indeed, can be understood by a very deep level of examination of each individual case and by clearly by conducting a detailed content analysis. Because the context in which actors operate determines the kind of power they utilize, it may not be clear whether soft power has substantial influence on a particular policy outcome without taking into account the nature of the context itself. And as Nye argues that the importance of soft power has been increasing. Due to what he calls as "democratization of technology," the information revolution has reduced the cost and facilitated the ease of global communication. He has also argued, as the technology improves and as non-state actors gain greater influence, the importance of soft power has grown. Alongside several authors as pointed out by Prof Jing Sun tend to reflect a love-hate attitude toward soft power. The concept is intuitively plausible but hard to define. This has led to two opposing tendencies: either to exaggerate soft power's utility or to dismiss it. Which position one takes depends on which aspect of the concept one pays attention to: its plausibility or its indefinability. Is there a middle way?

Given the nature of the subject a qualitative assessment is the more optimal way of addressing the issue. But therein lies the complexities too in a study like this as perceptions tend to dominate the narrative. The book therefore makes an interesting read and is quintessential for the scholars of international relations and policy –makers alike.

Dr Manish
Professor
Centre for International Relations
School of International Studies
Central University of Gujarat
Gandhinagar

Preface

The book is the product of the PhD thesis (2011-2016) conducted in the department of International Relations, Sikkim University.

The book examines India's projection of soft power and employment of attendant tools in case of its relations with Bangladesh. The core objective is to draw lessons from India's practice of soft power policies and to study its applicability in India's foreign relations vis-à-vis Bangladesh. Such an approach is underexplored when it comes to understand and interpret the relations between the two structurally asymmetrical countries, which ironically, is plagued by neglect, mistrust and suspicion. This has further been accentuated by excessive politicization of issues and the lack of innovative approach to better their relationship. The book thus aims at exploring one such approach, that is, the soft power approach in context of India-Bangladesh bilateral relations.

In this context, it is important to understand that the theory of soft power, since its inception, has been associated more with the rise/decline of the United States. Its application with regard to the developing countries has been given little importance. Hence, it remains to be seen whether the concept of soft power can be applied to the developing countries? And, this is more so in a situation when they are structurally asymmetrical neighbours. Equally important is that the studies on soft power has tended to focus more on, or, has been used as a 'power projection' tool. In other words, soft power is seen by some as another aspect of power, sometimes as corollary with hard power and sometimes as something quite opposite to it. The employability of soft power so far has not been studied in a bilateral context.

The book, thus, endeavours to locate soft power in a bilateral context taking three specific issues pertaining to water, border delineation, and the issue of trade and transit between India and Bangladesh. These issues flow from the partition of the sub-continent and have been resolved in the form of treaties and agreements. The book, therefore, examines whether soft power as a foreign policy tool was at all employed in the resolution of these contentious issues, and, whether application of soft power in any way contribute to the resolution of these disputes? And, if so, which elements of soft power contribute towards this end. Can this approach be further exploited in context of other impending disputes between the two countries? Or can the soft power approach be exploited in case of similar bilateral relations within the sub-continent or elsewhere? As such concluding an agreement/treaty has its own imperatives. As we shall see, in case of India-Bangladesh relations, the signing of the treaties and agreements on contentious issues of waters, border delineation, trade and transit have been achieved incrementally. These negotiations have run through various phases, with each phase having its own soft power imperatives. Also, resolution of one issue further led towards progress on another. This book, therefore, suggests ways and the means to find out the efficacy of soft power in improving the relations between India and Bangladesh.

Acknowledgements

Endeavour such as this requires help, support, encouragement and guidance of individuals more than one. I take this opportunity to extend my sincere gratitude and appreciation to all those who made this book possible.

First and foremost, I would like to express my deepest gratitude and thanks to Dr. Manish, Professor Centre for International Relations, Central University of Gujarat, Gandhinagar, for his motivation, enthusiasm, and his meticulousness. His profound insights and guidance have been instrumental in not only in shaping thebook but also in helping me grow as a researcher.

My heartfelt gratitude to the entire faculty of Department of International Relations, Sikkim University, Dr. Sebastian N, Dr. Teiborlang T. Kharsyntiew and Mr. Newton Singh for their constant encouragement, support and for their generous feedbacks and constructive criticisms.

I'm grateful to Sikkim University, specially the Library of Sikkim University, JNU and IDSA for allowing me to collect necessary materials for my study.

I would like to express my profuse thanks to Kalpaz Publication, New Delhi for taking interest in my work and bringing it to the academic arena.

I am especially indebted to SaradGurung, AfridaAainunMurshida, and RomanaLepcha for all the help they rendered throughout the course of writing this book.Last but not the least, this bookand my academic career would not have been possible without the patience, cooperation and unflinching support of my family. A heartfelt regards goes to my parents, my sister and my relatives, for always believing and encouraging me to pursue my dreams.

Komal Kaushik Baral

Abbreviations

ADB	Asian Development Bank
AGP	Asom Gana Parishad
AL	Awami League
APTA A	Asia Pacific Free Trade Agreement
ASEAN	Association for South East Asian Nation
BBIN	Bangladesh, Bhutan, India and Nepal
BCMC	Border Control Management Course
BHF	Bangladesh Heritage Foundation
BIMSTEC	Bay of Bengal Initiative for Multi Sectoral Technical and Economic Cooperation
BIPPA	Bilateral Investment Promotion and Protection Agreement
BJP	Bharatiya Janata Party
BNP	Bangladesh Nationalist Party
BOPs	Border Out Posts
BPC	Bangladesh Petroleum Corporation
BSF	Border security Force
BSTI	Bangladesh Standards and Testing Institute
BTV	Bangladesh Television
CBMP	Coordinated Border Management Plan
CEP	Cultural Exchange Programme
CII	Confederation of Indian Industry

DGFT	Directorate General of Foreign Trade
DTAC	Double Taxation and Prevention of Fiscal Evasion
DTH	Direct To Home
EEZ	Exclusive Economic Zones
FDI	Foreign Direct Investment
FTA	Free Trade Agreement
GBM	Ganges, the Brahmaputra and the Meghna/Barak
HuJI	Harkatul Jihad al Islam
IB	International News Broadcasting
ICCR	Indian Council for Cultural Relations
ICP	Integrated Check-Post
IDSA	Institute for Defence Studies and Analyses
IIMs	Indian Institute of Management
IITs	Indian Institute of Technology
INCB	International Narcotics Control Board
IPL	Indian Premier League
IPT	International Passenger Terminal
JBWG	Joint Boundary Working Group
JCE	Joint Committee of Experts
JMB	Jamaat-ul Mujahideen Bangladesh
JRC	Joint River Commission
LAD	Least Available Depth
LBA	Land Boundary Agreement
LCSs	Land Customs Stations
LDCs	Least developed Countries
LeT	Laskar-e-Toiba
LoC	Line of Credit
MOU	Memorandum of Understanding

NDA	National Democratic Alliance
NRL	Numaligarh Refinery Limited
OIC	Organization of Islamic Countries
PAF	Pakistan Air Force
BPDB	Bangladesh Power Development Board
PGCIL	Power Grid Corporation of India Limited
PIWTT	Protocol on Inland Water Transit and Trade
POW	Prisoners of War
RLP	River Linking Project
SAARC	South Asian Association for Regional Cooperation
SAFTA	South Asian Free Trade Agreement
SAPTA	South Asian Preferential Trade Agreement
SAPTA	South Asian Preferential Trading Arrangement
SEZ	Special Economic Zones
SOP	Standard Operating Procedure
TBT	Technical Barriers to Trade
TMC	Trinamool Congress
ULFA	United Liberation Front of Assam
UNEP	The United Nations Environment Programme

Chapter - I

Introduction

1. 1 Background

The year 2015 has ushered a new hope as far as India-Bangladesh relations is concerned. With the visit of Indian Prime Minister Narendra Modi to Bangladesh in June 2015, a positive and significant step has been taken towards improving their bilateral relationship. The signing of the 2015 Land Boundary Agreement (LBA) is an apt testimony of it. The land boundary problem drew importance immediately after the creation of Bangladesh. The land boundary agreements of 1974 and 2011 tried to solve the major issues pertaining to the boundary problems between India and Bangladesh, but in vain. This was primarily due to the lack of ratification in the Indian Parliament. Consequently, the land boundary problem continued to plague Indo-Bangladesh relations throughout the subsequent years. These problems, however, have been resolved by the recent conclusion of the LBA 2015. Under this particular agreement India agreed to transfer 111 border enclaves (measuring of 17, 160.63 acres) to Bangladesh while Bangladesh transferred 51 enclaves (measuring of 7, 110.02 acres) to India. The LBA has been implemented, and enclaves, adverse possessions and demarcation of the land boundary were implemented on August 01, 2015 in a time-bound manner (Chakravarty 2016: 211).

Subsequently, plethora of agreements concerning maritime cooperation, trade and transit (road, rail and waterways), cultural cooperation, and so on were also signed. Further, India also provided Line of Credit (LoC) worth US $ 2.0 billion to Bangladesh. The two countries have also reached an agreement on the energy and power sector. Apart from it, very recently on July 21, 2016, Asia's largest Integrated Check-Post (ICP) has also been inaugurated which is regarded as a landmark development towards strengthening Indo-Bangladesh bilateral trade as well as the border management process.[1] Thus, an effort has been made to give a fresh impetus to India-Bangladesh relations.

India-Bangladesh relations date back to the days before the creation of Bangladesh. Even before the creation of Bangladesh in 1971, Mujibnagar Government[2] had got a safe haven in India. Consequently, India pooled much of its resources to liberate Bangladesh (then East Pakistan). After the independence of Bangladesh, it was thought that its relationship with India would continue to remain peaceful and that their friendship would last forever. However, differences soon began to arise and their relationship started deteriorating further after the assassination of Sheikh Mujibur Rahman.

Against this backdrop, the book examines India's projections of soft power and employment of attendant tools in case of its relations with Bangladesh. While doing so, it will exploit the concept of soft power, cultural diplomacy, public diplomacy and economic aid and inducement. The core objective is to draw lessons from India's practice of soft power policies and to study its applicability in India's foreign relations vis-à-vis Bangladesh. Such an approach is underexplored when it comes to understand and interpret the relations between the two structurally asymmetrical countries, which ironically, is plagued by neglect, mistrust and suspicion. This has further been accentuated by excessive politicization of issues and the lack of innovative approach to better their relationship.

The book thus aims at exploring one such approach, that is, the soft power approach in context of India-Bangladesh bilateral relations. This approach has an advantage as India's links with Bangladesh are civilizational, cultural, social and economic. As we know, there is much that unites the two countries: a shared history and common heritage, linguistic and cultural ties. The question therefore arises: to what extent have both the countries explored their cultural similarities to foster their bilateral relationship? While doing so, an attempt is also made to understand as to why there exists numerous problems in India-Bangladesh relations, despite having cultural ties, and especially when India pooled much of its resources to liberate Bangladesh? Can the two countries hope to explore their cultural affinities and more importantly can they use it to better their relationship. In other words, can soft power be used as a tool to resolve the impending and 'enduring'[3] disputes between the two countries?

In this context, it is important to understand that the theory of soft power, since its inception, has been associated more with the rise/decline of the United States. Its application with regard to the developing countries has been given little importance. Hence, it remains to be seen whether the concept of soft power can be applied to the developing countries? And, this is more so in a situation when they are structurally asymmetrical neighbours. Equally important is that the studies on soft power has tended to focus more on, or, has been used as a 'power projection' tool. In other words, soft power is seen by some as another aspect of power, sometimes as corollary with hard power and sometimes as something quite opposite to it. The employability of soft power so far has not been studied in a bilateral context.

However, a close observation would suggest that soft power has been used in the South Asia to create an atmospherics. For instance, cricket diplomacy has been used in the past to mitigate tensions between India and Pakistan. The meeting of Pakistan's Prime Minister Yousuf Raza Gilani's with the then India's Prime minister Manmohan Singh during the 2011 World Cup semi-final in India closely followed the resumption of high-level diplomatic dialogue between the two countries after the 2008-Mumbai attacks. Similarly, India's aid and assistance to Nepal after the devastating April 2015 earthquake; and, India's assistance to Afghanistan in building Salma Dam and Afghanistan reciprocity in conferring the country's highest civilian honour 'Amir Amanullah Khan Award' to the Indian Prime Minister Narendra Modi are some instances of the employability of soft power in inter-state relations. In case of Bangladesh, however, the role played by India during its liberation movement, India's aid in various forms in the consequent years of Bangladesh's independence; has soft power ramifications. In fact, India and Bangladesh even signed a Treaty on Cultural Cooperation as early as December 30, 1972. Till date, India and Bangladesh have signed 89 agreements[4] between them mostly relating to trade and transit, water, line of credit, cultural cooperation and land boundary agreements.

The book focuses on three major issues pertaining to water, border delineation, and the issue of trade and transit between India and Bangladesh. These issues flow from the partition of the sub-continent and have been resolved in the form of treaties and agreements. The book will, therefore, examine if soft power as a foreign policy tool was at all employed in the resolution of these contentious issues, and, whether application of soft power in any way contribute to the resolution of these disputes? And, if so, which elements of soft power contribute towards this end. Can this approach be further exploited in context of other impending disputes between the two? Or can the soft power approach be exploited in case of similar bilateral relations within the sub-continent or elsewhere? As such concluding an agreement/treaty has its own imperatives. As we shall see, in case of India-Bangladesh relations, the signing of the treaties and agreements on contentious issues of waters, border delineation, trade and transit have been achieved incrementally. These negotiations have run through various phases, with each phase having its own soft power imperatives. Also, resolution of one issue further led towards progress on another. This book, therefore, will suggest ways and the means to find out the efficacy of soft power in improving the relations between India and Bangladesh.

1.2 Framework of Analysis

The term 'soft power' was first coined by the Harvard University Professor, Joseph Nye (1990), in his book, *Bound to Lead: The Changing Nature of American Power.*[5] Nye developed the concept further in his book, *Soft Power: The Means to Success in World Politics* (2004) (Purushothaman 2010: 2). Power in general is the ability to alter the behaviour of others to get what one wants. As Nye puts it, there are three ways to do that: coercion (sticks); inducement (carrots) and attraction (soft power). If one is able to attract others, Nye writes, "One can economize on the sticks and the carrots." Soft power, says Nye is thus "the ability to get what one want through attraction rather than coercion or payments (Nye 2004: X-XI)." In other words, soft power is the ability to affect others through the co-optive means of framing the agenda, persuading, and eliciting positive attraction in order to obtain preferred outcomes (Nye 2011: 20-21). This ability to affect what other countries want tends to be associated with intangible power resources such as culture, ideology, and institutions (Nye 1990: 166-67).

According to Nye, soft power of a nation has three primary sources: culture (in places where it is attractive to others), its political values (when it lives up to them at home and abroad), and its foreign policies (when they are seen as legitimate and having moral authority) (Nye 2004: 11). In other words, soft power is, in essence, the power of attraction[6] and it inheres in the attractiveness of a country's culture, political ideals and domestic and foreign policies. These assets are rightly called 'intangible' to the extent that one cannot 'hold' a nation's culture in one's hand as one might hold a gun or monetary instrument. However, what soft power does have in common with other power resources is that its effectiveness is increased when it is projected (Mukherjee 2014: 47-48)

As such, the concept of power holds utmost importance to the discipline of international relations. Most definitions of politics involve power. Most international interactions are political or have ramifications for politics. Thus, it is not surprising that power has been prominent in discussions of international interaction from Thucydides to the present day. The long history of discussions of the role of power in international relations, however, has failed to generate much agreement. Scholars disagree not only with respect to the role of power but also with respect to the nature of power (Baldwin 2013: 273). In the discipline of international relations, the concept of power is – rightly or wrongly – closely associated with theories of 'realism'. At the beginning of *Politics Among Nations*, Hans J. Morgenthau proclaimed that "international politics, like all politics, is a struggle for power." One of Morgenthau's core assumptions about human nature was that all men held an insatiable "lust for power". According to Morgenthau, "man is a political animal by nature" who "is born to seek power" (Morgenthau 1946: 168). He added that "whatever the ultimate aims of international politics, power is always the immediate aim" (Morgenthau 1954: 25). E. H. Carr concurred with Morgenthau, claiming that "politics are, then, in one sense always power politics." Carr argued that power was indivisible, yet he claimed that for purposes of discussion it could be divided into three categories: military power,[7] economic power, and power over opinion (Carr 1964: 109).

According to the 'realists', security of the state is attained and preserved through the maximization of power and the elements of national power include: geographical boundaries, large territorial size, the capacity for self-sufficiency in natural and industrial resources and a strong technological base, all of which contribute to a strong military capability (Morgenthau 1948: 113). In short, classical realists argue that power lies at the heart for the state's struggle which can be explained by their quest to maximize their own relative power which again is rooted in the sinful and power seeking nature of man. In fact, the realist conception of power can be briefly summarised as the ability of states to use material resources to get others to do what they otherwise would not (Barnett and Duvall 2005: 40). Also interesting it is to note that power is perceived more in material terms or in other words the realists' emphasis is on hard power.

Similarly, 'neorealism' (structural realism or defensive realism) developed by Waltz (1979) focuses on the role of power and capabilities. Kenneth Waltz's structural realism employs the notion of international anarchy and view states as basic units of the international system. The central concern of an anarchical international system is power. It is conceived as a self-help system with states primarily seeking survival and security (Waltz 1979: 117-18). Wars and conflicts are the usual consequences of this state of affairs as states seek power, resources and territory, often at the cost of other states. The desire to dominate other states increases as a state's power capabilities grow. Power indeed is the key factor in states' balancing behaviour (Purushothaman 2010: 1-2). Further, Waltz contends that the capabilities of states are much harder if power (or capability) is conceived as multidimensional. Thus, Waltz asserts that 'the economic, military, and other capabilities of nations cannot be sectored and separately weighed' (Waltz 1979: 131). Nevertheless, neo-realist approaches emphasize the *hard power* capacities of states, especially their military capabilities and economic strength. Like other realists, including Morgenthau and Waltz, Mearsheimer views power largely in military terms. For Mearsheimer, "calculations about power lie at the heart of how states think about the world around them. Power is the currency of great-power politics, and states compete for it among themselves. What money is to economics, power is to global relations (Mearsheimer 2001: 17)."

Neoliberals, on the other hand, have argued how states with convergent interests create international institutions and arrangements that effectively tame (state) power, highlighting processes of social choice and leaving the impression that institutions are the antidote to power (Barnett and Duvall 2005: 40). Scholars of liberal international relations theory typically stress that many important international outcomes cannot be adequately explained with reference to power, but instead are better understood by the salutary presence of democracy, particular configurations of domestic interests, liberal values, economic interdependence, or international institutions. Neo-realism emphasises the capacity of states to influence others to behave as it wants them to behave whereas the co-optive power of liberal-institutionalism aims at as Nye says "getting others to want what you want". In other words, liberal institutional approaches have emphasized soft power aspects with cultural attraction, ideology and international institutions as the main resources (Wagner 2005: 2).

Mainstream constructivists too, have pitted themselves against explanations in terms of power as they have attempted to demonstrate the causal significance of normative structures and processes of learning and persuasion (*Ibid.*, pp. 40-41). Arguing on constructivists stand Geun Lee contends:

The Constructivists focus ideational factors and emphasize on political culture, forms of government, history, domestic political trends and debates and show how these shapes the foreign policy of a state. However what is important to note is that though Constructivists in international relations recognized the power of ideas and norms, which is quite similar to soft power, their discussions did not develop into a new concept of power with concrete policy implications. Therefore, even though constructivist discussions of power in international relations contain many central elements of what Nye calls soft power, constructivist ideas have not developed into a systematic merge of separate constructivist discussions of ideational power. Consequently, while Nye's concept of soft power gained journalistic popularity, constructivist discussion of ideational power tended to be superseded by the concept of soft power even in the academia (Lee 2004: 2).

The argument that the nonmaterial assets of states can be important tools of influence in international relations is far from new. These assets have constituted an integral part of states' foreign policies for decades, if not centuries (Jowett and Donnell 1986: in Kushner 2006, 4). At academic level too, scholars have been quite comfortable with 'softer' variations of power, especially the idea that it can be exercised through influence and legitimacy. For instance, Steven Lukes (2005) argues that power need not be blunt or behavioural; it can operate socially in ways that subconsciously affect the formation of preferences. Similar inferences can be drawn from Gramsci's idea of 'hegemony', Bourdieu's 'symbolic power', Weber's 'authority', Foucault's 'disciplinary power', and Habermas' 'communicative power'.

Nonetheless, in contemporary mainstream scholarship and foreign-policy circles, it is Nye's account that has captured imaginations. Perhaps, this is because Nye does more than just call attention to soft power, he also treats it as a platform for action, arguing that actors have, can and should continue to find ways to effectively develop and use this power resource. In this way, Nye conceives of soft power in much the same way as many do hard power: as a tangible tool that can be amassed and deployed through concerted effort (Mattern 2007: 100-101).

Nye basically is critical of the realist notion of power which focuses more on hard power, particularly military power. Nye problematises the tendency to define power as the possession of resources that can influence outcomes. According to him, such an approach makes power appear concrete and measurable, but it is mistaken because it confuses the results of a power relationship with the means to that end. He says, "Analysts call this the 'vehicle fallacy' or the 'concrete fallacy'. But such concrete vehicles as bombs and bullets may not produce the outcomes you want. After all, the

United States lost the Vietnam War to a weaker and more determined opponent, and the richest politicians do not always win the elections. A player holding the highest cards can still lose the game (Nye 2008: 28)." Nye has a clear point here as in today's world it is difficult for the states to achieve their foreign policy objectives through the mere exercise of hard power. In fact, Nye's proposal of a new form of power can be seen as a logical consequence of some major changes that has occurred in the international system, especially in the post-Cold War era.

The post Cold war era coupled with globalization has forced us to relook the dynamics of international politics from a much wider prism. With the end of Cold War, there was a fundamental shift in the workings of international system. First was the diminishing of the gap between the domestic and international. These until then were seen as two different realms that were not interdependent or inter-related. However, happenings in the post Cold war proved how they were intimately linked to one another. Issues such as environmental problems, threat of terrorism and so on transcend domestic frontiers and become an international concern. Second was the growth of various non-state actors which had an effect on the foreign policy decision making of the states. In other words, we witness the depleting role of states or what is commonly called 'the retreat of states' (Strange 1996). States role thus shifted from its 'only actor' status to 'one of the actors'. Apart from it, the very notion of security underwent a dramatic transformation. Thus, in the post Cold War era we talk more in terms of non-traditional security. Power which is intimately linked to security also was seen from a different prism and that is how the discourses on soft power became prominent in the post Cold War era. In this regard Nye in his article "Soft Power" (1990) contends:

New elements in the modern world are diffusing power away from all the great powers. Thus, any successful strategy must incorporate both continuity and change. The great powers of today are less able to use their traditional power resources to achieve their purposes than in the past. On many issues, private actors and small states have become more powerful. At least five trends have contributed to this diffusion of power: economic interdependence, transnational actors, nationalism in weak states, the spread of technology, and changing political issues.

Nye highlighting the importance of soft power in the globalizing world and the world of information technology, says, "The countries that are likely to be more attractive and gain soft power in the information age are those with multiple channels of communication that help to frame issues; whose dominant culture and ideas are closer to prevailing global norms (which now emphasize liberalism, pluralism, and autonomy); and whose credibility is enhanced by their domestic and international values and policies (Nye 2004: 31-32)." Nye further asserts:

> The information revolution is creating virtual communities and networks that cut across national borders. Transnational corporations and nongovernmental actors (terrorists included) will play larger roles. Many of these organizations will have soft power of their own as they attract citizens into coalitions that cut across national boundaries. Politics then becomes in part a competition for attractiveness, legitimacy, and credibility. The ability to share information and to be believed becomes an important source of attraction and power (*Ibid.*, p. 31).

Another important aspect of soft power is its ability to shape international institutions and agendas, which actually can be seen as part of reference to legitimate foreign policies (Li 2009: 3). Hence, government policies at home and abroad are another potential source of soft power. At the same time Nye cautions that "government policies can reinforce or squander a country's soft power. Domestic or foreign policies that appear to be hypocritical, arrogant, indifferent to the opinion of others, or based on a narrow approach to national interests can undermine soft power (Nye 2004: 13-14)." Also, it is important to note that the success of soft power heavily depends on the State's reputation within the international community, as well as the flow of information between States. Thus, soft power is often linked to the rise of globalization and neoliberal theory. Popular culture and media is often identified as a source of soft power, as is the spread of a national language, or a particular set of normative structures. A nation with a large amount of soft power, and the goodwill so won, can inspire other countries to acculturate, thus avoiding the need for expensive hard power expenditures (Purushothaman 2010: 2). American popular culture that has been integrated into many other countries is a strong indication of the power of media in Public diplomacy. In West Asia, especially since 9/11, there has been a growing need to use soft power to change perceptions of US in the Muslim world. Hollywood is recognized as the key driver and U.S. made films and music is especially penetrating the youth in the Muslim world. In addition to this a review of Public Diplomacy strategies highlighted the internet as a major tool of leveraging soft power.[8]

For Nye, the U.S. was the archetypal exponent of soft power, home as it is to Boeing, Intel, Ford, the IPod, the Iphone, Microsoft, MTV, Hollywood and Disneyland, McDonalds, Starbucks and most of the major products that dominate daily life globally. The attractiveness of these assets and emblems of the American lifestyle is that they permit the U.S. to maximize its soft power and enhance their ability to attract and persuade others to adopt the American agenda. In fact, Nye feels that its subtly deployed soft power was as important to the U.S. as its hard power (Tharoor 2008: 36). This leads Nye to conclude "Those whose dominant cultures and ideals are closer to prevailing global norms which now emphasize liberalism, pluralism, autonomy; those with the most accessed multiple channels of communication and thus more influence over how issues are framed, and those whose credibility is enhanced by their domestic and international performance (Nye 2004: 90)." Indian scholar Shashi Tharoor also exemplifies Nye's contentions. He states: When France lost the War of 1870 to Prussia, one of its most important steps to rebuild the nation's shattered morale and enhance its prestige was to create the Alliance Francaise to promote French language and culture and literature throughout the world. French culture, as we all know, has remained a major selling point for French diplomacy ever since. The U.K. has the British Council; the Swiss have Pro Helvetia and Germany, Spain, Italy and Portugal have respectively Institutes named for Goethe, Cervantes, Dante Alighieri and Camoes. Today, China has started establishing Confucius Institutes to promote Chinese culture internationally. But soft power does not rely on governmental action alone. Hollywood and MTV have done more to promote the idea of America as a desirable, admirable society than governmental initiatives such as the Voice of America or the Fulbright Scholarships. Soft power, as Nye has pointed out, is created partly by governments and partly in spite of governments (Tharoor 2008: 36-37).

Joseph Nye has emphasized that it is not smart to discount soft power as just a question of image, public relations, and ephemeral popularity as it is a form of power; a means of obtaining desired outcomes (Nye 2004: 129). According to Nye, it is important to understand that soft power is not merely the same as 'influence'. After all, influence can also rest on the hard power of threats or payments. And soft power is more than just persuasion or the ability to move people by argument, though that is an important part of it (*Ibid.*, p. 130). In behavioral terms, soft power is attractive power. In terms of resources, soft power resources are thc assets—tangible and intangible—that produce such attraction (Nye 2008: 31). Equally important it is to understand that soft power is not good *per se*, and it is not always better than hard power. Nobody likes to feel manipulated, even by soft power. Soft power can be used for competitive purposes (*Ibid.*, p. 43). Whether that attraction in turn produces desired policy outcomes has to be judged in particular cases (Nye 2004: 6). But attraction can turn to repulsion if we act in an arrogant manner and destroy the real message of our deeper values (*Ibid.*, p. 7). What Nye means is that, like any form of power, soft power can be wielded for good or bad purposes, and these often vary according to the eye of the beholder (Nye 2008: 43).

1.2.a Hard Power and Soft Power

Joseph Nye makes a clear-cut distinction between how soft and hard power is used. Hard power is evident in the practices of threat, coercion, sanction, payment, and inducement, whereas soft power is demonstrated in attraction, persuasion, appeal and co-option (Nye 2004: 3). In Nye's words:

> Hard power can rest on inducements (carrots) or threats (sticks). But sometimes you can get the outcomes you want without tangible threats or payoffs. The indirect way to get what you want has sometimes been called 'the second face of power'. A country may obtain the outcomes it wants in world politics because other countries-admiring its values, emulating its example, aspiring to its level of prosperity and openness—want to follow it (*Ibid.*, p. 5).

In this sense, it is also important to set the agenda and attract others in world politics, and not only to force them to change by threatening military force or economic sanctions (*Ibid.*, p. 5). Thus hard and soft power is related because they are both aspects of the ability to achieve one's purpose by affecting the behavior of others. The distinction between them is one of degree, both in the nature of the behavior and in the tangibility of the resources (*Ibid.*, p. 7). Thus it is important to understand that hard and soft power sometimes reinforce and sometimes interfere with each other (*Ibid.*, p. 25). If having hard power traditionally meant enjoying the privilege of not having to adjust or learn, wielding soft power often requires learning and adapting to followers' needs. At the same time, Nye says that hard power remains an essential tool for effective leaders even in modern democratic societies. Contextual intelligence is necessary if leaders wish to understand the appropriate mix of hard and soft power skills in particular situations (Nye 2008: 141). In other words, though the use of force as a foreign policy tool is gradually losing ground it does not, however, mean that military force has, or will cease to remain an option. It will be one of the several strategies for influencing states, while not being the most important one. This combination of both hard and soft power has been often termed as smart power by scholars working in the area (Palit and Palit 2011: 1-2).

In fact, hard and soft power can be regarded as two extremities on a continuum of power (Wagner 2005: 2). They involve different ideas, interactions and institutions for foreign policy whether in the areas of security, politics or economics. Ideally, hard power strategies focus on military intervention, coercive diplomacy, and economic sanctions in order to enforce national interests resulting in confrontational policies vis-à-vis neighbouring countries while soft power strategies stress on common political values, peaceful means for conflict management, and economic co-operation in order to achieve common solutions (*Ibid.*, pp. 2-3). In contrast to military and economic power, soft power differs in its behaviours, primary currencies and government policies. Economic resources, however, have a middle position and are sometimes attributed to either hard or soft power strategies. India's economic sanctions against Nepal in 1988–89 and the closure of the border stations were a classical hard power strategy to exert pressure on Nepal in the controversy over the renewal of the trade and transit treaty. India's aid programme and her unilateral economic concessions for the least developed South Asian Association for Regional Cooperation (SAARC) members are good examples for a soft power approach (Wagner 2010: 335).

Yet a country relying solely on soft power without hard power assets can find its weaknesses exposed easily. This happened to India in 1962, when China inflicted a humiliating military defeat on it, tarnishing New Delhi's hard-won soft power position in the world, especially among other developing countries in the nonaligned movement (Paul 2014: 157). In other words, soft power without hard power holds no importance and in T.V Paul's words (speaking in Indian context) states, "Indeed, soft power without hard power is a chimera, and they should not be seen in oppositional terms, especially for an aspiring global power." In other words, soft power can bring reputation, credibility, and legitimacy to a state's power position in the global system if it is developed and exercised in conjunction with hard power resources (*Ibid.*, p. 157).

Nye recognizing the interplay between hard and soft power professes for a combination of the two types of power which he calls as 'smart power'. Nye developed the concept of 'smart power'[9] in 2004 to counter the misperception that soft power alone can produce effective foreign policy. Nye defines smart power as the ability to combine hard and soft power resources into effective strategies. He further contends, unlike soft power, smart power is an evaluative as well as a descriptive concept. Soft power can be good or bad from normative perspective, depending on how it is used (Nye 2011: 22-23). Nye says, "A smart power narrative for the twenty-first century is not about maximizing power or preserving hegemony. It is about finding ways to combine resources into successful strategies in the new context of power diffusion and the 'rise of the rest' (*Ibid.*, pp. 207-208)." He further asserts smart power is neither hard nor soft. It is both (Nye 2004: xiii). Thus, soft power is not a substitute but should be seen as a complementary strategy with hard power. The challenge is to find the right mix between both strategies in order to achieve smart power.[10]

1.2.b India's Soft Power vis-à-vis Bangladesh

The concept of soft power is an artifact of the post-Cold War world, as is the rise of India. Both have grown in prominence during the same period, and observers have increasingly drawn a link between the two (Mukherjee 2014: 46). The growing consensus in the IR literature is that India possesses considerable soft power resources arising from its universalist culture, democratic political institutions and tradition of leadership among developing nations (Malone 2011: 35). Various scholars have commented on the soft power capacities of India. As pointed out, "India continues to have tremendous potential for soft power because of its culture and civilizational links—its large diaspora, popular films, music, art and historical and cultural links with several countries around the world all contribute to its soft power (Purushothaman 2010: 4)." Among the various commentators who have enumerated India's soft power resources, Tharoor is perhaps the most enthusiastic. He says:

> When India's cricket team triumphs or its tennis players claim Grand Slams, when a Bhangra beat is infused into a western pop record or an Indian choreographer invents a fusion of Kathak and ballet, when Indian women sweep the Miss World and Miss Universe contests or when Monsoon Wedding wows the critics and Lagaan claims an Oscar nomination, when Indian writers win the Booker or Pulitzer prizes, India's soft power is enhanced (Tharoor 2007: 25).

In a similar vein, Indian foreign policy analyst C. Raja Mohan in 2003 argues:

> The spiritualism of India has attracted people from all over the world, and its Gurus have travelled around the world selling yoga and mysticism. Bollywood has done more for Indian influence abroad than the bureaucratic efforts of the Government. From classical and popular music to its cuisine, from the growing impact of its writers and intellectuals, India now has begun to acquire many levers of soft power (Mohan 2003: 46).

Blarel speaking on India's soft power states:

In the last decade, India's soft power has mainly been defined in opposition to hard power considerations. In fact, soft power has now become an active element of India's diplomacy in parallel with the development of its hard power resources. India has progressively understood that these two dimensions of power should not be placed in opposition to one another, especially for an aspiring global power. Similarly, as India's hard power capabilities, notably in the economic and military realms, have increased over the last decade, it became important to develop in conjunction a soft power strategy to give legitimacy and credibility to India's leadership role in the world (Blarel 2012: 32).

Clearly, India's soft power resources are multi-faceted – they include sports, music, art, film, literature, and even beauty pageantry. To this list, others have added India's anti-colonial history, democratic institutions, free press, independent judiciary, vibrant civil society, multi-ethnic polity, secularism, pluralism, skilled English-speaking workers, food, handicrafts, yoga, India's status as a responsible nuclear power, the rapid growth of the information technology sector in places such as Bangalore, and the existence of a large Indian diaspora in certain western countries (See Nicolas Blarel, (2012), "India's Soft Power: From Potential to Reality, David Malone (2011), "Soft Power in Indian Foreign Policy", Uma Purushothaman, (2010), "Shifting Perceptions of Power: Soft Power and India's Foreign Policy", C. Raja Mohan (2003), "Indian Diaspora and 'Soft Power'"). Yet, when it comes to the current study, it is important to note that all aspects of India's soft power cannot deemed to be fit in its relations with Bangladesh. However, some of India's major soft power components that can be explored vis-à-vis Bangladesh are as follows:

1.2.b.(i) ***Culture*** Culture is the most important source of soft power. India is at a very advantageous position as far as culture is concerned and has historically enjoyed much soft power. According to T.V. Paul and Baldev Nayar, Indian culture offers one of the most dynamic alternatives to Western cultural values (Paul and Nayar 2003: 59). In the last decade, Indian diplomats have started emphasizing the appealing and also 'familiar' nature of India's culture. India has a long history of civilisational and cultural links with countries in Central Asia, South Asia, South-East Asia and the Middle-East (Blarel 2012: 29). Karan Singh, president of the Indian Council for Cultural Relations (ICCR) stated that 'soft power is important and the idea behind is to project India as a plural multicultural society and to achieve the goals of political diplomacy' (Shukla 2006: 335). Until 2009, the ICCR has set up 22 cultural centres in 19 countries. Numerous activities ranging from film festivals to book fairs and art events illustrate India's new endeavours to use soft power in her foreign policy Wagner 2010: 335). The Indian government has also encouraged the use of Hindi abroad by organising an annual and rotating World Hindi Conference and by offering Hindi classes in its different centres (Blarel 2012: 31).

As pointed out earlier, culture can be an important component of soft power vis-à-vis Bangladesh as India's links are civilization, cultural, social and economic. There is much that unites the two countries – a shared history and common heritage, linguistic and cultural ties, passion for music, literature and the arts; with Bangladesh, India shares not only a common history of struggle for freedom and liberation but also enduring feelings of both fraternal as well as familial ties (Mantoo 2015: 331). As such West Bengal will always play a pivotal role when it comes to India-Bangladesh relations. India and Bangladesh have in fact tried to use their cultural affinity in their bilateral relationship. Till date three agreements on cultural cooperation has been reached coupled with various academic, scientific and technological cooperation. In addition, MOU on Cooperation between Doordarshan and Bangladesh Television (BTV) was also signed in 2011 and during the 2015 Modi's visit to Bangladesh, it was agreed that Doordarshan and BTV will enter into an agreement to allow BTV to join Prasar Bharati's DTH platform.[11] More recently, on August 2016, India launched a new state-run radio service in bid to further strengthening the existing communication with Bangladesh.[12]

Further, Indian popular culture like Bollywood which is continually gaining popularity worldwide is another source of India's soft power. Commenting on it, C. Raja Mohan contends that Bollywood has done more for Indian influence abroad than the bureaucratic efforts of the Government (Mukherjee 2014: 46). India's film industry is probably the largest and farthest reaching medium for Indian culture. It is today the world's largest film industry, surpassing Hollywood with an annual output of over 1000 movies. Thanks to satellite TV and internet, Bollywood movies and Indian soap operas have reached a growing global audience that has become increasingly familiar with Indian society and culture. India's most successful and long-lasting exports, yoga, is now practiced around the world as a form of exercise, and Indian cuisine, with its distinctive use of spices, has become popular worldwide (Blarel 2012: 29-30). Undoubtedly, from classical and popular music to its cuisine, from the growing impact of its writers and intellectuals, India now has begun to acquire many levers of soft power (Mukherjee 2014: 46).

1.2.b.(ii) ***Economic Assistance*** While economic power is usually considered a hard and material asset, a country's economic assistance programme and its economic development model could also be interpreted as a soft power resource to the extent that its accomplishments prove attractive to others. The recent global successes of Indian information technology firms such as Infosys Technologies and Wipro, the achievements of other multinational companies such as the Tata Group and the Reliance Group; and the now global reputation of the Indian Institute of Management (IIMs) and Indian Institute of Technology (IITs) have contributed to the development of a new image of India as an economic powerhouse (Blarel 2012: 30). India in its relations with Bangladesh needs to effectively use its economy on the one hand and on the other needs to improve its image by giving economic assistance to Bangladesh in various sectors like building infrastructure, energy etc. As we shall see, economic inducement has often been used by India in its relations with Bangladesh ever since the independence of Bangladesh in 1971. The various credit line allocated to Bangladesh by India in 1974, 1999, 2011 and 2015 respectively is a clear employability of economic inducements as soft power.

1.2.b.(iii) ***Sports*** Sports as a soft power, is continually gaining importance among foreign policy practitioners and academicians alike. For instance, Lesley Masters in "The Olympics, International Geo-politics and Soft Power" (2012) contends:

The Olympics, however, offers numerous opportunities for diplomatic engagement. It provides an opportunity for parties to engage in a context outside of formal political processes, where protocols and adhering to 'political correctness' may inhibit dialogue.

Similarly, Jonathan Grix and Donna Lee (2013), speaking in context of China, South Africa and Brazil in their article 'Soft Power, Sports Mega-Events and Emerging States: The Lure of the Politics of Attraction' highlights "the possibilities that hosting a sports mega-event offers countries like China, South Africa and Brazil to practise public diplomacy in order to both project and boost their soft power in the international system (Grix and Lee 2013: 521)."

Regarding India-Bangladesh, one most important commonality that can bind the people of two nations is cricket as the craze for the game is quite high in both the countries. Cricket has proved to be a strong soft power resource for India, with cricket diplomacy having notably positive effects in reducing Indo-Pakistani tensions. Pakistani Prime Minister Yousuf Raza Gilani's meeting with Indian Prime minister Manmohan Singh during the 2011 world cup semi-final in India closely followed the resumption of high-level diplomatic dialogue between New Delhi and Islamabad after the 2008 Mumbai attacks. On another level, the creation in 2008 of the rich and internationally-popular Indian Premier League (IPL) has reinforced the narrative of India's rise (Blarel 2012: 29-30). An article by Amrut Thobbi entitled "How cricket diplomacy and politics marry in India" aptly encapsulates the role of cricket diplomacy in foreign policy. Thobbi states—"Call it soft diplomacy or cricket diplomacy, many politicians, national or otherwise; have used Indian cricketers' popularity to weave meaningful relations with the cricket-mad country."[13] Cricket has also fostered strong relations between India and some other Asian nations beyond its immediate neighbourhood. However, it is to be remembered that cricket vis-à-vis India-Bangladesh relations will be seen more as a soft power potential in the coming years rather than trying to decipher its role in the resolution of, for instance, the Farakka dispute or for that matter the conclusion of Land Boundary Agreement 2015. Logically too the evolution of cricket in Bangladesh is just a recent phenomenon.

1.2.b.(iv) ***Public Diplomacy*** In the most commonly used definition Signitzer and Coombs (1992: 138) understand the public diplomacy as: "a way, with which the government and the private individuals and groups can directly or indirectly influence those public opinions and positions, which directly influence the foreign politics decisions of another government (Signitzer and Coombs 1992: 137-147)." In 1996 Edmund A. Gullion a former diplomat defined public diplomacy as "the means by which governments, private groups and individuals influence the attitudes and opinions of other peoples and governments in such a way as to exercise influence on their foreign policy decisions."[14] According to Nye "public diplomacy does not focus on specific policy issues (a task better suited to lobbying); neither is it ideological in its content (like propaganda). Rather, it focuses on "building long-term relationships that create an enabling environment for government policies (Nye 2004: 107)." Building on such conceptions of public diplomacy the study will review India's public diplomacy towards Bangladesh and will demonstrate as to how India should focus on five key elements of public diplomacy as propounded by Nicholas J. Cull which are Listening, Cultural diplomacy, Exchange diplomacy, International news broadcasting (IB) (Cull 2008: 616). Thus India's policy home and abroad will be critically analysed along with its neighbourhood policy. One key inference in this regard is "The Gujral Doctrine". In the words of Christian Wagner:

The *Gujral doctrine* represented a new regional approach that was pursued by successive governments irrespective of their political affiliation. It emphasised intergovernmental relations instead of political interference, non-reciprocity instead of tit-for-tat, and the promotion of common economic interests instead of divergent concepts like national security. As such, India's South Asia policy since the 1990s shows a shift from a *hard power* strategy of military and diplomatic interventions to a *soft power* approach that emphasises inter-governmental co-operation, negotiated settlements and economic collaboration. The changes can also be seen as attempt to change India's image from a regional bully to a benign hegemon (Wagner 2005: 13-14).

In consonance the recent India's neighborhood policy under Prime Minister Narendra Modi, and his policies often termed as 'Modi Doctrine', will also be analysed and efforts will be made to find out whether the doctrine has elevated India's image at the global level and whether India's neighbourhood policy has helped in improving Indo-Bangladesh relations.

What is evident, however, is the fact that India has a plentitude of soft power resources when it comes to bettering its relations with Bangladesh. It, therefore, has to follow a carefully thought out strategy for optimizing its soft power leverage in the region. Financial limitations must be offset by cultural and educational advantages, with country-specific variations wherever required (Palit and Palit 2011: 25). Equally important is, as Wagner says in context of India, to find ways to transform its soft power capacities into capabilities (Wagner 2010: 4). Thus, the book will focus on finding ways wherein India can develop its 'soft capacities' into concrete tool of diplomacy to improve its relations with Bangladesh. Attempts will also be made to draw inferences from the global experiences or how countries have been using soft power to achieve their foreign policy objectives along with India's own efforts to harness its soft power potentials and its employability with other countries. In doing so, the focus is made on the employability of soft power in India-Bangladesh relations with "A Soft Use of Power Approach" as propounded by Mingjiang Li at its base. Li in this regard contends:

If culture, ideology, and values can be used for coercion, and military and economic strength can be used for attraction and appeal, a better approach to soft power is how the resources of power are used rather than associating sources of power as soft or hard. In essence, soft power lies in the soft use of power to increase a state's attraction, persuasiveness, and appeal (Li 2009: 7).

In other words, by seeing India's soft power with the lens of how it uses its capability instead of focusing on the resources of power, the book contends that we can then better understand how culture, values, and institutions can be used to improve its relations with Bangladesh. As such India's hard power capabilities which it used to liberate Bangladesh qualify as soft power. Lastly, the book will also decipher soft power implications (if any) in the historical engagements between India and Bangladesh. Thereby, effort will be made to find means and ways to make these soft power resources into concrete tool of diplomacy towards Bangladesh. In doing so inferences will be drawn from the past experiences and examples of the employability of soft power in foreign policies will be studied.

1.3 Scope of the Study

The current study seeks to test the employability of soft power in the relations between India and Bangladesh. As known, India-Bangladesh relations carry strong historical and cultural overtones. Both share a common history, culture and language. Until the partition of India in 1947, Bangladesh had formed an integral part of the geographical, ethnic, cultural and political entity known from ancient times as Bang (now Bengal). In other words, India and Bangladesh share not only common script and language, but also many sub-national features born of centuries of interaction between different cultural and spiritual influences and local tribal traditions and political experiences (Biswas 2016: 50). In addition, India's role in the birth of Bangladesh is well known. Yet, within a few years, this relationship started turning sour. The question arises every now and then, what went wrong? Why have India and Bangladesh become estranged and distant? This is a relationship which has really suffered because of a sense of mistrust and neglect (Sobhan 2008: 1).

Further, the nation-building process also has played a major role in Bangladesh distancing itself from India. One of the main reasons for it has been the role of changing nature of 'identity' formation in Bangladesh. If Bengali identity played an important role in the creation of Bangladesh, it was Bangladeshi identity which became important after the formation of Bangladesh. Bengali nationalism gives salience to the linguistic feature and as such is regarded as being closer to West Bengal and India, whereas in Bangladeshi nationalism, the religious aspect is accorded greater salience. However, the divide between the two forms of nationalism is somewhat artificial. For the overwhelming number of those who believe in Bangladeshi nationalism are the ones who are steeped in the Bengali culture and almost all those who believe in Bengali nationalism are never forgetful about their

Islamic identity (Dubey 2013: 79-80). Apart from it, the geographical realities (India's overwhelming geographical presence) feed to its security dilemma vis-à-vis India. Sharing of common borders also creates a scope for generating a horde of disputed issues like illegal migration, cross-border criminal and terrorist activities and so on. Moreover, as a lower-riparian country, Bangladesh remains highly dependent on India for its sufficient and regular flow of water (Biswas 2016: 51).

Both India and Bangladesh view each other from a negative prism. Bangladesh as seen by India is a source of an unending flow of illegal migrants, as a haven for fundamentalists and terrorists and a sanctuary for Indian insurgents in the north-east; a troublesome, non-cooperative neighbour, most difficult to engage (Mukharji 2007: 558). On the other hand, Bangladesh sees India as a giant neighbour without the attributes of a good neighbour, and hence to be treated with caution (*Ibid.*). On the Bangladesh side, there is a feeling that they have been neglected and ignored, that Bangladesh does not figure on the Indian list of foreign policy priorities (Sobhan 2008: 2). Further, there are many contentious issues between India and Bangladesh, a general overview of which is espoused in the succeeding section. The seeds of discontent between the two countries lie in host of issues of which principal ones should be noted as they are of enduring nature.

1.3.a *Water disputes* Among the most contentious and complicated problems that caused a great deal of acrimony between the two countries is the sharing of the waters of the Ganges/ Farakka barrage construction by India. India and Bangladesh share 54 rivers between them. Despite setting up a Joint River Commission for Water Management as early as 1972, tensions between the countries on how to share water resources remain a problem.[15] The core of the problem lies in the sharing of waters for five dry-season months between January and May. Sheikh Mujib and Indira Gandhi had agreed that the technical experts of the two countries should find an amicable solution to the issue of sharing of these waters. But after the death of Mujib, the issue became increasingly tied up in political knots. Moreover, Bangladesh tried to internationalize the issue, without any conspicuous success (Dutt 2008: 142). The basic agreement was signed in 1977 by the Janata Party government in New Delhi for a five-year period regulating the flow to Bangladesh during the dry season. But India's proposal to build a link canal was strongly opposed by Bangladesh while India disapproved Dhaka's attempt to bring Nepal into what it regarded as a bilateral issue. India remained worried about the adequate flow during the lean months to Bihar and U.P. as well as about the fate of Calcutta port if it were denied sufficient water. On the other hand, Bangladesh alleged that it faced the threat of ruin during the lean season because of insufficient waters available to it from India during this period (*Ibid*., p. 142-43).

In November 1977, the two countries proposed a five year agreement on water sharing. However, the basic issue remained unaddressed, leading to its lapse in 1982. Finally a comprehensive bilateral treaty was signed by the Indian Prime minister H. D. Deve Gowda and his Bangladeshi counterpart Sheikh Hasina on December 12, 1996. This treaty established a thirty year water sharing arrangement with guaranteed minimum quantities of water supply for Bangladesh, whose rights as a lower riparian country was recognized (Dutta 2010: 4). Though the Farakka issue has been resolved by the Ganges Water Treaty 1996, the question of other rivers such as Teesta and Feni has come to the fore and are bound to create problems in India-Bangladesh bilateral relations, if they continue to remain unresolved.

1.3.b ***Border Issues*** India and Bangladesh share almost 4096 kilometers of land border. Officially 6.1 kilometers of land [at three sectors viz. Daikhata-56 (West Bengal), Muhuri River-Belonia (Tripura) and Lathitila-Dumabari (Assam)] is considered as disputed. But the border disputes between India and Bangladesh are by no means confined to demarcation problems. It is linked with other problems like illegal migration of people and goods and other cross border criminal activities (*Ibid*., p. 7). The porous border makes it easy for terrorists to move at will. Bangladesh is also a transit point for Indian jihadis to go across the border and thence for training to Pakistan (Mukharji 2007: 559). Other problems related to the border were the transfer of the enclaves and the question of 'adverse possession'. With the conclusion of the LBA in 2015 major problems pertaining to the border has been resolved. Yet there are other problems such as illegal migration, security concerns and the problems associated with the fencing of the border which needs immediate attention.

There were also the unresolved problems related to the India-Bangladesh maritime boundary and the New Moor Island (Dixit 2001: 207). The issue of demarcating territorial waters led to serious differences between the two countries. Questions of ownership over a new born island known as South Talpatty in Bangladesh and New Moore/ Purbasha in India spotted by a satellite picture in 1975 in the estuary of Haribhanga River on the border of the two countries has been a source of contention since its discovery. In order to settle the above dispute Bangladesh proposed sending a joint Indo- Bangladesh team to determine the flow of channels of the river on the basis of existing International Law of the Sea. But the Indian counterpart sent forces to establish claims by stationing naval troops on the island in 1981. After initial resentment by Bangladesh, India agreed to resolve the issue through negotiations. Most of the years, the sovereignty over the island nation remains undecided and many reports of the press and media suggest that Bangladesh views India with suspicion in its activities over the disputed piece of landmass on the breast of an international water (Dutta 2010: 7-8). However, cooperation on maritime issues showed positive signs during the Indian Prime Minister Modi's visit to Bangladesh when India responded positively to resolve the maritime dispute. India's decision to opt for international arbitration to settle her maritime boundary with Bangladesh was a similar gesture of goodwill. It signified a deliberate, a priori relinquishment of its claims on the disputed waters, nearly 80 per cent of which have gone to Bangladesh (*The Hindu*, May 11, 2015).

1.3.d *Trade and Transit* Trade disputes also have adversely affected India-Bangladesh relations. There are pressing concerns in Bangladesh regarding the large bilateral trade deficit with India and the large volumes of informal imports from India across the land border which avoid Bangladeshi import duties. Bangladesh's bilateral trade deficit with India has been increasing rapidly on average at about 9.5% annually. Political discontentment in Bangladesh tends to stem from the huge trade gap, supported by the fact that India has a lot of non-trade barriers for Bangladeshi exports. Even though exports from Bangladesh are growing at a healthy pace, there is no sign of reducing this trade gap (Dutta 2010: 1). Further, Indian concessions under the South Asian Preferential Trade Agreement (SAPTA) in line largely with Bangladeshi demands have made little impact (Mukharji 2007: 565).

Both India and Bangladesh desire transit facilities through each other's territories for trade. India wants transit facilities to reach its eastern and north-eastern states more expeditiously. Bangladesh desires transit facilities to Nepal and Bhutan to augment its exports. Both sides have reservations about granting these facilities not primarily due to economic considerations. The reservations are based on political considerations and security perceptions (Dixit 2001: 207-208). Apart from it, the proposed gas pipeline from Myanmar to India via Bangladesh has also been declined by Bangladesh (Mukharji 2007: 566). However, many breakthroughs were achieved during Indian Prime Minister Modi's visit to Bangladesh. In the said visit, 'Agreement on Coastal Shipping', 'Protocol on Inland Water Transit and Trade (renewal)', 'Agreement on Dhaka-Shillong-Guwahati

Bus Service', 'Agreement on Kolkata-Dhaka-Agartala Bus Service' and 'Memorandum of Understanding on Use of Chittagong and Mongla Ports' were reached upon between India and Bangladesh, which obviously signals positive signs for the future. In addition, foundation Stone for Rehabilitation of Kalaura-Shahbajpur section of Bangladesh Railways and for the Construction of Khulna-Mongla Railway line were also unveiled in the said visit.[16]

This book, however, limits itself to the three issues pertaining to water, land and trade and transit to test the applicability of soft power in India-Bangladesh bilateral relations.

1.4 Survey of Literature

The section gives a brief survey of the literature used for the purpose of the study. The section is divided into two parts, first relates to the literature on conceptual aspects and theoretical framework, that is, the concept of 'power' and 'soft power'. The succeeding section will give a brief overview of the existing literatures pertaining to India-Bangladesh relations.

The two books *Discourses of Power: From Hobbes to Foucault* by Barry Hindess (1996) and *Power* edited by Steven Lukes (1986) probe into the concept of power from various dimensions. The former starts with the 'Two Concepts of Power'. It subsequently deals with power in relation to Hobbes' *Leviathan* (1651) and *Locke's Second Treatise on Government* and his *Essay Concerning Human Understanding* (both published in 1689). The book also discusses Locke's concept of political power and morality and Luke's perspective of power wherein he contrasts his own 'radical' perspective with the 'liberal' account of power. Lastly the book ends with Foucault's views on power, domination and government. Similarly, Luke's book deals with various aspects and views on power. For instance, Max Weber's talks about the domination in relation to economic power and authority; Robert Dahl talks about power as the control of behavior while Hannah Arendt talks about 'communicative power'. Apart from it the book offers various other forms, dimensions and perceptions by other scholars which makes us understand the various aspects and dimensions of power which is integral to understand as well as build the concept of 'soft power'.

Soft Power: The Means to Success in World Politics (2005) by Joseph Nye Jr. is an important contribution as it gives us an understanding of the concept of 'soft power'. In the book Nye defines soft power as "the ability to get what you want through attraction rather than coercion or payments," which "arises from the attractiveness of a country's culture, political ideals, and policies." However, Nye contends that soft power is much more than "image, public relations and ephemeral popularity," as soft power can attain foreign policy objectives. Further, Nye contends that seduction is always more effective than coercion, and many values like democracy and human rights, and individual opportunities are deeply seductive. This book also highlights as to how transnational issues such as terrorism, environmental problems and so on needs to be dealt multilaterally. One important aspect which Nye highlights in the book is that Soft power is more difficult to exert as many of its resources lie outside the purview of the governments, and, more importantly, their effects depend heavily on acceptance by the receiving audiences. Moreover, soft-power resources often work indirectly and sometimes take years to produce the desired outcome.

In the book Nye divides 'power' into three general categories. According to Nye, to achieve desired outcomes, one can coerce with threats, induce with payments, or attract and co-opt to get people to want what one wants and soft power is basically associated with the co-optive power. Nye adds that the information age has greatly expanded the effectiveness of the third type of power owing to the mobility of information and propaganda. Soft power holds importance especially in the contemporary times as the possession of superior economic and military power is frequently not enough to attain one's foreign policy objectives.

According to Nye, personal contacts are another important channel for soft power. Travel by tourists and business people facilitate such contacts. The half million foreign students studying in the U.S. is a powerful resource. Further, immigrants are also a powerful soft power factor. Further, he says that internal policies can have an impact on soft power. Efforts to promote human rights and democracy have noticeably enhanced U.S. influence, while capital punishment and weak gun control laws have undermined it in Europe. Apparently, military, economic and soft power influence abroad can both enhance and hinder soft power. Highlighting on the limits of soft power Nye says, "all power depends on context –who relates to whom under what circumstances but soft power depends more than hard power upon the existence of willing interpreters and receivers. Moreover, attraction often has a diffuse effect, creating general influence rather than producing an easily observable specific action."

Commenting on U.S economic power Nye contends that U.S' economy does not only provide economic strength but also the soft power of economic influence. Immigration flows, Hollywood films, multinational corporations, foreign students, books, music, internet websites, Nobel laureates, scientific achievements –all are sources of attraction and influence. One important aspect which Nye highlights in the book is that Soft power is more difficult to exert as many of its resources lie outside the purview of the governments, and, more importantly, their effects depend heavily on acceptance by the receiving audiences. Moreover, soft-power resources often work indirectly and sometimes take years to produce the desired outcome.

The book titled, *The Future of Power* (2011) by Joseph Nye Jr. highlights the fundamental shift in the workings of international system in the contemporary times with the rise of various non-state actors and with the rise of new economies including Asian countries. The book discusses various issues ranging from the growth of non-state actors to the rise of the People's Republic of China (PRC). More importantly, the book highlights the tri-level nature of the international system which he illustrates through three-dimensional chessboard. At the highest level, the world is viewed from the traditional, state-centric perspective that gives importance to military power. In this regard the world according to Nye remains unipolar and the U.S. "is likely to remain supreme for some time". On the second level, however, where economic power is the marker of the system, Nye contends that the system is multipolar in a sense that power is more evenly distributed between the U.S. and other powers, such as Europe and China. Finally, the bottom level of the chessboard represents the realm of transnational relations that cross borders and are outside of government control, and it includes non-state actors as diverse as bankers... and terrorists.

In the book, Nye espouses three variants of power namely hard power, soft power and smart power (which is the combination of hard and soft power). Besides, the book highlights on the power shifts taking place, that is, power transition and power diffusion. Power transition, in simple words, refers to the shift in power from one country to another. However, in this context the question of declining American power becomes important. On the other hand, power diffusion refers to the rise of non-state actors in international system and its growing role and importance. In other words, the states are not the sole authority as individuals and private organizations, NGO's, and terrorists now play a critical role in world politics.

On the question of U.S decline Nye states that U.S can surpass China not only because U.S has a stronger hard power capabilities but also because it has more soft power capabilities than China. What Nye professes is that, it is not possible for the states to achieve its foreign policy objectives merely by using its hard power capabilities; nor can it achieve its goals by acting alone. What he contends is that in this changed international system, nations must use soft power to build networks and institutions to respond to shared threats. It is no longer sufficient to think exclusively of wielding power over others, rather we must instead think of using power to accomplish goals with others. To Nye an ideal foreign policy of 21st century would be the combination of hard power and soft power. What he contends is that the countries with better stories will prevail in the 21st century. Thus, Nye calls for the policy makers and scholars for the need of re-adjustment and proper employment of smart power to attain the foreign policy objectives.

Soft Power: China's Emerging Strategy in International Politics (2009) edited by Mingjiang Li analyses and examines domestic and international view of China's soft power potentials. It also offers Chinese perspectives on soft power and the impacts and implications of China's emerging soft power strategy in world politics. Apart from the conventional approaches on soft power, the book provides other sources of soft power such as domestic politics, social relations and so on and tries to move beyond Nye's conception of soft power, though not completely disagreeing with his concept. The book is helpful as it probes into the complexities and ambiguities inherent in the concept of soft power. The book analyses the potential resources, strengths, and weaknesses of China's soft power from various perspectives, such as—foreign policy strategy, political economy, culture, history, and education. The book also offers various case studies that highlight China's relations with South Korea, Australia, Southeast Asia, and Africa and Beijing diplomacy in international climate change negotiations.

It is evident from the book that in China, however, the popularity of the concept of soft power among Chinese political leaders, scholars, journalists and pundits has been striking. Its prevalence in the Chinese media is by no means an insignificant issue. Some of the main questions raised by scholars on soft power are worth contemplating. For instance, one scholar argues that the complex relationship between hard power and soft power still needs to be scrutinized and better understood. It is argued that Nye's approach to soft power does not provide clear cut answers to some notable puzzles. For instance, where is the exact boundary between hard power and soft power? Does soft power include a laundry list of anything other than material factors, such as morality of the citizens, national image, national cohesion, domestic political stability, leadership, and innovation? How do we measure soft power? More importantly, how do we know that soft power, as defined by the existing approach translates into policy outcomes? Concerning the relation between hard power and soft power, some Chinese analysts seem to be more willing than Nye to emphasize the inseparability of hard power and soft power. They argue, for example: "Soft power and hard power are mutually complementary to each other. Soft power can facilitate the growth of hard power, whereas hard power can demonstrate and support the increase of soft power." The study is critical of Nye's dichotomy of hard power and soft power, arguing that, depending on the context, any source of power can be both hard and soft, and that China's soft power is best illustrated in the 'China model', multilateralism, economic diplomacy and good-neighborly policy.

Due to the inherent flaws in the concept of soft power, scholars like Mingjiang Li have offered an alternative approach to the concept of soft power. Li's concept of soft power is best encapsulated in what he calls 'A Soft Use of Power Approach'. Li contends: "If culture, ideology, and values can be used for coercion, and military and economic strength can be used for attraction and appeal, a better approach to soft power is how the resources of power are used rather than associating sources of power as soft or hard. In essence, soft power lies in the soft use of power to increase a state's attraction, persuasiveness, and appeal. In other words, by seeing soft power with the lens of how a state uses its capability instead of focusing on the resources of power, we can then better understand how culture, values, and institutions can be brought into the discussion of soft power. Culture and values contain social principles or normative guidelines on how power should be exercised.

Moving beyond Nye conceptualization, it is also argued that the source of soft power comes from three dimensions: institutional power, identifying power and assimilating power. Institutional power refers to a state's ability to propose or build new international institutions or arrangements. Identifying power refers to a state's ability to influence other states through the latter's recognition of its leadership role. Finally, assimilating power refers to the attraction of a state's cultural values, ideology and social system. Yan Xuetong believes that soft power lies in political power that is exclusively found in political institutions, norms, and credibility, rather than in culture. Zhu Feng argues that soft power has little to do with sources of power but it is all about whether the international community accepts a nation's policies and strategic choices, as well as to what extent those choices accord with most nations' interests.

The book offers a comprehensive understanding of the importance of soft power in China's international politics. Unlike Joseph Nye's primary focus on the efficacy of soft power in achieving foreign policy goals, Chinese discourse frequently refers to a domestic context and evinces a mission for domestic purposes. However, soft power, as expounded by Chinese analysts, is still a weak link in China's pursuit of comprehensive national power and largely perceived as a tool for defensive purposes, including cultivating a better image of China to the outside world, correcting foreign misperceptions of China, and fending off Western cultural and political inroads in China.

The second set of literature deal with India and Bangladesh relations. Various primary sources were surveyed for the purpose of the study, prominent among which are the Ganges Water Treaty 1996 and The Land Boundary Agreement 2015. Apart from it, various treaties, MOUs, agreements were also surveyed. In addition, the secondary sources which hold utmost importance for the purpose of the study are as follows.

J. N. Dixit's book titled *Liberation and Beyond: Indo-Bangladesh Relations* (1999) gives us insightful account of India's former Foreign Secretary, J. N. Dixit who was not only a witness but a participant in the processes leading to the creation of Bangladesh. This book is an analytical account of the political processes and policy orientations of leaders and governments who were involved in the East Pakistan crisis and the breakup of Pakistan. As such the book probes into various aspects related to Indo-Bangladesh relations including the genesis alienation among the East Pakistanis; how India gets involved into the Bangladesh crisis, the birth of Bangladesh and so on. The book is important in a sense that it gives us the author's experiences with Mujibur Rahman and also sheds some light into Mujib's personality and psyche as well as his attitude towards India. The book is divided into three parts: the road to separation, the actual conflict, and Indo-Bangladeshi relations, with the author's thoughts and a prognosis; with Chapter 'Five' basically dealing with the documentation of atrocities by the Pakistan Army. This is also the first book which provides analytical and insightful details regarding the motivations of India in supporting the liberation war, the complexities and its political dimensions.

Similarly Harun-ur-Rashid's *Bangladesh-India Relations: Living with a Big Neighbour* (2010) gives us personal account of his experience as a delegate in Foreign Services. If Dixit's book gives us the Indian side of the story, Rashid's provides us with the Bangladeshi perspectives. Since the author is himself a diplomat and has played a key role in many bilateral negotiations with India on issues, such as the Ganges water dispute, sea boundary in the Bay of Bengal, air services agreement, trade agreement, land border disputes and a host of other issues, we get a very insightful analysis from his personal experience. The book gives us a holistic account of India-Bangladesh relations since the emergence of Bangladesh in 1971. The author highlights Bangladesh's insecurity owing to the dominance of India in the region and argues that Bangladesh has often felt strains and stresses to live with a big neighbour. However, the author acknowledges that 'India factor' looms large in Bangladesh foreign policy. Besides, Rashid also tried to probe into the psychological factors that have impinged Indo-Bangladesh relations and also highlights as to how the attitudes of political leaders of both the countries during the first four decades have had a negative impact on India-Bangladesh relations.

The major themes dealt in the book are: causes of mistrust between India and Bangladesh, impact of India's security interests on Bangladesh, critical appraisal of main issues in bilateral relations during the first 38 years, and future directions of India-Bangladesh relations. The book is interesting in a sense that it gives an appraisal of Bangladesh's foreign policy towards India from 1971-2009, under various governments. In crux, the book has tried to probe into complex, sensitive, and multidimensional nature of Indo-Bangladesh relations.

Another book, *Four Decades of India-Bangladesh Relations: Historical Imperatives and Future Direction,* edited by Smruti S. Pattanaik (2012) is basically an outcome of a bilateral dialogue between the Institute for Defence Studies and Analyses (IDSA), New Delhi and the Bangladesh Institute for International and Strategic Studies (BIISS). The book is important for the current study, in a sense that it gives both Indian and Bangladeshi perspectives. While doing so, the book provides a historical background of the Indo-Bangladesh relations along with the issues that have put their relations into a backburner. It contextualizes Indo-Bangladesh relations into wider perspectives and explores areas wherein the two can cooperate. The book consists of thirteen chapters and deals with entire gamut of bilateral relations ranging from water, trade and transit to the energy issues.

P. Sukumaran Nair's book, *Indo-Bangladesh Relations* (2008) highlights the importance of India in Bangladesh's foreign policy. The book is divided into six main chapters. The first chapter discusses the factors and reasons which led to the breakup of Pakistan and the birth of Bangladesh. The second chapter deals with India-Bangladesh relations since its birth, till the assassination of Sheikh Mujibur Rahman. The chapter is important for the current study as it outlines the reasons for the rise of hostilities between India and Bangladesh. The third chapter probes into the nature of relationship between the two countries in the post-Mujibur period. It also deals with the domestic political factors on the eve of Zia's assumption of office, his principles of state policy and his inclination towards Islamic policy. The next chapter deals with nature of economic relations between the two countries and the impediments in Indo-Bangladesh economic relations. Since, trade and transit is an area of focus for the current study, the chapter gives important insights in this regard.

The fifth chapter entitled 'Disputes between India and Bangladesh' focuses on the Farakka dispute between the two countries. Farakka as the chapter demonstrates were among the contentious issues even before the creation of Bangladesh. The chapter is important in a sense that it provides phase wise negotiations between India and Bangladesh on Farakka. Chapter six, deals with the problems of refugees and minorities. The author gives account of the genesis of refugee influx into India from Pakistan since 1947, Chakma problem and its impact on India-Bangladesh relations. Apart from it, the 'Tin Bigha' issue and New Moore island dispute has also been dealt in this chapter. In short, the book is helpful for its brief overview on Indo-Bangladesh relations.

Y. M. Bammi's book *India-Bangladesh Relations: The Way Ahead* (2010) recounts the personal experiences and views of a Lt. General who participated the 1971 Indo-Pak war. The book gives a brief overview of the geography and history of Bangladesh as a backdrop and then proceeds to the pertinent aspects in regard to India-Bangladesh relations. The strategic importance of Bangladesh to India, security perceptions of Bangladesh and the major issues in Indo-Bangladesh relations have been dealt with. The book also provides a chronological review of Bangladesh's foreign policy towards India. Apart from it, the author has incorporated the views of a large cross-section of eminent personalities of both the countries and an attempt has been made to substantiate the existing relations. The final chapter, 'The Way Ahead' basically deals with the author's suggestions and an action plan for the future.

Indo-Bangladesh Relations (1982) by S. S. Bindra basically deals with the Farakka Barrage dispute between the two countries. Since the Farakka dispute is dealt at length by the author, it gives us a complete understanding on the issue. Apart from it the book also focuses on Indo-Bangladesh Treaty 1971, Border Agreement of 1974, coup in Bangladesh and its impact on India-Bangladesh relations etc. The book probes into the India-Bangladesh cooperation on social, cultural and economic fields. This is of critical importance for the current study as it has soft power connotations. Another important aspect which the book touches is the genesis and the reasons for the rise of anti-India feelings in Bangladesh. Besides, Indo-Bangladesh relations in the immediate post-Mujib era have been dealt. The book also probes into the nature of economic relations after 1974, how the border problems arose, the problem of illegal migration and New Moore controversy and so on.

Another book *Bangladesh: Promise and Performance* edited by Rounaq Jahan (2000) deals with the potentials of Bangladesh as a country and its performance till late 1990s. The book as such does not deal with Indo-Bangladesh relations, nonetheless it is helpful to understand the domestic milieu of Bangladesh. The highlight of the book lies in the depiction of the changing nature of identity formation in Bangladesh which is of critical importance to India-Bangladesh relations. Apart from it the book also deals with the Chakma problem and highlights as to how 'cultural pluralism' has become an emerging challenge in Bangladesh. The book also highlights on the role NGOs and civil society in democratic development of the country. Moreover, the question of Bangladesh economy and its various aspects and limitations has been dealt at length by the author. Besides, the book also raises various pertinent issues such as poverty, human development and the problems inherent in building a responsible civil society.

1.5 Research Questions

(a) Has soft power been employed in the resolution of Ganges Water dispute between India and Bangladesh?

(b) Can we find the elements of soft power in the negotiations on border issues and the recent conclusion of the LBA?

(c) Can trade and transit be an effective soft power tool when it comes to India and Bangladesh relations?

1.6 Methodology, Chapters, and Research Limitations

The study is primarily descriptive, where historical-analytical method is followed. The study looks into certain historical developments in India-Bangladesh relations and analyzes it in broader framework of soft power. It as such probes into three main contentious issues between India and Bangladesh, namely, water, border and trade and transit and provides a derivative understanding of the employability of soft power. The negotiations on these issues will be analysed and inferences will be drawn from it. It is a qualitative study, wherein both primary and secondary sources have been used. Primary source consist of various interviews and treaties, government documents and reports. Apart from it, various books, articles and online journals have been used for the purpose of study. The study looks into major problems which have been solved in India-Bangladesh Relations and efforts will be made to decipher the elements of soft power in it.

The book unfurls in six chapters. The introductory chapter lays out the theoretical bases of soft power in the context of India-Bangladesh relations. The second chapter will delineate a brief history of the creation of Bangladesh and India's role and involvement in the Bangladesh liberation movement. The main thrust of the chapter is to demonstrate as to how the pertinent problems between India and Bangladesh have historical roots. The third, fourth and fifth chapter will deal with the three major issues-water, border disputes and trade and transit respectively, which have hampered India-Bangladesh relations. All these will be studied in the soft power context. The last chapter will delineate the major findings of the research and will substantiate the research questions. However, the study has few limitations. For instance, issues such terrorism, informal trade and migration which are pertinent problems in Indo-Bangladesh relations have not been dealt in this study.

Notes

1. http://www.idsa.in/idsacomments/indo-bangladesh-border-banijya-basati-lakkhi_gsen_020816
2. Bangladesh Government in exile created by those Awami League members who fled to India after the arrest of Mujib.
3. Enduring conflicts are those kinds of conflicts whose solutions are generally hard to achieve and which take years to get resolved.
4. Refer to Annexure I
5. In the book Nye disputed the then-prevalent view that America was in decline. He pointed out that the United States was the strongest nation not only in military and economic power, but also in a third dimension that he called soft power
6. In *The Future of Power* (2011) Nye says "Attraction is more complex than it appears. It can refer to drawing attention—whether positive or negative—as well as creating alluring or positive magnetic effects. The production of soft power by attraction depends upon both the qualities and efforts of the agent and how they are perceived by the target which is critical for the creation of soft power. What produces attraction for one target may produce revulsion for another. When an actor or action is perceived as malign, manipulative, incompetent, or ugly, it is likely to produce revulsion."
7. According to In E. H. Carr military power is the most important form of power in international politics. Carr explained that "the supreme importance of the military instrument lies in the fact that the ultima ratio of power in international relations is war".

8. http://thenewdiplomats.blogspot.in/2011/03/how-crucial-is-soft-power-to-successful.html
9. See also Ernest J. Wilson, III (Mar., 2008), "Hard Power, Soft Power, Smart Power" Annals of the American Academy of Political and Social Science, Vol. 616
10. See Ernest J. Wilson, III (Mar., 2008), "Hard Power, Soft Power, Smart Power" *Annals of the American Academy of Political and Social Science*, Vol. 616 and Nye (16 January 2009), "Get smart" *International Herald Tribune*
11. http://www.thedailystar.net/online/bangladesh-india-joint-declaration-93490
12. http://theindianawaaz.com/india-launches-moitreee-radio-to-strengthen-communication-with-bangladesh/
13. https://cricket.yahoo.com/news/how-cricket-diplomacy-and-politics-marry-in-india-115315188.html
14. http://fletcher.tufts.edu/Murrow/Diplomacy/Definitions
15. http://isnblog.ethz.ch/global-voices/india-bangladesh-water-disputes-and-river-diplomacy
16. http://www.thedailystar.net/online/bangladesh-india-joint-declaration-93490

Chapter - II

India-Bangladesh Relations: Historical Trends and Patterns

2.1 Introduction

The elements of soft power between India and Bangladesh are rooted in the very history of the sub-continent. Both shared a common history, culture and language long before the creation of Bangladesh. India provided moral, emotional and material support to Bangladesh' freedom struggle movement; gave refuge to millions of refugees and even the government in exile which had fled to India during the East-Pakistan crisis, got a safe haven in India. The values of secularism and democracy were among the common threads that binded India with Bangladesh especially during the tenure of Awami League (AL) in Bangladesh. After the army took over the power in Bangladesh, there was a general trend of bilateral disputes turning into conflicts. The chapter tries to encompass these aspects. However, as we shall see the three contentious issues, namely the water, the problem of boundary delineation, and the issue of trade and transit, which the thesis tries to study, flow from the first partition in 1947 and secondly with the creation of Bangladesh in 1971.

This chapter thus is divided into two main sections. The first section proceeds with a brief account of the partition of India. It subsequently deals with the events leading to the creation of Bangladesh with special emphasis on the rise of 'Bengali nationalism' and the factors that entangled India into the East Pakistan crisis. The second section will deal with India-Bangladesh bilateral relations until the Mujib era. The section is important on two counts: First, it will delineate the factors that ended the honeymoon phase of Indo-Bangladesh relations and the subsequent rise of hostilities between the two countries, which impinge their bilateral relations in the coming years. Secondly, the section will demonstrate India's employability of soft power in its relation with Bangladesh in the initial years of Indo-Bangladesh relations.

2.2 Section-I

The history of Bangladesh is closely intertwined with that of India and Pakistan. The end of the British Empire in India in August 1947 resulted in the creation of two separate states, India and Pakistan.[1] During the Indian freedom movement, the Muslim League advocated the creation of Pakistan, based on religious lines; the Indian National Congress rejected the 'Two-Nation' theory for a 'secular' state. Many Muslim leaders such as Muhammad Ali Jinnah, Allama Mohammad Iqbal, Liaquat Ali Khan and others were wary of predominantly Hindu majority rule and demanded safeguards through separate electorates. In order to press for their demands, they formed the Muslim League in December 1906. Their claim for separate electorates was accepted by the British in the Government of India Act of 1909.[2] Over time this policy helped to unify the Muslim community in a communal and political sense and sowed the seeds for the idea of Pakistan (Paul 2005: 6).

Never before had the communal question assumed a dangerous dimensions in the country as it did in the 1920s, after Khilafat and Non-cooperation movements (1919-22). In the years between 1923 and 1926, there were as many as 72 communal riots against 16 in the course of 20 years from 1900. The Hindu-Muslim problem, Mahatma Gandhi announced in March 1925, was an 'insoluble puzzle' and he would keep out of it (Datta 2002: 5035). During the 1930s the idea of a separate, independent Muslim state began to take shape in the country (Islam 1981: 55).

The division between the Hindus and the Muslims was well articulated by figures like Allama Iqbal. This poet-philosopher is credited with conceiving, articulating, and finally selling the idea of a separate Muslim polity to the Muslim League leadership, thus giving a more potent objective to the Muslim community than constitutional rights and representation in the civil services. In fact, Iqbal's view of nationalism was both ideological (creating a Muslim community on the basis of Islam) as well as territorial (bringing this community within the territorial framework of a polity). According to Iqbal a community based on Islamic ideology was not possible without a polity (*Ibid.*).

The Government of India Act of 1935 was equally pivotal in the rise of Muslim separatist nationalism, with the League under Mohammad Ali Jinnah deciding to contest elections for limited self-governing provincial governments in 1937. The overwhelming electoral victory of the Congress Party in six provinces and the party's decision of not forming coalition governments with the Muslim League – which had not fared well even in the separate Muslim constituencies – disillusioned Jinnah, who then began to propagate the merits of the two-nation theory. The Congress Party's rejection of Jinnah's demand that the League be recognized as the sole party of Indian Muslims (because the Congress itself had a substantial Muslim membership) and the misdeeds of some Congress provincial leaders embittered Jinnah and his followers even further (Paul 2005: 6-7).

Hindu-Muslim dichotomy exploded further in the 1940s, and the weakness of the secular ideology – the emblem of the desire to create a world beyond religious divisions became all too clear. Finally, the colonial government's conciliatory policy towards the Muslim League bore fruit during the Second World War, and stiffened Mohammad Ali Jinnah's resolve to achieve a Muslim homeland (Singh 1987: 238). Consequently, in March, 1940 the Muslim League voiced the demand of Pakistan. The Lahore Resolution of the Muslim League (1940) demanded an independent status for "areas in which Muslims are numerically in a majority, as in the north-western and eastern zones of India." These were to consist of five provinces: Sind, Baluchistan, North-West Frontier Province, and the Punjab in the northwest and Bengal in the east (Spate 1948: 7). Further, the May 1944 Gandhi–Jinnah talks and the June 1945 Simla conference of top Congress and Muslim League leaders failed to break the deadlock between them (Paul 2005: 7). The emergence of Pakistan was a logical consequence of these events (Islam 1981: 56).

It is important to note that the establishment of a separate homeland for Indian Muslims was also visualized by the Bengali masses (especially peasants) as emancipation from the exploitation and oppression of the ruling Hindu classes. Thus class consciousness of the Bengali Muslim peasantry was transformed into positive support for the Pakistan movement by populist leaders such as Maulana Bhashani and A.K. Fazlul Huq. But the peasants were not alone in their demand for the creation of Pakistan. Members of the decaying Muslim aristocracy, represented by Dacca-Murshidabad Nawab, and the professional middle class, represented by H.S. Suhrwardy—both numerically very small, also resented Hindu domination and competition and, therefore, supported the demand for Pakistan (Ahmed

1971: 4). The Hindu-Muslim divide became all the more serious with the passage of time and it eventually culminated into the partition of India into two states, India and Pakistan in August 1947.

2.2.a Post-Partition: Creation of Sub-Nationalism

In hindsight, one can say that Pakistan was born with a temporary sense of national identity. Various Muslim groups in the subcontinent were able to suspend their regional, ethnic, and linguistic identities. Religion as a way of life had become the predominant force as a basis for nationalism, other ethnic factors being temporarily pushed aside. But, this certainly did not mean that regional and other ethnic identities had been assimilated by this newfound sense of Muslim nationhood (Islam 1981: 57). It is important to note that barring the small urban elites, the overwhelmingly rural Muslim masses did not share common characteristics of race, language or culture. The one characteristic they had in common was the dislike for the Hindu domination which can be described as a logical consequence flowing from their Muslim-ness (Qureshi 1969: 557-558).

However, the sense of Muslim national identity became less important, once the objective of Pakistan was achieved and the external 'enemies' of the Muslim nation—the Hindus and the colonial regime were removed from the domestic political scene. Territorially the Muslims had achieved the status of a nation. But the question that remained: how could a sense of national identity be sustained in the absence of visible external threats to the Muslim nation? As the time would demonstrate, during the post independence era, the sustenance of Pakistani national identity and the process of national integration would be greatly influenced by two sets of factors: regional-ethnic diversity and the policies of Pakistani power elites (Islam 1981: 57).

It is important to note that ethnic differences or similarities per se do not necessarily lead to balkanization of a multiethnic state. They are a necessity but not a sufficient condition of dismemberment or disintegration of a country (Nordlinger 1972: 60). Bengali Muslim nationalism, as such, is the product of many complex forces (Qureshi 1972/1973: 568). In the words of G. W. Choudhury:

> The rise of Bengali sub-nationalism within Pakistan, however, had its origin in a number of factors-political, economic, cultural, sociological, etc. that had been operating since Pakistan was created in 1947. Of all the provinces which constituted Pakistan, it was Bengal which gave the most solid support to Mohammed Ali Jinnah in his struggle for the establishment

of a separate Muslim state in the sub-continent. Yet, within a very short period, the Bengalis began to have second thoughts. Although they were the majority group in Pakistan, they suffered from a deep-rooted fear of domination by the minority group of West Pakistan. In a democracy, the majority should not have any fear of domination, nor should they have to ask for safeguards, such as regional autonomy, reservation of places in the civil service and the army and guarantees that the economic development of their region would not be neglected nor their culture threatened. But for two decades the majority Bengali group did feel obliged to seek these guarantees; and when they were not granted, Bengali sub-nationalism began to gather momentum until ultimately it became a national movement for the creation of a separate state (Choudhury 1972: 242).

Similarly, Nasir Islam contends:

Bengali nationalism grew in response to the changing nature of ethnic-group inter-relations in Pakistan. It originated as ethnic conflict aimed at changing the 'dominant-subordinate' relationship between East and West and the distribution of power within the society. It began as demands for language rights and economic equality as a reaction to the central government's policies to impose Urdu on Bengalis, to reduce Bengali representation (both political and administrative) in the central government, and to increase economic disparity (Islam 1981: 62).

2.2.b Factors Leading to the Creation of Bangladesh

There were various inter-related factors for the growth of Bengali nationalism. After its independence, the capital of Pakistan and the seat of the Central Government of Pakistan was located in Karachi in West Pakistan although the majority of Pakistan's population (56%) lived in East Pakistan, a much smaller territory in size than that of West Pakistan. Further, in March 1948 Jinnah announced that Urdu should be the state language of Pakistan (Rashid 2002: 14).

2.2.b.(i) ***Imposition of Urdu*** Pakistani government wanted to have Urdu as the only state language of Pakistan (Islam 1981: 62-3). Nowhere in their thinking did Bengali, the language of more than half of the total population, figure even as the second national language (Callard 1971: 8). It may be noted that Bengali was the language of an overwhelming majority in East Pakistan. Only a small remnant of aristocratic elites, some urban groups, and refugee settlers from Bihar spoke Urdu. Even in West Pakistan, only 7-8 percent of the population spoke it (Islam 1981: 62-63). Moreover, the people in East Pakistan were not only Bengali speaking people but they were very proud of the richness and traditions of their language. Since Urdu had been declared the sole state language, the Bengalis felt that this would provide a greater edge to the Urdu-speaking people in every sector of life and society, including job opportunities in Pakistan (Rashid 2010: 3). It also created an impression that the other languages were non-Islamic (Callard 1971: 8).

The effort of the Central Government to impose Urdu as the national language and the denial of representation on the basis of population by the West led the Bengalis toward a complete distrust of the central government (Sayeed 1967: 72-73). The language issue as such initiated resentments and agitations especially among the students and intellectuals of East Pakistan. Consequently, demand was made to make Bengali as the official language and medium of instruction of the Eastern wing and made one of the state language of Western wing along with Urdu (Bammi 2010: 22). The disillusionment of people of the East Pakistan over the language issue gradually led to the language movement.

Bengali Language Movement The Language Movement of 1952 was the first major movement in Pakistan that was completely secular in character. It highlighted the link between cultural rights and emancipation from autocratic political bondage *(Ibid.*, p. 104). Another important thing which the movement did was that it sparked a renaissance of Bengali culture and an emphasis on secular ideas as opposed to Islamic ideology (Bhattachargee 1973: 82-110). As a result, the Bengali Language Movement brought a significant change in the literature of this region, especially in the field of poetry. The movement, however, was already there in embryonic form as early as 1948, that is, less than a year after Pakistan was born. One simply has to recall the historic words of Dr. Mohammad Shahidullah (1855-1969), a great scholar of Bengali language and literature and a widely revered Muslim. In one of his Presidential addresses delivered at a literary conference held in Dhaka in 1948, he said that the Muslims in East Pakistan were more Bengalis than Hindus or Muslims. He said that Nature had seen to it (Chowdhury 1997: 103).

The 1952 Language Movement inspired all including the Bengali writers to create a significant body of writings, where not only the issue of Bengali language and literature but of Bengali nationalism in a wider context occupies a central position (*Ibid.*). The Bengali poets responded to it by declaring their love for Bengali language and culture with passion. They did so in a way where the note of protest and rebellion was explicit against all forms of authoritarianism and tyranny. This poetry was nationalistic in a new way. Firmly rooted in the soil, it spoke against communalism and autocracy in no uncertain fashion. It also strove to achieve a certain level of technical excellence, notwithstanding its rich emotional content (*Ibid.*, p. 104).

On the other hand, the Bengali intellectuals began to produce literature emphasizing the distinction between culture, religion, and politics. They took to preaching rational, liberal, and secular ideas. They began to reinterpret the history of the nationalist movement emphasizing its class nature rather than its religious foundations. The Muslim League was looked upon as a political organization of landlords, the two-nation theory was refuted, and lack of participation on the part of Muslims of Bengal in the Bengali Nationalist Movement in the first decade of the twentieth century was attributed to their lack of education and backwardness (Islam 1981: 63). University students, professors, journalists, writers, and artists played an important role in reviving the Bengali culture as a reaction to the government's policy to impose Urdu or Islamization of the Bengali language. The nationalist slogan of 'Jai Bangla' was coined during this renaissance period (Islam 1981: 63).

In spite of the fact that Bengali was recognized later (1956) as one of the official languages, (Choudhury 1972: 247) the earlier decisions by the west Pakistani leaders and actions of the Pakistani political elite had made them look discriminatory, domineering, and un-trustworthy in the eyes of Bengali Muslims (Khan 1985: 843). Moreover, the Pakistan from time to time kept proposing to Islamize the language by changing its script or eliminating certain letters with a view to bringing it closer to *Urdu*. This in turn led to the sustenance of their resentments towards the central authority (Choudhury 1972: 247). Thus the Bengalis began to make demands for a weaker center and for stronger provinces in the future constitutional set-up of the country. This was the beginning of the demand for regional autonomy (Sayeed 1967: 72-73).

The language movement in general symbolised the antagonism against West Pakistan (Rahman 2002: 4558). It inevitably led to the struggle for autonomy and, in course of time, to the mass non cooperation movements of 1969 and 1970 led by Bangabandhu Sheikh Mujibur Rahman. Finally, it led to the Liberation War of 1971 (Chowdhury 1997: 104). In this regard, Philip Oldenburg in his article 'A Place Insufficiently Imagined: Language, Belief, and the Pakistan Crisis of 1971' contends, "if Bengali nationalism can be traced to the language issue, and was significantly rooted in it, then the Pakistani insistence on Urdu was one of the causes of the breakup of Pakistan (Oldenburg 1985: 727)."

2.2.b.(ii) ***Economic Factors*** It is now a well-documented fact that economic policies in Pakistan led to a sharp increase in regional and social disparity. Business interests, civil servants, landlords, and middle classes benefited from national economic policies. Agricultural workers, landless peasants, and industrial workers were excluded from sharing the benefits of the development plans. Most of these people were concentrated in relatively backward regions of the country, particularly in the Eastern Wing (Jahan 1972: 60). A report by a panel of experts to the Pakistan government's planning commission provides documentation of the increasing economic disparity between the two regions. In 1959-60, the per capita income in West Pakistan was 32 percent higher than in the East. Over the next ten years the annual rate of growth of income in West Pakistan was 6.2 per cent, while it was only 4.2 percent in East Pakistan. As a result, by 1969-70 the per capita income in the West was 61 percent higher than in the East (Mason, et al. 1971: 4). Further, as G. W. Choudhury illustrates:

> At the time of independence, gigantic efforts were made to speed up economic growth. But, tragically, the rate of economic growth in the development plans was much slower in East than in West Pakistan....The bulk of the country's revenue was spent in West Pakistan because the federal capital was there. Moreover, a high percentage of the budget was spent on defense, which was all concentrated in West Pakistan. A much larger share of development expenditure as well as of foreign aid and loans went to the West. East Pakistan earned most of the country's foreign exchange by exporting its jute; yet most of the foreign exchange was spent on the industrialisation of West Pakistan. Whether it was revenue or development expenditure, foreign assistance and loans or foreign exchange, East Pakistan did not get its fair share, though the majority of the country's population lived there (Choudhury 1972: 245-246).

In addition, the economic policies of the Pakistani government concentrated wealth in the hands of small industrial elite based in West Pakistan and transformed East Pakistan into a captive market for West Pakistani manufactured products. This virtually created a situation of internal colonialism, leading to a vertical ethnic stratification, by which a class character was imposed on ethnic differentiation (Islam 1981: 64). This colonialism was manifest in the unequal exchange, via foreign trade mechanisms, of primary products for manufactured goods. Moreover, West Pakistanis controlled industry and commerce in both wings (Oldenburg 1985: 711-712).

There seemed to have been a direct relationship between the economic disparity between the two wings and the demand for regional autonomy. As the disparity became greater, the demand for autonomy grew stronger. The students, politicians, economists, the press, and the intellectuals effectively utilized the economic argument to mobilize mass support for regional autonomy in the East Wing. The elitist political system of Pakistan was hardly responsive to the growing unrest and the demands for sharing economic and political power. The dominant elites who largely belonged to West Pakistan always reacted with selective coercion or bureaucratic persuasion but never by political accommodation. In short, conflicts and distrust, rather than compromise and confidence, marked the political process (Islam 1981: 60).

By the beginning of the 1960s, if not earlier, the conditions for Bengali disillusionment with the concept of Pakistan were already present, and at least a few political leaders and intellectuals were thinking in terms of relative autonomy, if not independence (Schuman 1972: 290-291). Many moderate East Pakistani leaders, like Nural Amin[3] and others, who also wanted to live in a united Pakistan, strongly urged the government to accelerate the economic development of East Pakistan and thereby remove the most serious grievance of the Bengali separatists. Unfortunately, this advice was not taken seriously. Instead the government in West Pakistan accused the Western powers, particularly the Americans, of encouraging secession in East Pakistan. President Bhutto in particular made these wild accusations; so did the controlled press in West Pakistan (Choudhury 1972: 245).

In fact, the situation that existed in post independence Pakistan could be compared to that which prevailed in undivided India when Jinnah convinced the Muslim intelligentsia and the masses that their rights and interests were not safe under Congress rule in India. He catalogued the list of Muslim grievances under Congress rule; whether these allegations were all true or not, the important thing was that the Muslims believed in Jinnah's version of their plight. Similarly, Sheikh Mujib and his party were highly successful in convincing the emotional Bengalis that their interests and rights were not safe with a government controlled and directed from West Pakistan. This ignited the younger and more militant sections of the Awami League to start a movement for secession (*Ibid.*, p. 246).

2.2.b.(iii) ***Political Factors*** Pakistan began its political career under a parliamentary system modeled on Westminster and under a federal constitution. But neither the parliamentary system nor the federation was genuine. The constitutional form sand trappings of democracy only provided a cloak for rule by the few who were able to concentrate power in their own hands. During eleven years (1947-58) of so-called parliamentary democracy, there was not a single general election, and the provincial elections were described as 'a farce, mockery and a fraud upon the electorate' (*Report of the Pakistan Electoral Reforms Commission*, 1956 in Choudhury 1972: 242).

The emergence of the all-powerful ruling elite had a great impact on the separatist movement in East Bengal. The ruling elite composed of senior bureaucrats, none of whom was East Bengali. Until 1958 they were supported indirectly by the army and after 1958, army support was direct and open. There was a cabinet and a parliament, but the political order in Pakistan could be called 'an oligarchy under a democratic constitution' wherein Bengalis had no share. Except during the short interval of thirteen months of H. S. Suhrawardy's cabinet in 1956-57, the Bengalis had hardly any role in national affairs. Every vital decision, whether it related to political or defense or economic or diplomatic matters, was in the final analysis made by the ruling elite, composed of West Pakistani civil and military officer (Choudhury 1972: 243).

The fact, that the bureaucracy and the military were dominated by the non- Bengalis, reinforced the alienation of the Bengali people from the central government. One very important cause of the failure of nation building in Pakistan, therefore, is the political system which came to be established there over the years. Three features of this political system intensified Bengali alienation: authoritarianism, centralisation and non-Bengali domination of the central government (Ahmed 1971: 9). Bengali representation in the national bureaucracy remained extremely weak. According to one estimate, nine years after the creation of Pakistan, only 51 top level policy-making positions were occupied by the Bengalis in the Central Secretariat out of a total of 741 such positions. Bengali representation in the army was minimal as 98 percent of the officer corps of the army, navy, and air force was composed of West Pakistanis (Islam 1981: 63).

In provincial matters, the situation was no better for the Bengalis. Even in their own province, all the key posts in the administration were held by West Pakistanis who had direct access to the central ruling clique. The country had, in theory, a federal constitution, but in practice the provincial government was entirely subordinate to the centre, particularly in financial and administrative matters. The Bengalis found a new ruling group set over them in place of the former British officials. The civil and military officials from West Pakistan stationed in East Bengal never bothered to develop any real bonds with the local population. There were few social contacts; the West Pakistani officials considered themselves to be socially superior to the Bengali Muslims (Choudhury 1972: 243). In fact, most of the West Pakistani leaders were of the opinion that Bengali Muslims were 'inferior Muslims' because of their culture and traditions (Rashid 2010: 3-4). The result was bitterness and a widening gap.

It must be pointed out, however, that at the time of independence the Indian civil service left behind by the British Raj contained only one Bengali officer. Similarly, the Bengalis were very poorly represented in the army because the British authorities had considered them to be a non-martial race. There were therefore some historical reasons for the preponderance of West Pakistani civil and military officers in East Bengal. But after independence nothing was done to rectify the situation, and, in the absence of a genuine democracy, with the country run by an oligarchy of civil and military officials, the Bengalis found themselves in the position of a colonial people (Choudhury 1972: 243-244). Moreover, the Muslim League disintegrated into many regional groups. All the political groups operated on regional bases. After the death of Jinnah and Liaqat Ali, no Pakistani leader could claim support of a national majority. The politics became fragmented, particularly in West Pakistan, where the landlords had extended their funds to the provincial and national political arenas (Sayeed 1967: 87).

Between 1950s and 70s, the Central Government of Pakistan went through a number of political changes including imposition of Military Rule and experiments with various forms of Governments, first under Ayub and then Yahya Khan. All this while East Pakistan continued to be discriminated and deprived of allocations of funds for industrial and infrastructural development and agriculture. Its quota in the civil services, armed forces and other job avenues also continued to be less, as the policy makers were mainly Punjabis or Afghans who looked down upon Bengali Muslims as inferiors, and had no common bond with them (Bammi 2010: 23-24).

Responding to the culminated grievances, Sheikh Mujibur Rahman in 1948 formed a students' organization called the Chhatra League. In 1949, Maulana Abdul Hamid Khan Bhasani and some other Bengali leaders formed the East Pakistani Awami League (AL), a party designed mainly to promote Bengali interests. Mujib became the president of the Awami League in 1966 and emerged as leader of the Bengali autonomy movement (Bammi 2010: 24). In fact, Mujib's metamorphosis from an organization man to a charismatic leader came in the 1960s. After H.S. Suhrawardy's death in

1963, the Awami League suffered a leadership vacuum. As Mujib remained in the background with the organization, Nawabzada Nasrullah Khan from West Pakistan was made the party President to play up the Awami League's national image. But Nasrullah's unimaginative leadership did nothing to improve the League's strength. After the election of 1965, when Mujib saw the Awami League slipping in popularity, he felt the need to revitalize the party and decided to step forward as the leader. Soon after assuming the party presidency, he launched the Six Points movement, which not only brought the Awami League into the limelight again but made Sheikh Mujib a popular hero (Jahan 2005: 41).

The Six Point Charter on the autonomy for East Pakistan propounded in 1966 by Awami League's Party's Chief, Sheikh Mujibur Rahman, immediately captured the imagination of the Bengali intellectuals, bureaucrats and students of East Pakistan. Soon after the Six Points Charter, a political movement started in East Pakistan to realize the demands in accordance with the Charter. Sheikh Mujib earned the name of 'Bangabandhu' (the Friend of Bengal) from the people of East Pakistan (Rashid 2002: 15).

The Six Points were as follows (Rashid 2010: 4-5):

1. The establishment of a federal form of government with Parliament to be supreme point of power, directly elected by universal adult suffrage.
2. The federal government would control only defense and foreign policy, leaving all other subjects to the federating states of East and West Pakistan.
3. The two wings would have separate (but freely convertible currency) currencies or if one currency, separate fiscal policies to prevent the flight of capital from East to West Pakistan.
4. The federal government would have no power of taxation. It would share in state taxes for the needs of foreign and defense affairs.
5. Each of the federating states would have the power to enter into trade agreements with foreign countries. They would also have full control over their earned foreign exchange.
6. The states would have their own militias or para-military.

The Pakistani leadership of the West considered the demands counter to national integration of the country. They felt that if accepted, these measures would further strengthen and enhance Bengali ethnic and linguistic unity (Bammi 2010: 25). Further, the military regime and some political leaders in West Pakistan were wary of the Six Points Charter as it threatened their power base (Rashid 2002: 16). To muzzle the growing popularity of Mujib, Rawalpindi charged Mujib Rahman with sedation and for hob-knobbing with India and started the Agartala Conspiracy case.[4] As no charges could be proved, the case was finally dropped (Bammi 2010: 25).

The Agartala Conspiracy Case was, in fact, the greatest fiasco on the part of Ayub's government. It was thought that by involving Sheikh Mujib and others in such a case and publicizing them as agents of India they could be coerced into making an end to the demands for regional autonomy and to liquidate the political position of the supporters of the six points. But it had the opposite effect, and as the trial opened and its proceedings began to appear in the newspapers, the spurious character of the conspiracy case became evident. This negative reaction was evident not only in East Pakistan but also in the West. No single factor contributed so greatly in the raising the personal popularity of Sheikh Mujib and discrediting the central government (Umar 2006: 198). The Agartala Conspiracy Case was critical on two counts: On the one hand, it instead of destroying Mujib's support, helped to build it by magnifying his role as a champion of Bengali rights, (Jahan 2005: 41) and on the other, it widened the wedge between Dhaka and Rawalpindi.

2.2.b.(iv) Other Determining Factors

On November 12, 1970, a major cyclone hit East Pakistan and devastated nearly 8000 sq km of mid-coastal low-lands and outlying islands, killing nearly 250,000 people. Not only the relief program was slow, but Yahya arrived in Dacca after two days of his visit to China and left in a day. His seemingly indifference to the worst natural disaster and indifference to the plight of the Bengali victims further created great deal of animosity between Dhaka and Rawalpindi (Bammi 2010: 25). Further, Yahya Khan turned down Indian aid saying that what came from other sources was enough and that Pakistan did not need India's assistance. This despite the fact, that due to geographical proximity, India would have been the speediest source of relief. The cyclone was in fact used by certain West Pakistani politicians and military rulers to postpone the scheduled general elections. Zulfiqar Ali Bhutto, President of the People's Party of Pakistan, advocated postponement by a few months. He had support from certain segments of the military and its intelligence which had accurately assessed that the election would bring Mujibur Rahman to supreme power on the basis of a genuine mandate of the people. Apart from using the cyclone as an excuse, riots and disturbances were perpetrated by the government in Khulna, Dhaka and some other district headquarters of East Pakistan (Dixit 1999: 32-33).

The final breaking point came after the 1970 elections of Pakistan in which Awami League won a clear majority which empowered Mujib to be the Prime Minister of Pakistan (Bammi 2010: 25-26). It was clear by the end of December 1970 that the Yahya regime and Zulfiqar Ali Bhutto were not going to allow Mujibur Rahman to form the national government or to commence drafting a new constitution responsive to the aspirations of the people of East Pakistan. Public and polemical exchanges between leaders of East Pakistan and Zulfiqar Ali Bhutto characterized events during December, 1970 and January 1971. Bhutto's non cooperative attitude prevented Yahya Khan from setting in motion even the procedure to convene the National Assembly and create a democratic Government in Pakistan (Dixit 1999: 34). On March 1, 1971, General Yahya Khan indefinitely postponed the session. This in turn threw the country into a constitutional crisis. The Awami League responded by launching an unprecedented non-violent, non-cooperation movement which resulted in the entire administration of East Pakistan coming to a virtual standstill. Even the government bureaucracy complied with the non-cooperation movement. Indeed, the movement demonstrated that the Bengali nationalists had total allegiance and support of the Bengali population (Jahan 2005: 68).

The Yahya regime in turn initiated political negotiations with the Bengali nationalists but at the same time thousands of armed forces flew in from West to East Pakistan, thus consolidating for a military action (*Ibid.*). As talks were moving towards anticipated failure, Mujibur Rahman made his famous speech at the Ramma Maidan on March 7, 1971 in which he said "The struggle now is for liberation and self-rule; the struggle this time is for independence." There have been reports that Mujib was reluctant to take this categorical public position as negotiations were to continue till March 25. He wanted to wait for the final outcome without adopting any decisive position on breaking away from Pakistan. It was the student leaders of the Awami League sharing the dais with him who virtually compelled him to make a declaration for freedom (Dixit 1999: 39).

Having failed to reach to a settlement between Bhutto and Mujib, the Pakistani military began their crackdown in Dhaka and other places in East Pakistan on the night of March 25, 1971 (Bammi 2010: 26). Citing reasons for the military crackdown Sisson and others in their book *War and Secession: Pakistan, India, and the Creation of Bangladesh* (1990) contend:

Preparation for military action was prompted by serious concern about the security of the armed forces and by mistrust of the Awami League's commitment to a united Pakistan. The senior officers, including Yahya, felt that the army had lacked leadership and direction in East Pakistan. This had begun, in their view, with Gen. Yaqub Khan's unwillingness to use sufficient force to implement his own plan to reinstitute law and order in the east and his subsequent resignation on 7 March. In their judgment, it was this softness and lack of will that had encouraged the Awami League and its supporters in the excesses to which they had gone. The lack of central direction had also been accompanied by the development of a siege mentality within army units. When the troops returned to their barracks after the abortive crackdown in early March, cantonments had become increasingly isolated in pockets cut off from rations and supplies, without central command providing focus and direction. Because of their physical and emotional isolation, the military command feared, the forces in East Pakistan would at best become prisoners in their cantonments and ultimately be forced to leave East Pakistan without a fight unless preemptive action were taken; at worst they would have to fight a civil war in which they were pitted against Bengali troops, police, and guerrillas while lacking effective centralized command and lines of supply. Such an eventuality was unthinkable to the military (Richard et al. 1990: 132-133).

Bhutto left for Karachi on March 25, 1971 the day on which Yahya Khan had promised to reconvene the postponed session of the National Assembly. Orders for military operations were directed not only against the Awami league and its youth wing but also against the East Bengal Regiment of the Pakistani Army and the East Pakistani Rifles. Similarly, East Pakistani police barracks in all the major cities were proposed to be surrounded by West Pakistani forces and neutralized (Dixit 1999: 40). Three provisions were given highest priority: (1) the Awami League and its supporters were to be treated as rebels; (2) East Pakistani units of the military forces were to be disarmed along with the police; and (3) the top leaders of the Awami League and antigovernment student leaders were to be arrested (*Ibid.*, p. 132).

General Tikka Khan was given instructions to launch a district-wise military operation against the Awami League and the people of East Pakistan on the evening of March 25. Yahya Khan flew out of Dhaka within a couple of hours of giving these orders. Lt. General Tikka Khan now had 70,000 troops under his command in East Pakistan. West Pakistani troops outnumbered the troops of the East Bengal Regiment, the East Pakistani

Rifles and the East Pakistani Police force. Tikka Khan launched his genocidal operations with brutal precision. His troops attacked and killed all the personnel at the regiment headquarters of Dhaka police at Rajabagh. There was military resistance from the Bengali personnel of these military and para-military organizations, but in vain as they were up against an overwhelming force which included armour and artillery (Dixit 1999: 41-42).

Pakistani troops also attacked the campus of the Dhaka University and the Bengali troops at all the major metropolitan centres of East Pakistan. The worst carnage was at Jagannath Hall in Dhaka University and the girls' hostel there. Hundreds of students were killed. The university building was seriously damaged. Mujib went underground sometime around midnight on March 25, 1971. A pre-recorded broadcast by him declaring East Pakistan as a newly independent country called Bangladesh went on the air from a clandestine radio station established by the Awami League at Rangpur and Rajshahi districts in the north-western part of the country. Simultaneously the battalion commander of the East Bengal Regiment at Chittagong, Major Ziaur Rahman (who became President of Bangladesh in 1976-77), briefly captured the Chitagong radio station and broadcast a declaration announcing the establishment of free Bangladesh and appealing to all Bengali military and para-military personnel to resist the Pakistani army. In fact, Ziaur Rahman's broadcast came a little earlier than Mujib's broadcast. He was the first Bengali military officer of the Pakistan army to declare his loyalty to the new country (Dixit 1999: 42). Meanwhile the genocide continued.

India was closely monitoring the situation. Prime Minister Indira Gandhi in a series of statements in both Houses of parliament between March and May, 1971, expressed growing concern about developments in East Pakistan and India's support for the restoration of the democratic processes in Pakistan. Mrs. Gandhi also strongly criticized the military action of the Government of Pakistan. Her views had the unanimous support of all political parties and unqualified support of Indian public opinion (*Ibid.*, p. 43). In April an Indian parliamentary resolution demanded that the Government of India should support the people of East Pakistan in their liberation movement and supply aid to the rebels there.[5]

By the middle of April, the liberation struggle in Bangladesh had become an operational fact. It however took nearly seven months for the world at large to acknowledge this struggle as a political reality. Even India was cautious in publicly proclaiming its support for the break-up of a neighbouring country through military means till August-September 1971, though by the end of May, 1971, the inner deliberations of the Government of India considered supporting the liberation struggle as unavoidable (Dixit 1999: 46). According to J. N. Dixit – "political and psychological factors characterizing the East Pakistan crisis made India's involvement in the liberation struggle inescapable. The point to be underlined is that India's support to the liberation struggle of Bangladesh was not a pre-planned, conspiratorial strategic move but a politico-strategic response to the continuous threats which Pakistan had been posing against the unity and territorial integrity of India right since the partition of the country in 1947 (*Ibid.,* p. 46)."

In the immediate aftermath of the military crackdown and the arrest of Sheikh Mujibur Rahman, senior leaders of the East Pakistani Awami League escaped to India and sought Indian support for the establishment of a government in exile which was named 'Mujibnagar'. Elaborating on these developments, Dixit writes:

> The first formal step India took was to allow the establishment of such a government in exile under the leadership of Syed Nazrul Islam and Tajuddin Ahmed. The second move was to give refuge to East Bengali military and para-military personnel who escaped to India as they were particular targets of the extensive military crackdown. India assured support for the fulfillment of the aspirations of the people of East Bengal and urged the Government of Pakistan to release Sheikh Mujibur Rahman and to negotiate a peaceful political settlement of the crisis. Meanwhile efforts were made to appeal for international support and arms aid to the liberation struggle… The Mujibnagar Government operating from the Indian Border was provided with headquarters at the Camac Street in Calcutta. The Indian Ministry of External Affairs opened a full-fledged secretariat in Calcutta to liaise with the Mujibnagar Government under Nazrul Islam and Tajuddin Ahmed. The secretariat was headed by one of the senior officers of the Indian Foreign service, Mr. A. K. Ray, who had been Deputy High Commissioner in East Pakistan, and was Joint Secretary in charge of the Pakistan division at the headquarters when the crisis blew up (Dixit 1999: 43-47).

Wary of the growing involvement of India, the Pakistan Air Force (PAF) launched a pre-emptive strike on India. However, the plan failed to achieve the desired success and was seen as an open act of unprovoked aggression against India. Indira Gandhi declared war on Pakistan and in aid of the Mukti Bahini, then ordered the immediate mobilization of troops and launched the full scale invasion. This marked the official start of the Indo-Pak war (Trivedi 2008: 105).

On December 3, 1971, a full-scale war broke out between India and Pakistan. The Indian army, supported by Mukti Bahini units also established operational bases in Pakistan on the east, west, and the north. The outcome of the conflict on the eastern front after December 6 was not in doubt, as the Indian military had all the advantages. Its force was considerably larger, much better armed, more mobile, and had complete control of the air and sea. It had established excellent logistical supply lines right up to the border and had ready access to the rivers and roads in East Pakistan. The Pakistani forces, in contrast, were cut off from the outside world and had insufficient supplies. The Pakistanis also had to deal with a basically hostile local populace, while the Indians, acting through the Mukti Bahini and the Awami League, had excellent local intelligence that gave them a deciding advantage over the Pakistanis. In addition, most Pakistani units had been involved in a difficult struggle against the rebel forces for six months and were both physically and emotionally exhausted (Richard et al. 1990: 214). It is also believed that India's external intelligence agency; the RAW played a crucial role in providing logistic support to the Mukti Bahini during the initial stages of the war. In fact, RAW's operations in East Pakistan, was the largest covert mission in the history of South Asia (Trivedi 2008: 106).

The war lasted barely two weeks from December 3-17, 1971. On December 16, 1971 Pakistan's commander, Lieutenant General A.A.K. Niazi, with his troops, surrendered to Lieutenant General J.S. Aurora, the Indian commander of the combined Indian and Mukti Bahini forces at the Dhaka Stadium, signaling the birth of Bangladesh.[6] On the western front too, India pushed back the Pakistani forces from Jammu and Kashmir from the Rann of Kutch. India had captured strategic locations in Jammu and Kashmir and about 5000 square kilometers of Pakistan territory in southern Punjab and Sind, when it declared a unilateral ceasefire in the western sector on December 16, 1971 (Dixit 1999: 93-94).

Highlighting India's role in the freedom struggle of Bangladesh Robert Jackson aptly encapsulates:

Both officially and unofficially, India played a critical role in mobilizing support for Bangladesh. The genocide and the resultant influx of the ten million refugees in West Bengal and neighboring states created unofficial sympathy. The press, political parties, and voluntary organizations in India pressed Prime Minister Indira Gandhi to immediately intervene in Bangladesh when the Pakistan army cracked down in March 1971. The Indian government initially declined to intervene but gave moral and financial support to the Bangladesh Government in exile as well as the freedom fighters. It also sponsored a systematic international campaign in favor of Bangladesh. And finally in December 1971, when the ground was well prepared, Bangladesh was liberated as a result of direct Indian army intervention (Jackson 1975: 75).

The military crackdown by the Pakistani forces resulted in nearly ten million refugees, mostly Hindus and Bengali Muslims fleeing to Indian states of Assam, Tripura and Meghalaya, which resulted in a massive relief and human problem. Though world opinion was gradually turning against Pakistan for the genocide being carried out by her Army against her own nationals, United States, China and few other countries continued to side with Pakistan. The crackdown by the Pakistani army and their supporters was not restricted to Mukti Bahini, but also on the innocent and un-armed civilians, Muslims and Hindus – men, women and children of all ages (Bammi 2010: 27). In the liberation struggle nearly 3 million people including intellectuals and students were massacred and more than 2, 00,000 women were raped. On the Indian side, the Indian Armed Forces sacrificed 1521 lives, while another 4061 all ranks were wounded during the liberation struggle (*Ibid.*, p. 28). Over 9,000 Pakistani soldiers were killed (*The Hindu*, July 28, 2012) with India taking 93,000 prisoners of war (POW), the largest number of soldiers taken prisoner in world history, and only comparable with the Russian army capturing the entire corps of Field Marshal Von Paoli at the battle of Stalingrad (Dixit 1999: 93-94).

Bangladesh was thus born on December 16, 1971. India recognized Bangladesh as a sovereign country on 6 December while the armed conflicts between India and Pakistan continued. Bhutan and Burma (now Myanmar) accorded recognition to Bangladesh soon after 16 December, 1971 (Rashid 2010: 6). The new nation was named Bangladesh on 10 January 1972 and became a parliamentary democracy under a constitution which enshrined four basic principles of nationalism, secularism, socialism and democracy (Bammi 2010: 29).

2.3 Section II

2.3.a The Emergence of Bangladesh & India-Bangladesh Relations under Mujib

Bangladesh's emergence was a major historical event in the sub-continent. With the major chunk of its territory surrounded by the India and its whole hearted material and moral support for the Liberation War, Bangladesh was bound to have intimate ties with India. Further, its domestic challenges made it imperative to establish close links with India in the immediate years of independence. Two macro-level challenges which Bangladesh faced immediately after coming into existence were, domestically to ensure politico-economic consolidation, and to gain international recognition for its sovereign existence (Dixit 1999: 130).

Mujibur Rahman sent three requests to Mrs. Gandhi immediately after assuming charge. First, he desired Indian personnel with experience in district administration to come and serve in Bangladesh on deputation for a period of three to six months till Bangladesh civil servants could replace them. Second, he wanted a part of the Indian armed forces to remain in Bangladesh for about a year more to neutralize pockets on anti-Bangladesh resistance within the country. Third, that India should render across the broad economic assistance and help create a Bangladeshi national airlines and shipping. He desired that India undertake the repair of main roads, bridges and railway communications. India was prompt in responding to these requirements. (*Ibid.*, pp.131-132). Consequently, India gave commodity assistance to the tune over US $ 32 million. Another about $ 12 million of aid was given to Bangladesh to meet its foreign exchange requirements. The Indian Railway Board and the Corps of Engineers of the Indian Army repaired 247 bridges and restored 1, 714 miles of railway tracks. Sappers from the Indian Army and the engineers from the Public Works Department restored river communications and repaired all the major airfields of Bangladesh between 1972 and 1973 (Dixit 1999: 181). Besides India's assistance to Bangladesh to address its food security was of prime importance. In fact, by November 1972, India had supplied 931,000 tons of food to address the food crisis in Bangladesh (*Asian Recorder*, June10-16, 1972 in Nair 2008: 50). Apart from it, India also decided to give at least Rs. 100 crores (around $ 133 million) immediately to Bangladesh for reconstruction. Both the governments also finalized a detailed agreement which envisaged an annual trade of Rs. 1,000 crores (around $1.3 billion) (*The Statesman*, December 8, 1971).

To strengthen the relations with India, the Foreign Minister of Bangladesh Abdus Samad Azad, paid an official visit to India from January 5-9, 1972. Sheikh Mujibur Rahman, the Prime Minister of Bangladesh on the invitation of India visited India between February 6-8, 1972. While addressing a mammoth gathering of the people of Calcutta, he expressed gratitude on behalf of the Government and people of Bangladesh to the neighbouring states of West Bengal, Tripura, Meghalaya and Assam, for the hospitality and assistance given to millions of Bangladesh citizens and for the moral and material support given by the Government and the people of India to the struggle for liberation. In a joint statement issued in New Delhi on February 8 after talks between Mrs. Indira Gandhi and Mujibur Rahman, both the leaders agreed that Indian forces would withdraw from Bangladesh by March 25, 1972 and every means would be adopted to ensure the return of all refugees from India. They also expressed their determination to promote in every possible way the cooperation between the Governments and people of the two countries inspired by a vision of lasting peace, amity and good neighbourliness (*Foreign Affairs Record* 1972: 36-38).

Subsequently Indian Army was withdrawn thirteen days ahead of the schedule and Mrs. Gandhi visited Dhaka on March17, 1972. The joint communiqué issued after the end of the visit contained the efforts which the two countries would make so as to strengthen the bonds of friendship. Firstly, it was decided that regular consultations shall be held between the officials of the Ministries of the Foreign Affairs, Defense, Planning Commissions and the Ministries and departments dealing with economic, commercial, cultural and technical affairs of the two countries. Secondly, a Joint Rivers Commission comprising of experts of both the countries on a permanent basis to carry out a comprehensive survey of the river system shared by the two countries, formulate projects concerning both the countries in the field of flood control and implement them. Efforts were to be made so that the water resource of the region can be utilized on an equitable basis for mutual benefit of the people of the two countries. Thirdly, the joint communiqué reviewed the progress of deliveries of supplies of food grains and other commodities under the economic assistance programme and recognized the need to accelerate deliveries under this programme in view of the urgent economic need of the rehabilitation programmes in Bangladesh. Fourthly, both the Prime Ministers approved the principles of the revival of Transit Trade and the Agreement on border trade. Fifthly, both the Prime Ministers desired for science and technological cooperation. Thus, experts and officials of both the countries would hold consultations and exchange information on peaceful uses of nuclear energy, technological and scientific research for industrial development and utilization of the future space research for communication purposes. Sixthly, efforts were to be made towards cultural cooperation between the two countries (Bindra 1982: 17-19).

The two countries in order to extend their cooperation to another level signed the Indo-Bangladesh Friendship Treaty on March 19, 1972. New Delhi also extended cultural cooperation to Bangladesh in consonance with the spirit of article[7] of the Indo-Bangladesh treaty. Thus, a cultural cooperation agreement was signed between the two countries in the field of culture, education, science and technology on December 30, 1972 (*Asian Recorder*, June10-16 in Nair 2008: 51). Further, a treaty of cooperation in the field of atomic research and development was signed in Dhaka on August 27, 1973. Besides, India also offered 100 scholarships annually to Bangladesh nationals for higher studies and research. In this regard, it was agreed by both the countries agreed to encourage collaborations between the respective societies, universities and research institutions (Nair 2008: 51).

However, the 1972 friendship treaty which India and Bangladesh had signed began to be criticized. Soon the signing of the treaty was seen by many as either unnecessary or as something imposed by India on Bangladesh. In this regard S. A. Zafar in his article 'Indo-Bangladesh Relations: Problems and Prospects' argues:

The Indian attitude towards Bangladesh and other smaller neighbours stems from its expansionist policy and hegemonic aspirations arrogantly perceived to have been bestowed upon it by history. India's perception of having taken over the mantle of power in 1947 from the departing British Raj has imparted to it an egoistic notion of the responsibility to ensure the security of South Asia; which explains why India has been pressurising the smaller countries of the region not to establish any security links with countries outside the area. India does not tolerate even the mutual help and assistance that the other nations of the subcontinent want to render to each other to overcome their security problems. It also developed a doctrine parallel to the Monroe Doctrine during the ethnic crisis in Sri Lanka in early 1980s. It was in this context that India had earlier imposed the Treaty of Friendship on Bangladesh in 1972, Article 9 of which, implying mutual defense in the case of any attack on the Dhaka regime, would have enabled India to militarily intervene in support of its protégé Mujib or anyone else supporting the Indian supremacy in order to ensure that Bangladesh remains an Indian backyard (Zafar 1993: 90).

In similar vein Harun ur Rashid contends – "Although there were genuine concerns for Bangladesh at that nascent stage, the questions often asked are: was it necessary to conclude a Treaty for such a long period? Could those concerns have been addressed without a Treaty? My short answer to both the questions is that a Treaty for the 25 year period was not needed (Rashid 2010: 12)." On the other hand Ishtiaq Hossain refuting allegations on India argues that the sources close to Sheikh Mujibur Rahman suggest an entirely different story. Rather than being pressured, Sheikh was the one who approached Mrs. Indira Gandhi on such a treaty, and on his insistence, the Friendship Treaty was signed during the Indian Prime Minister's first visit to Bangladesh. He further contends:

> Mujib's insistence on signing the treaty may be explained in two ways. First, Mujib wanted to show by signing the treaty that Bangladesh was truly sovereign and independent. He believed that the act of signing a treaty would demonstrate that Bangladesh was capable of managing its own affairs and making decisions on its own. Second, it is argued by many in Bangladesh that Mujib may have wanted Indian support in any future political upheavals in his country. Article 9 of the Indo-Bangladesh Friendship Treaty provides for mutual consultations between the two signatories in order to remove a threat if either of them is attacked. It is interesting to note that the clause does not limit this to an 'external attack'. Therefore, it is argued that this 'attack' could also apply to an attempt to capture power in Bangladesh by any quarter hostile to India, using means other than political. In this scenario, the treaty could be invoked and Indian troops invited into Bangladesh. In fact, during the army coups and counter coups of November 3-7, 1975, there were reports of Indian troop movements along the Bangladesh borders. It is also alleged that Brigadier Khalid Musharraf, who briefly held power during the November 3-7, 1975 period, was about to invoke the treaty when he was toppled and killed (Ali 1973, in Hossain 1981: 1116).

J.N. Dixit recounting his personal experience recounts:

> Mujibur Rahman asked Mrs. Gandhi as to what kind of document should be issued at the end of her visit. Mrs. Gandhi turned to T. N. Kaul and asked what it should be like. Kaul said normally a joint communiqué is issued summarizing the decisions taken by the Prime Ministers. Mujib interjected, saying: "Didi, what is better than a communiqué?" Kaul said: "A joint declaration." Mujib persisted, and inquired what was better than a joint declaration, upon which D. P. Dhar said "a bilateral treaty of friendship and cooperation." Then Mujibur Rahman ventured that he would like to have both a joint declaration and a bilateral treaty if Mrs. Gandhi would agree. Mrs. Gandhi responded by saying that she would go by whatever the Prime Minister of Bangladesh desired (Dixit 1999: 151-152).

Nevertheless, within months after the signing of the Treaty a few opposition parties in Bangladesh were annoyed because they believed that the Treaty demonstrated mistaken set of priorities between the two countries. This view has led many to conclude that India's assistance to Bangladesh during the Liberation War was motivated primarily to assert its dominance in South Asia. A smaller Pakistan without the territory of Bangladesh would hardly be a match for India (Rashid 2010: 16).

This was perhaps the beginning of the change of the Bangladeshi perceptions towards India and the inherent bilateral problems only compounded to it. The next issue in dispute in Indo-Bangladesh relations in the immediate post-1971 years was the trade pact signed between the two countries in 1972. The central feature of this pact was the creation of ten miles of free trade zones on both sides of the border, designed ostensibly to promote closer trade relations between Bangladesh and India. Taking advantage of the free trade zones, smugglers on both sides of the borders became active. Jute, food stuffs, relief goods, and other essentials from the hinterland in Bangladesh were collected inside the free trade zone and then smuggled into India. Similarly, consumer goods, medicine, tobacco, etc., found their way into Bangladesh from India (Hossain 1981: 1116-1117). In this regard, S. A. Zafar states, "that medicines and low quality consumer goods were dumped by India in Bangladesh. This process inflicted heavy economic losses on the Bangladesh government and raised the cost of living in the country by 50 per cent. Consequently, people pressed Mujib to cancel the trade pact which, on the aggregate, was causing Bangladesh through the massive smuggling, a loss of 15 billion takas annually according to official estimates, three times more than Bangladesh earned from exports during the same period (Zafar 1993: 91)."

The increases in the cost of living index were partly blamed on the trade pact with India, and there was strong public pressure on Mujib to cancel it. Some clauses of the Indo-Bangladesh Friendship Treaty had already created suspicions in Bangladesh, and the concept of a free trade zone in the trade pact further fueled rising fears of Indian domination. The Mujib administration tried desperately to contain smuggling, but with no success. These efforts came to naught because all the conditions for the activity, that is, extreme shortage of supply of goods, mounting inflation and rapid erosion of the internal purchasing power of money, artificial over-valuation of currency, illegal transfer of capital and so on, were present in Bangladesh during the immediate post-1971 years (Hossain 1981: 1117).

The issue of Prisoners of War (POW) became another issue of contention in Indo-Bangladesh Relations in its immediate years. In this regard Harun ur Rashid states:

One can see the merit in the transfer of the thousands of Pakistani prisoners of war to India because of the reasons of their personal safety. However, by transferring 195 prisoners of war accused of war crimes, genocide and crimes against humanity from the custody of Bangladesh government, India held the key to trial of the prisoners of war. Furthermore, the very fact that India had the custody of all Pakistani prisoners of war strengthened the hands of India in dealing with Pakistan after 1971 war. This move of transfer of the prisoners of war was not appreciated by many in Bangladesh. Many argue that if these Pakistani prisoners of war had not been moved, Bangladesh would have been able to set the pace of the trial of 195 prisoners of war. This in turn would have given Bangladesh a great leverage in settlement of disputes with Pakistan. By agreeing to transfer them to the Indian custody, Bangladesh faced practical difficulties in putting them to trial in the absence of prisoners of war in Bangladesh soil (Rashid 2002: 26-27).

On the Indian side, it is argued that India had advised Bangladesh that holding of war crimes trials was its sovereign discretion; India would go along with whatever decision Bangladesh took. According to India, Bangladesh had two options; the prisoners should either be released after resumption of contacts with Pakistan under appropriate agreements, or kept in Bangladesh if it insisted on holding them for a long time (Dixit 1999: 148).

Further, there was the thorny question of weapons and military stores captured by the Indian Army from the Pakistanis during the liberation war. The Indian military advisers were not very enthusiastic about returning the weapons and other material captured from the Pakistanis. They felt that returning these weapons to Bangladesh would become the basis for Bangladesh's future dependence on the Pakistani weapon systems rooted in Pakistan's membership of military alliance arrangements with the US and others (*Ibid.*, pp. 144-145). Apart from it, the improper behavior of the Indian soldiers during and after the war also came to fore. There were reports that some of the elements in Indian army were greedy and unscrupulous in their conduct and forcibly took away foreign made cars and other consumer goods as 'booty' from Bangladesh. It was alleged that a big carpet was looted from a University residential hall in Dhaka, and many private and public owned cars from Bangladesh were taken to India, including military hardware (Rashid 2010: 8). More so a section of anti-India element in Bangladesh felt that Rakhi Bahini[8] had been created to challenge the Bangladesh Army and the part played by Freedom Fighters and that it could be used as a disguise by the Indians to re-enter Bangladesh (Bammi 2010: 30-31).

It was also alleged that India interfered in the day to day administration of Bangladesh. It may be recalled here that it was on Mujib's request that the Indian government had deployed Indian administrators to manage the day to day administration in Bangladesh. It was believed that the Awami

League was a puppet in Indian hands. They did not like the Indian advisers coming to Bangladesh to advise the Government at the time of preparing the Five-Year Plan, Budget etc (Bindra 1982: 23). It was also believed in Bangladesh that the Indian advisers in most cases was found to be less qualified than his/her counterpart in Bangladesh. Furthermore, the attitude of many of the Indian advisers was perceived to be arrogant to Bangladeshi officials, as they behaved as if Bangladesh officials were somewhat 'inferior' to them in terms of competence, experience and skill. In fact, the appointment of Indian advisers led many bureaucrats to believe that the move was a pretext on the part of India to influence the decisions of the Bangladesh Government. Thus, from the very beginning, this perception did not seem to advance a healthy and balanced relationship between the two nations (Rashid 2010: 9-10).

The print media of both the countries also played a major part in creating a negative attitude amongst each other. Indian newspapers like Amrit Bazar Patrika, Hindustan Standard and Jugantar (Bengali Paper) had published derogatory references and cartoons about Bangladeshi leaders. A cartoon of Moulana Bhashani standing naked but refusing to accept clothes supplied by Marwaris had appeared in one of the Calcutta newspapers. The same newspaper in an editorial called Bhashani 'Badmash'. This created strong resentments among the people of Bangladesh (Bindra 1982: 23). On the other hand the media in Bangladesh too had become critical of India and as such much anti-Indian news began to be published. This played a critical role in shaping negative perceptions towards India.

The most pertinent factors however, that impinged Indo-Bangladesh Relations, during the initial years was the failure to resolve the three crucial bilateral issues between them. They were (a) Sharing of the Ganges waters on a permanent basis and the Farakka issue; (b) the delimitation of sea boundary in the Bay of Bengal and (c) re-drawing the land boundary between the two countries.

2.3.b Sharing of the Ganges waters

The problems of sharing of the Ganges waters were among the most contentious issues since the birth of Pakistan. As noted earlier, various negotiations and consultations at various levels had taken place between India and Pakistan over the Farakka issue. Although communications on the question were initiated in 1951, it was not until 1960 that both India and Pakistan agreed to meet to discuss the matter. Between 1960 and 1970, ten meetings at the expert and secretary levels were held between the two countries but in vain (Hossain 1981: 1118). When the talks commenced between India and Bangladesh on the issue, India was at its final stage to build a barrage at Farakka (11 miles from the Bangladesh border in the West) on the Ganges River to divert its water to flush the silt of the Hoogly river bear Kolkata (Rashid 2010: 29). The barrage, 7,229 feet long and with 108 spans, proposed to divert 40,000 cusecs of water from the Ganga into the Bhagirathi-Hoogly river during the lean period. Bangladesh felt that if such a huge quantum of water was diverted during the dry season, there will obviously be serious shortage of irrigational water which would make the seven northern districts of Bangladesh a desert. Moreover, the barrage would also disrupt the agriculture pattern, water transport, fish wealth etc. of Bangladesh. A section of the people feared that India, by not providing water to them, wanted to cripple the economy of Bangladesh for ever so that it would always be subservient to India (Bindra 1982: 23).

However, the most important step in this direction was taken in 1972 when the prime ministers of both countries agreed to establish on a permanent basis a Joint Rivers Commission (JRC) to be composed of experts drawn from the two countries. The chief aim of the JRC was to "carry out a comprehensive survey of the river systems shared by both the countries in the fields of flood control and implement them" (*India-Bangladesh Joint Declaration* March 19, 1972). Although not specifically entrusted with Farakka, the JRC nevertheless assisted in the negotiations between India and Bangladesh. A joint declaration issued following Mujib's visit to New Delhi in May 1974 called for a mutually agreed solutions on Farakka issue (*Bangladesh Documents*, Vol. 2, no. 4, in Ishtiaq Hossain 1981: 1119). Similarly, in July 1974, at a Ministerial level meeting with Bangladesh, India agreed once again that mutually accepted solution would be arrived at before operation the barrage (Rashid 2002: 35).

The two sides also expressed their firm support of a mutually beneficial agreement before the Farakka Barrage was commissioned in 1975. But differences soon arose over the question of the augmentation of the fair weather flow of the Ganges. Bangladesh proposed augmentation through storage in the Ganges basin, while the Indian proposal included augmentation of water through diversion of water from the Brahmaputra by excavating a 200-mile link canal to the Ganges and the construction of two dams in the Brahmaputra basin at Dihang and Subansari (Majlis 1978: 134). The Indian proposal for constructing a link canal through Bangladesh territory was not accepted by Dacca authorities on the grounds that the "diversion of the Brahmaputra water during the lean months would cause adverse effects on its down streams and the excavation of a link canal (through Bangladesh) would cause problems in Bangladesh (*Bangladesh Documents*, Vol. 2, no. 4, in Ishtiaq Hossain 1981: 1119).

Apart from it, the two countries also differed over the amount of water to be funnelled into Bangladesh. During the dry season (March-May) the average discharge below Farakka is estimated to be only 55,000 cusecs (cubic feet per second). India maintains that it needs 40,000 cusecs of water to flush the Hooghly River, leaving the rest for possible use by Bangladesh. But Bangladesh demands the entire amount of 55,000 cusecs during the dry season to flush the Padma, which flows out of the Ganges further downstream into Bangladesh (Hossain 1981: 1119-1120). Moreover, India's proposal to commission the Farakka Barrage as a test-run to divert the waters during the dry season (April and may) was not welcomed by Bangladesh (Rashid 2010: 31). The sharing of Ganges water remained unsolved during the Mujib era.

2.3.c The Problem of the Maritime Boundary Demarcation

Another problem which grappled India-Bangladesh relations immediately after Bangladesh's independence is the dispute over the maritime boundary demarcation. Disagreement arose mainly when the Bangladesh government in 1974 signed contracts to share production with six oil companies, granting those oil and natural gas exploration rights in its territorial waters in the Bay of Bengal. The Bangladesh line moved toward the south from the edge of its land boundary, while the Indian line took a southeasterly direction, thus creating an angle within which lie thousands of square miles of the bay claimed by each country as its economic zone (Rahman 1984: 1308). This overlapping has become a critical problem between the two neighboring countries. Thus the delimitation of maritime boundaries became an all-important matter for Bangladesh and India. The concave nature of the Bangladesh coast made the resolution of the issue difficult. Bangladesh's position is that no rigid principle can be applied in the present case and that the basic guideline is equity. India, on the other hand, applies the principle of 'equidistance' in delimiting the boundary, ignoring the physical features of the coast (*Ibid.*).

2.3.d The Problem of Land boundary Demarcation

The problem of land boundary demarcation became another major irritant in India-Bangladesh relations. In the case of the Indo-Bangladesh border, several villages or pockets of land were located in one country but occupied by citizens of the other. Known as 'in adverse possession', there were 111 such enclaves in India's possession, and 51 in Bangladesh. Under the 1974 agreement between Indira Gandhi and Sheikh Mujibur Rahman, it was agreed that these enclaves would be handed over to the respective sides (Banerjee 2001: 1505). The problem of Dahagram, Berubari and Angarpopta enclaves were previously between India and Pakistan. But after the liberation of Bangladesh, this problem too like others would be settled amicably, it was felt. Under the agreement while the Berubari union would remain in India, Bangladesh would retain the Dahagram and Angarpota enclaves. To connect Dahagram with Paubari Moaza in Bangladesh, India would lease in perpetuity land corridor (Teen Bigha) measuring 178 metres by 85 metres to Bangladesh. It was also agreed to define the border more accurately at certain points and the demarcation of the land boundaries between the two countries would be completed (*Foreign Affairs Record* 1974: 92-96). However, the Land Boundary agreement could not be ratified in the India Parliament and as such, the boundary problems remained unresolved.

In spite of some contentious issues and anti-Indian feelings prevailing in the minds of some sections of people of Bangladesh, there were some positive trends in Indo-Bangladesh relations worth recalling. In this regard, a brief reference to India's economic assistance to Bangladesh during 1972-73 is called for. India gave commodity assistance to the tune of Rs 25 (around $ 32 million) to 30 crore (around $ 39 million). Another Pound 5 million ($ 12 million) of aid was given to Bangladesh to meet its foreign exchange requirements. The Indian Railway Board and Corps of Engineers of the Indian Army repaired 247 bridges and restored 1,714 miles of railway tracks. Sappers from Indian Army and engineers from the Public Works Department restored river communications and repaired all the major airfields of Bangladesh between 1972 and 1973 (Dixit 1999: 181).

Both countries also signed various cultural, scientific and trade agreements. To develop the cultural ties between the two countries India and Bangladesh on September 27, 1974 signed a two year protocol for exchange programmes in fields of culture, education, information and sports. India offered to give scholarships, send eminent musicians to conduct short term courses in Bangladesh, in classical music and dance. The protocol also provided for exchange of visits by academicians, scientists, educational, literary figures, cultural troops and sportsmen. In addition, a treaty was also signed by the two countries on August 27, 1973 in Dhaka which provided for exchange of information between the two countries on atomic research and literature published by the two atomic energy commissions (Bindra 1982: 24-28).

As we shall see in the succeeding chapters, trade and economic inducements have often been used to propel India-Bangladesh relations. This trend, however, was evident even in the early years of Bangladesh independence. The trade relations between the two countries got a major boost, when on May 16, 1974 a number of agreements on wide ranging economic and trade cooperation between India and Bangladesh emerged from the five day high-level discussions between the two countries. In addition, India agreed to extend three credits totaling Rs. 41 crores ($ 52.6 million) to Bangladesh. It was also agreed to set up a ministerial-level commission for closer cooperation in the production, trade, technical development, manufacture and promotion of jute (*Foreign Affairs Record* 1973: 269-270). To further boost the trade between the two countries, a trade protocol was signed on December 17, 1974 which provided the facilities to both the countries in switching over to trade in freely convertible currency from January 1, 1975 (Bindra 1982: 26).

However, the honeymoon phase of Indo-Bangladesh relations came to an end by the spring of 1973. The symptoms which confirmed this were the instances where, certain leaders of the Awami League, such as Khondakar Mushtaq Ahmed, started questioning India's motivations in Bangladesh' liberation movement. In fact, the events from second half of 1972 not only gave inkling to it but also showed that the Indian expectations proved to have lacked a clear understanding of the deep undercurrents in the psyche of the Bangladesh power structure under Sheikh Mijibur Rahman. Indian anticipations also lacked in political realism as the latter developments proved. Bangladesh's attitude under Mujib though not expressed overtly and clearly, were quite different from Indian expectations (Dixit 1999: 156-175). Mujib, in fact, did not want to be overly dependent on India and that he was a puppet of India. This can be deduced from the fact that he declined Indian aircraft but chose British aircraft to return to Bangladesh from London on January 10, 1972 after his release from prison in Pakistan and this was not tolerable to India. It is also believed that in the early 70s, India wanted to use the Bangladesh territory under the Friendship Treaty to transport security forces to Arunachal Pradesh but Bangladesh refused it (Rashid 2010: 24).

Mujib was also conscious that if Bangladesh earned sufficient recognition from important countries and developed the minimum required levels of bilateral political, economic and technological relations, he would have to depend less on India's substantive support and assistance. In keeping with this approach, he was clear in his mind that he did not wish to be over-dependent on India. He also (quite logically) did not wish Bangladesh to be dubbed a client State of India, as was being anticipated by many political observers and analysts from different parts of the world. He was of the view that while pending disputes and issues should be resolved amicably through political dialogue, there was not going to be any compromises on the part of Bangladesh on issues which could affect Bangladesh's vital interests as perceived by him. He also wanted to consolidate his own leadership and the Awami league's sway over Bangladesh politics. Further, he wanted to focus on the political consolidation and economic reconstruction of Bangladesh. For this he felt that he had to gain recognition from important countries, particularly from US, China and Pakistan. By June 1972 he had decided to compromise on the question of release of prisoners of war and the holding of war crime trials in order to establish relations with Pakistan (Dixit 1999: 156-157).

Another important thing to note is that, during his last year, though secular in policy, Mujib showed inclination to move towards political Islam. He revived the Islamic Academy banned since 1972 for suspected collusion with Pakistani forces, banned manufacture and sale of alcohol, banned gambling. He replaced his trademark salutation of 'Joy Bangla', with 'Khuda Hafiz'. He also sought membership of the Organization of Islamic Countries (OIC) and travelled to Lahore in 1974 to attend the summit (Bammi 2010: 31). India perceived it as Bangladesh shifting from its secularist orientation to being a pro-Islamic country (Rashid 2010: 24). It was also Mujib's assessment that Bangladesh should re-assert not just its Bengali linguistic and cultural identity but its Muslim identity as well if the country were not to be swamped by identification with West Bengal and India. He was therefore keen for Bangladesh to be acknowledged as an important Muslim country of South Asia (Dixit 1999: 157-158). Further, Mujib decided to recruit some of the repatriated civil and military officers from Pakistan into the service of Bangladesh (Rashid 2010: 25). He did so despite the fact that many of them did not support liberation struggle of Bangladesh (Dixit 1999: 158). This was not comfortable to India as it perceived many of them as 'pro-Pakistan' (Rashid 2010: 25).

Still there were hopes that India and Bangladesh would be able to solve their bilateral problems amicably. However, a study of the joint statements and communiqués issued at the end of official level discussions between January 1974 and middle of 1975 reveals that most of these talks remained inconclusive and ended in an impasse. There was no major interaction between India and Bangladesh between April and August of 1975. It is also pertinent to note that both Sheikh Mujibur Rahman and Mrs. Indira Gandhi were embroiled in domestic crisis at this particular time (Dixit 1999: 207). Despite all these India-Bangladesh relations during the Mujib era can be deemed to be fairly successful. However, if both the countries had cooperated and had been sensitive to each others' concerns and priorities and only if they had shown a serious political concern, probably then the contentious issues would have been dealt in a proper manner. It can be said that the depth of the friendship between Mrs. Gandhi and Mujib could have been used to deal with the pertinent problems but it wasn't to be. In fact, some critics argue that the failure to resolve some of the key issues with India, coupled with the introduction of one party government in the country, was viewed by some quarters as one of the principal factors which were exploited by Bangabandhu Sheikh Mujib's political opponents and culminated in the tragic assassination of Mujibur Rahman on August 15, 1975 (Rashid 2010: 57).

The assassination of Sheikh Mujib marked a qualitative change in Bangladesh's attitude towards India. The successive regimes followed policies which were not compatible with India. Islamisation became a recurring phenomena in Bangladesh in the consequent years and India factor became all the more pertinent in the domestic milieu, which was often used by the leaders for their own political gain (Bhardwaj 2003: 269). Indian motives and intentions were openly questioned, and two parallel developments led to India losing its special relationship with Bangladesh: the frequent military interventions and the rise of an Islamic identity in Bangladesh (Datta 2016: 7).

Conclusion

The rise of Bengali nationalism as the chapter demonstrates is the product of many forces, right from cultural, economic, political and social. The policies of Pakistan towards its eastern side continually disillusioned the Bengali populace which became vocal with the rise of Sheikh Mujibur Rahman into the political scene. Awami League's 'six points charter' captured the mind of the common masses as well as the students and the Bengali intelligentsia. The final reason for the partition of Pakistan was the 1970 general elections wherein despite gaining the majority the Awami League was not allowed to form the government in Pakistan. Further negotiations failed and Islamabad resorted to the military for the resolution of the issue.

The political imperatives compelled India to intervene in the East Pakistan crisis. Bangladesh was liberated with the active support of Indian military aided by Mukti Bahini and other rebel forces who in turn were aided by the local populace. The point to be noted is that though India used its hard power to liberate Bangladesh, the military for the people of Bangladesh proved to be a soft power. This aspect is aptly substantiated by Mingjiang Li's 'A Soft Use of Power Approach' mentioned in the preceding chapter. India had intervened in Bangladesh on humanitarian grounds and the fact that Indian military took barely two weeks to secure Bangladesh's independence definitely improved India's image not only in Bangladesh but at global level at large. Viewed in this light India's use of soft power vis-à-vis Bangladesh can be seen right at the start. It can also be argued that the Indian aid to the Bangladeshi government in exile; providing logistics to its refugees (despite its weak economy); India's efforts to garner international support to its freedom struggle and recognition can all be viewed from the soft power prism. Thus, Mujibur Rahman, after his release, before going to Dhaka arrived at New Delhi where he expressed his profuse thanks and gratitude to Mrs. Indira Gandhi and the people of India for all the assistance and sacrifices made by them in liberating Bangladesh.

Even after the liberation, India provided various economic aids and assistance to Bangladesh which is a clear case of the employability of soft power by India. The joint communiqué issued in March 1971 contains provisions for cultural cooperation between the two countries. The September 1974 protocol which had its validity for two years envisaged for exchange programmes in fields of culture, education, information and sports. Further, various scholarships and exchange visits were offered under the protocol. Thus, what is evident is the fact that we find enough soft power implications even in the initial years of India's relation with Bangladesh. However, India's soft power was short-lived. There arouse numerous issues in the immediate years of Bangladesh independence that squandered India's soft power. As Nye says, soft power is difficult to wield and easy to lose. The Indo-Bangladesh Friendship Treaty on March 19, 1972 was perhaps the beginning of the change of the Bangladeshi perceptions towards India. The Friendship Treaty was criticized on numerous grounds and India's assistance to Bangladesh in Bangladesh' liberation war began to be seen from *real politik* perspective. The other issues which impinged India-Bangladesh relations were the question of the Prisoners of War, the Trade Pact 1972, India's alleged interference in the day-to-day administration of Bangladesh, and so on. However, the most pertinent issues that impinged India-Bangladesh relations was to resolve the three main bilateral disputes, namely, the Farakka issue, the land boundary problems and the delimitation of sea boundary in the Bay of Bengal.

After the independence of Bangladesh, especially in the post -Mujib era, there was the advent of Islamic undercurrents. The military regime which captured power in Bangladesh gave prominence to Bangladeshi (religious) nationalism which in turn impinged India-Bangladesh relations. Simultaneously, a major trend was witnessed in Bangladesh's foreign policy. The AL government with its emphasis on secularism and democracy became closer to India and began to be termed as 'pro-India' while the non-AL government continued Islamisation process and as such began to termed as 'anti-India', the trend is still strong today. Thus, the question of 'regime compatibility' became and still is an important yardstick in Indo-Bangladesh bilateral ties. Another important factor in India-Bangladesh relations pertains to the use of 'India factor' in domestic politics of Bangladesh. As we shall see in the succeeding chapters, the politicians in Bangladesh have often used the 'India factor' and the contentious issues between the two countries for their political gains. As such the negative propaganda of India began to continually be entangled into the domestic politics of Bangladesh.

Understandably neither India nor Bangladesh made efforts to use soft power as a concrete tool in foreign policy decision making. Such soft elements in foreign policy were unimaginable at that point of time. Though agreements signed between the two countries called for cultural cooperation and academic exchanges and so on, they were not regarded as primary. Moreover, India did little to improve its deteriorating image. If both countries had used their cultural affinities, the euphoric atmosphere created out of the independence of Bangladesh and had used the Indira-Mujib friendship and had shown wisdom to deal with their problems in an amicable manner perhaps India-Bangladesh relations would have a better beginning.

Notes

1. http://www.nationalarchives.gov.uk/education/topics/the-road-to-partition.htm
2. The British were sympathetic to separate constituencies for Muslims which they hoped would weaken the incipient nationalist movement, spearheaded by the Congress Party.
3. Nurul Amin referred to as the Patriot of Pakistan, was a prominent Pakistani leader, jurist, national conservative, and Party Chairman of the Muslim League. Amin became a trusted lieutenant of Mohammad Ali Jinnah in East Bengal, fighting for the rights of Bengali Muslims in British India. Amin took an active part in the Pakistan Movement, organising the Bengali Muslims, while he continued to strengthen the Muslim League in Bengal. Amin was later appointed by Jinnah as the Chief Minister of East Bengal.

4. The 1968 Agartala conspiracy refers to the case wherein Sheikh Mujibur Rahman and several East Pakistani officials and political leaders were tried on charges of plotting with India to secure the separation of East and West Pakistan
5. http://www.globalsecurity.org/military/world/war/liberation-war.htm
6. http://www.globalsecurity.org/military/world/war/liberation-war.htm
7. Annexure II
8. Rakkhi Bahini was an elite para-military force formed on 8 February 1972 by the government led by Sheikh Mujibur Rahman after the liberation war of Bangladesh.

Chapter - III

The Issue of Water Sharing between India and Bangladesh

The water dispute between India and Bangladesh is an outstanding example of an interstate conflict - two state actors striving to acquire scarce water resource (Swain 1996: 193). In fact, water is considered to be one of the most crucial security issues in the contemporary times. The United Nations Environment Programme (UNEP) reported in 1999 that 200 scientists in 50 countries identified water shortage as one of the most distressing problems for the new millennium. The World Water Council believes that by 2020 we shall need 17 percent more water than is available, if we are to feed the world (Kirby 2000: 146-147). Consequently, as Michael Klare states, "There is a new geography of conflict – a reconfigured cartography in which resource flows rather than political and ideological divisions constitute the major fault lines. Just as a map showing the world's tectonic faults is a useful guide to likely earthquake zones, viewing the international system in terms of shared water systems provide a guide to likely conflict zones in the twenty-first century (Klare 2001: 163).

The chapter, therefore, shall deal with one of the major contentious issue, that is, the sharing of water resources between India and Bangladesh. The water sharing problem between India and Bangladesh is by no means confined to Ganges. Among the most prominent are the issues revolving around the sharing of waters between Teesta, Feni, Dharla, Dudhkumar, Manu, Muhuri, Khowai and Gomti. Yet the primary thrust of the chapter is to understand the Ganges water or the Farakka dispute between India and Bangladesh. This is because the Farakka dispute has been contentious since the partition days, when Bangladesh was part of Pakistan and which has now been resolved in the form of the Ganges Water Treaty 1996. The chapter is divided into two major sections. The first section deals with the phase wise negotiations on the Ganges water dispute till the eventual conclusion of the Ganges Water Treaty in 1996. As we shall see, the negotiations on Farakka went through four phases; the first phase (1971-77), the second phase (1977-82), the third phase (1982-90) and the last phase (1990-96). The main thrust of the chapter, however, is to decipher whether soft power did play a role in the resolution of the Ganges water dispute.

Though the Farakka is essentially a federal issue, the chapter demonstrates how the state government (West Bengal) used soft power in the form of the Bengali connection to resolve the Farakka issue. Further, the chapter demonstrates as to how other soft power strategies such as economic inducement and trade were often employed by India to improve its bilateral ties with Bangladesh, including the progress on the Ganges water or the Farakka issue. The second section will delineate the other three issues – Teesta, Tipaimukh dam and the River Linking Project, which are the current problems with regard to water. While doing so efforts will be made to understand the nature, issues and complexities involved in these issues.

3.1 Section-I

3.1.a Water Dispute between India and Bangladesh

India and Bangladesh share 54 rivers between them. Out of them, three major rivers of the region, namely the Ganges, the Brahmaputra and the Meghna/Barak (GBM) have a common terminus into the Bay of Bengal and thus form a river system. India and Bangladesh depend heavily on the waters from the GBM system. Thus, the dwindling supply of water in the dry season has become one of the key issues between India and Bangladesh. The situation is particularly critical for Bangladesh, as about 80% of its annual fresh water supply comes as trans-boundary inflows through 54 common rivers with India.[1]

As we are aware one of the most contentious and complicated problems that caused a great deal of acrimony between the two countries is the sharing of the waters of the Ganges and the Farakka barrage construction by India to harness its waters (Ray 2012: 8). The Ganges water dispute originated in 1950, when India planned to construct a barrage at Farakka, 18 kilometres upstream from the East Pakistan border (Swain 1996: 191). This was done to divert the Ganges water and to keep the Calcutta port operational during the dry season. It was thought that by increasing the river flow, the port could be kept from deteriorating from silt deposition.[2] The plan to divert water via the barrage to the Bhagirathi-Hooghly became a source of political tension, mistrust and apprehension between India and Pakistan and later between India and Bangladesh (Joy and Paranjape 2007: 49).

Rising from the Himalayas, the Ganges flows through the Indian province of Uttar Pradesh, Bihar and Bengal, before entering into Bangladesh. Among its several tributaries from the north are the river Gandhak and Kosi whose headwaters lie in Nepal (Bindra 1982: 66). The Ganges which navigates a 2,500-km long journey through India and Bangladesh originates in Gangotri, on the Southern slope of the Himalayan range in India and moves in the southeast direction towards Bangladesh. The mainstream of the Ganges bifurcates into two channels, which are known as Bhagirathi-Hooghly in India and Padma in Bangladesh. In Bangladesh the Padma covers a distance of around 120 km and then moves towards the south-east and joins the Brahmaputra in the heart of Bangladesh and their combined flow then runs south to empty into the Bay of Bengal. This geographical feature divides India and Bangladesh as upstream and downstream riparian states.[3] Thus, the problem over the Ganges is typical of conflicting interests of 'up-stream' and 'down-stream' riparian states.[4]

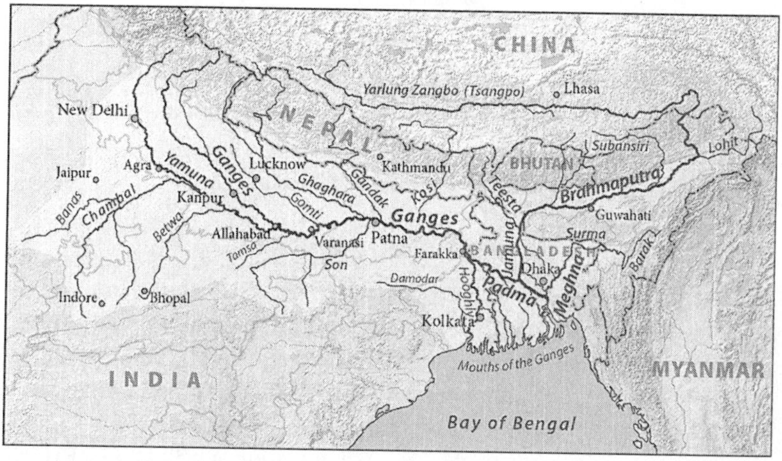

Source Wikimedia.org

Map 2: The Major Rivers of India and Bangladesh

Issues such as control of barrage gates, quantity of water to be released, sharing mechanism, augmentation measures, availability of water etc., became the focal points of tension and conflict between the two states. The question whether to treat Ganges-Brahmaputra-Meghna basin as a single unit, the feasibility of constructing a reservoir in Nepal to augment the flow, or whether to treat Farakka barrage as a 'barrage' or as a 'dam' also become contentious (Joy and Paranjape 2007: 49). Though the Ganges/ Farakka issue has been resolved by the conclusion of the Ganges Water Treaty in 1996, the Teesta water dispute has come to the fore along with some of the common rivers that flow between India and Bangladesh. Despite setting up a Joint River Commission for Water management as early as 1972, tensions between the countries on how to share resources remain a problem (Ray 2012: 9).

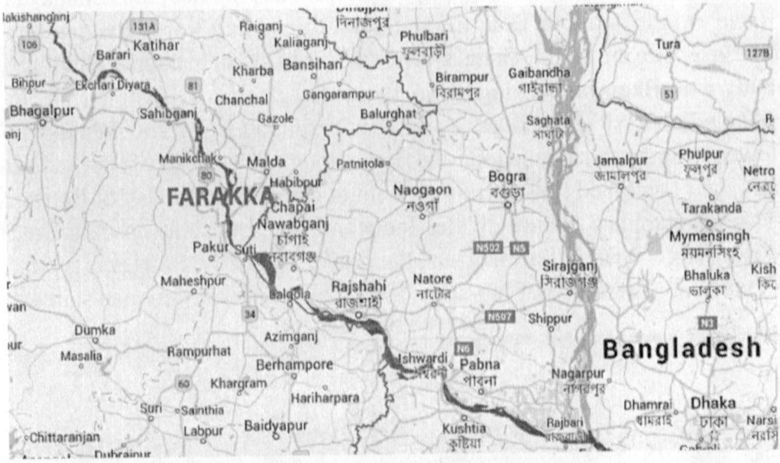

Source: http://archive.dhakatribune.com/bangladesh/2015/may/03/farakka-under-fire-india

Map 3: Location of Farakka

3.1.b The Origin of Ganges/Farakka Problem

The Farakka barrage scheme was the result of a long and continuous study from the middle of the last century itself. Continuous investigations were undertaken and committees of engineering experts were appointed from time to time much before the partition of India to formulate measures to maintain the Hooghly waterway condition. As far back as 1858, a barrage across the Ganges was planned by Sir Arthur Cotton, a well known British engineer. According to him, "if additional water were thrown into the Hooghly and kept flowing from it during the dry season, such an additional scour might just make the difference of preventing the Hooghly from being silting up (Bindra 1982: 68)." The same opinion was voiced in successive reports by Sir Arthur Cotton, 1853, Harcourt-Vernon, 1896, Stevenson-

Moor Committee, 1916–19, Sir William Willcocks, 1930, (Joy and Paranjape 2007: 49) T.M. Nag in 1939 and A. Webster in 1946 (Bindra 1982: 69). Walter Hensen's report to the Government of India in 1957 also recommended the construction of a barrage across the Ganges to augment the flow of the Bhagirathi-Hooghly so as to save the Calcutta Port (Joy and Paranjape 2007: 49). Dr. Hensen declared that the proposal for the construction of barrage across Ganges was the best technical solution of the augmentation problem. It, in fact, was the most purposeful measure with which the long term deterioration on the Bhagirathi-Hooghly could be stopped (Bindra 1982: 69).

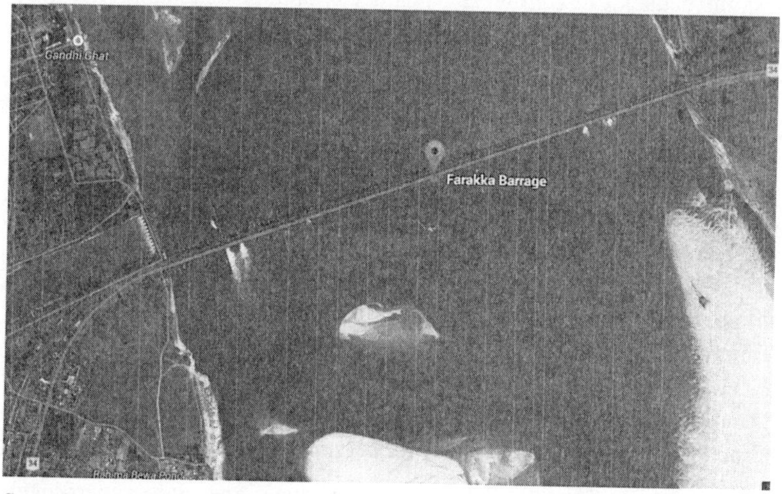

Source: https://sandrp.wordpress.com/2014/06/27/ganga-in-peril-building-more-barrages-will-finish-it-off/

Map 4: Google Image of the Farakka Barrage

After the partition of the sub-continent, the idea of constructing a dam at Farakka had been first mooted among official circles in India in 1950 (Crow et al. 1995: 1688). The then Pakistan government drew the attention of the government of India to the press reports of India that New Delhi had decided to construct a dam at Farakka in Murshidabad district. Pakistan apprehended that it might have adverse effects on East Pakistan and requested India in a letter dated October 29, 1951, to consult it before operating any such scheme. India replied on March 8, 1952, that the project was under preliminary investigation and described Pakistan's concern over its probable effects as purely hypothetical (*Ibid.*). Thus from the period from 1951 the discussions on the Farakka between India and Pakistan commenced.

The first round of expert-level meetings between India and Pakistan was held in New Delhi from June 28 - July 3, 1960, with three more to follow by 1962.[5] While the meetings were still in progress, New Delhi formally informed Islamabad, on January 30, 1961, about its intention to go ahead with the plan to build a barrage (Tiwary 2006: 1688). The plan included a 38 kilometer canal of 40,000 cubic feet/second capacity, to take off from the barrage to supplement the waters of the Bhagirathi-Hooghly at the lower point. The official reason, as mentioned earlier, was that the diversion would make the current of water strong enough to flush off the silt and clear the port of Calcutta, situated on the Hooghly River. Besides this, the demands of a growing Calcutta city and the agricultural needs of the state of West Bengal induced the Indian government to go ahead with the project (Swain 1996: 191).

It is imperative to mention that Calcutta is a premier Indian port situated on the banks of Hooghly river –also known as Bhagirathi in the upper reaches. The Bhagirathi-Hooghly water way, through which ships of all nationalities have pass to reach Calcutta port, is sustained by the supply of water from the Ganges. These supplies have dwindled over the years because of silting of the waterways at an alarming rate and the port is threatened with extinction which has serious repercussions for India at various levels (Bindra 1982: 67-68). It may be also be noted that 90 percent of the length of Ganges lies exclusively in India and if the course of the river along the Indo-Bangladesh boundary is also included then more than 98.50 percent of the length lies in the Indian territory (*Ibid*., p. 70).

In 1963, India and Pakistan agreed to have one more expert-level meeting to determine what data was relevant and necessary for the convening of a minister-level meeting. The meeting at which data needs were to be determined, the fifth round at the level of expert, was not held until May 13, 1968.[6] These meetings, at the level of secretary, commenced on December 9, 1968 and a total of five rounds were held in alternating capitals through July 1970. Throughout these meetings, the different strategies became apparent. As the lower riparian, Pakistan professed for "substantive talks on the framework for a settlement for equitable sharing of the Ganges waters between the two countries." India in contrast, professed concern at data accuracy and adequacy, arguing that a comprehensive agreement was not possible until the data available was complete and accurate (*Ibid.*).

The period 1950-71 was fruitless as far as negotiations on Ganges water sharing are concerned. There is a widespread belief that from 1950 to 1971 Islamabad deliberately neglected the Farakka issue as it was more interested in working on its own water sharing formula with India over the Indus river basin than in resolving the Farakka problem. The argument can be justified to an extent given Islamabad's overall policy of discrimination and neglect towards East Pakistan and its interests (Hossain 1998: 15). Nevertheless, the July 1970 meeting was significant in the sense that for the first time India recognized the Ganges as an international river, and, therefore, accepted the principle of sharing of its water. Some agreements on the quantity of water to be released were also expected in the next meeting. However, the next meeting was never held because of the emergence of Bangladesh independence struggle (Tiwary 2006: 1688).

3.1.c Negotiations on Farakka

3.1.c.(i) First Phase (1971-77)

After the independence of Bangladesh in 1971, it was expected that this dispute would be resolved to the mutual advantage of both neighbours under the euphoric atmosphere of independence, and especially due to the active association of India in the liberation war (Tiwary 2006: 1688). It is interesting to note here that soft power did play an important role even in the independence of Bangladesh. The Mujibnagar Government had got a safe haven in India along with the millions of Bangladeshi refugees. India army intervention when seen from Mingjiang Li's perspective, which he calls 'A Soft Use of Power Approach', also qualifies as a soft power. India had intervened in Bangladesh on humanitarian grounds and the fact that Indian military took barely two weeks to secure Bangladesh's independence definitely improved India's image not only in Bangladesh but at global level at large.

India's employability of soft power is also evident in the immediate years of Bangladesh's independence. Even after the creation of Bangladesh, India continued to provide various aids and other assistance to Bangladesh for its reconstruction and development. The three requests[7] of Mujibur Rahman that he made immediately after assuming charge of Bangladesh was also fulfilled by Mrs. Gandhi (Dixit 1999: 131-132). Not only that, India also decided to give at least Rs. 100 crores (around $133 million) immediately to Bangladesh for reconstruction. Both the Governments also finalized a detailed agreement which envisaged an annual trade of Rs. 1,000 crores (around $1.3 billion) (Bindra 1982: 16). All these have soft power connotations.

The soft power initiatives employed by India in turn created a congenial atmosphere and this initiated cooperation in all major areas including the water issue (Tiwary 2006: 1688). This was evident from the statement issued by B.M. Abbas, Advisor to the Prime Minister of Bangladesh on Flood control, Irrigation and Power on January 17, 1972 when he officially visited New Delhi, wherein he said- "a new vista has opened up for a free and frank discussion between Bangladesh and India on the Ganges and Brahmaputra river systems (Bindra 1982: 80)." The soft power that India had earned was, however, short-lived and was undermined by the Indo-Bangladesh Friendship Treaty signed on March 19, 1972. Though Article VI[8] of the Treaty laid down the provisions for the progress on water, it came under scrutiny from various sections. Soon the signing of the treaty was seen by many as either unnecessary or as something that was imposed by India on Bangladesh. It was also argued that the Friendship Treaty was aimed to keep Bangladesh as a client state of India (Zafar 1993: 90).

The Ganges river dispute gradually became a dominant issue influencing the political relation between the two countries in coming decades (Tiwary 2006: 1688). The crux of the issue lay in the sharing of the Ganges water during the five dry-season months (January-May). During the rest of the year, there is more than sufficient water for both the countries. In 1975 the dry season average minimum discharge to Farakka was estimated at only 55,000 cusecs (cubic feet/second). India asked for 40,000 cusecs while Bangladesh needed all 55,000 cusecs (Swain 1996: 192). Bangladesh complained that there was a 'unilateral diversion' of the waters of the Ganges by India at Farakka. Farakka barrage was seen as a case of a larger and more powerful country disregarding the legitimate interests of a smaller and weaker neighbour. That view has since been widely prevalent in Bangladesh, cutting across all kinds of divisions and became a significant factor in electoral politics. Thus, when Bangladesh was afflicted by drought or by floods, the responsibility was put at India's door and 'Farakka' was blamed for all ills (Iyer 1999: 1512).

The perceptions on the Indian side were entirely different. At the official level, a fairly common view was that Bangladesh was extremely rigid and unreasonable on this issue; that it had greatly over pitched its water needs and was claiming a disproportionate share of the waters in relation to the relevant criteria (contribution, cultivable area, etc.); that it tended to exaggerate the adverse effects of reduced flows; and that it had blown the dispute up into a big political issue in domestic politics, making intergovernmental negotiations difficult. A further complication was that there was a feeling at the level of the state governments in India that in its negotiations with Bangladesh the central government had failed to pay adequate heed to the interests of the states (some of which are very large entities) and tended to be generous to Bangladesh at their cost (*Ibid.*, p. 1512). This in fact, also points at the domestic imperatives that complicate the India-Bangladesh bilateral ties.

While the cooperation on Farakka was not up to the mark areas like trade were showing some positive signs. Perhaps India and Bangladesh were trying to build trust on economic sphere and were hoping that the cooperation would spill over to the political sphere subsequently. On March 28, 1972, the two countries initiated a three tier trade agreement[9] of the approximate value of Rs. 100 crores (around $133 million). It further provided for border trade for people living within a 16 kilometer belt of the border between West Bengal, Assam, Meghalaya, Tripura and Mizoram on the one hand and Bangladesh on the other (Bindra 1982: 25). This was important step in the sense that a lot of negative perceptions had already been generated that in turn was impacting Indo-Bangladesh relations in an unconstructive way. Thus, the border trade was actually a step to generate people to people contact in the border areas and as such can be seen from a soft power perspective.

Simultaneously, progress was made on the water issue. The most important step towards formulating a comprehensive plan was taken during Mrs. Gandhi's visit to Bangladesh in March 1972, when India and Bangladesh agreed to establish the Joint River Commission (JRC) on a permanent basis (Tiwary 2006: 1688). Consequently, both the countries signed in Dacca on November 24, 1972, the status relating to the JRC, formalising the working of high powered expert's body; the members of which were drawn from both the countries. Under the agreement, the commission was directed to formulate details, proposals on advance flood warnings, and study flood control and irrigation projects on the major river systems shared by both countries. In addition, the commission was to examine the feasibility of linking the power grids of Bangladesh with the adjoining areas of India for the equitable utilisation of water resources to the mutual benefit of the two countries. After the signing of the Statutes the meeting of the JRC started in Dacca on March 28, 1973 (Bindra 1982: 80).

Further efforts were made to strengthen the Indo-Bangladesh ties through closer economic ties. Consequently, on May 16, 1974, a number of agreements on wide ranging economic and trade co-operation between India and Bangladesh emerged from the five-day high-level discussions between the two countries. As a form of inducement, India agreed to extend three credits amounting to Rs. 41crores (around $ 50.7 million) to

Bangladesh. Thus, what is evident here is the fact that economic assistance as a form of soft power was constantly used by India to build a partnership with Bangladesh. In 1974, at a ministerial level meeting with Bangladesh, India agreed that a mutually accepted solution would be arrived at before operating the Farakka barrage. The phase of bonhomie was, however, short lived as India and Bangladesh had diverging interest and strategies for the development of the Ganges water resource (Tiwary 2006: 1688). Nevertheless, what is evident is the fact that India did employ soft power strategies to deal with the Farakka issue and that India's use of soft power became inapt to solve the bilateral dispute regarding water at that point of time.

The Farakka issue became one single issue to dominate the relationship between the countries which no political leader could ignore (Tiwary 2006: 1688). In May 1974, the Prime Minister of Bangladesh, Sheikh Mujibur Rahman, visited India and efforts were made to strengthen their bilateral relations. On the very first day of the summit Indira Gandhi and Sheikh Mujib met for seventy minutes without aids. The talks covered the sharing of the Ganges waters, trade between the two countries and the sub-continental affairs (Bindra 1982: 32). During his talks with Indian Prime Minister Indira Gandhi, Mujib demanded that the water issue be resolved quickly. The Joint River Commission (JRC) was entrusted the responsibility of finding a solution and the commission accordingly took up the augmentation issue (Tiwary 2006: 1688).

The JRC sought to explore all possible options of augmentation for optimum utilisation of their jointly available water resources in order to find a mutually acceptable formula for sharing waters in the lean season. Despite intense negotiations on augmentation from June 1974 onwards, the Joint River Commission was unable to reach an agreement on augmentation of the lean season flow of the Ganges (Pandey 2012: 269). In fact, vastly differing perceptions held by the two sides prevented the JRC from arriving at any agreed solution (Tiwary 2006: 1688). New Delhi suggested augmentation at the lower Ganges from the Brahmaputra in view of the limited storage potential on the Ganges and rapidly growing demands for agricultural requirements within India. Bangladesh on the other hand, continued to insist on augmentation within the Ganges basin. Two ministerial-level meetings took place in February and April 1975 but failed to break the impasse on augmentation (Pandey 2012: 269).

Negotiations of Farakka were not proceeding as desired but cooperation on other spheres showed some positive signs. On September 27, 1974 a two year Protocol was signed for exchange programmes in the fields of culture, education, information and sports. India offered to give 100 scholarships and fellowships to Bangladeshi nationals every year for higher studies and research in India. In addition, India agreed to send eminent musicians and dancers to Bangladesh to conduct short-term courses in Bangladesh in classical music and dance. The protocol also provided for exchange of visits by academicians, scientist, educational, literators, sportsmen, cultural troupes and sports teams. In fact, during Sheikh Mujib period, Indo-Bangladesh co-operation in the trade, science, culture and educational fields were in high spirits (Bindra 1982: 28).

On April 21, 1975, the Farakka barrage went on a test operation for 41 days under a temporary agreement on the utilisation of the Ganges waters which was signed on 18 April. Under the agreement signed in Dacca, India was allowed to draw upto a specified volume of water for its feeder canal for the benefit of Calcutta port. The daily withdrawal ranged between 11,000 cusecs in the last ten days of May 1975. The remaining flow of water would be received by Bangladesh. It was further agreed that the joint teams consisting of experts of the two countries would observe the effects of the Farakka withdrawal in Bangladesh and on the Hooghly river, at the appropriate places in both the countries. A joint team was also to be stationed at Farakka to record the discharges into the feeder and the remaining flow for Bangladesh. The teams had to submit their report to the Governments for consideration (*The Tribune*, April 21, 1975 in Bindra 1982: 82-83). India, however, continued to withdraw water from the Ganges after the expiry of the June 1975 Agreement. Bangladesh did not publicly protest about these withdrawals until early 1976. Bangladesh accused India of a breach of the agreement due to its continuing withdrawal at the end of the 40-day period, while India blamed Bangladesh for non-cooperation in collection of data and information required to finalise the joint assessment, as per the provisions of the 1975 Agreement. (Pandey 2012: 270).

Mujib's Assassination and its Aftermath

The assassination of Sheikh Mujib in August 1975 was a serious blow to the already problematic India-Bangladesh relations and the Farakka issue became increasingly tied up in political knots (Dutt 2008: 142). Simmering tensions came to the fore, resulting in mutual distrust and later into an open conflict (Pandey 2012: 270). After the assassination of Mujib the Bangladesh Government started maligning India at every opportunity, accusing it of taping all the waters of the Ganges. The Farakka issue which had received enough publicity through controlled press and other media became the kingpin in the relations between India and Bangladesh. Highlighting the dispute was natural for the new rulers of Bangladesh and they adopted the same tactics, which were employed by the Pakistan Government and had been avoided by the Government of Sheikh Mujibur Rahman. Creating tension with India too was in fvour of the Bangladeshi rulers as it diverted the attention of its subjects away from its urgent problems (Bindra 1982: 83-86).

In the post Mujib era, there was a general reluctance on the part of the then Indian government to negotiate with the new military regime under Major General Zia-ur Rahman who came into power through a series of military coups and counter-coups in November 1975 (Tiwary 2006: 1688). Indira Gandhi did not favour military regimes in India's neighbourhood and thus, made little efforts to evolve even a working relationship with General Zia-ur Rahman. Moreover, Zia-ur Rahman followed policies which were completely opposite to Mujib's regime (Pandey 2012: 270). Nevertheless, by 1976, the new Bangladesh government took initiatives to open negotiations with India on the Farakka issue. New Delhi's response was rather cool, perhaps because of the killing of Sheikh Mujibur Rahman. Dhaka decided to put pressure on New Delhi by raising the Farakka issue at a number of international forums. For example, Bangladesh tried to raise the Ganges water issue at the thirty-second meeting of the Economic and Social Commission for Asia and the Pacific, the seventh Islamic Foreign Ministers' Conference at Islamabad, and the Summit Conference of the nonaligned countries at Colombo. Bangladesh also raised the Farakka issue at the thirty-first session of the United Nations General Assembly in September 1976 (Hossain 1998: 136).

Through letters dated 21st and 26th August and 8th September 1976 addressed to the Secretary General, Bangladesh requested the inclusion of the agenda in the General Assembly in the thirty first session of an item "situation arising out of unilateral withdrawal of the Ganges waters at Farakka." On September 24, 1976, the General Assembly, on the recommendation of its General Committee, decided to include the item in its agenda and to allocate it to the Special Political Committee for consideration (Bindra 1982: 90). India, however, opposed the decision contending that the issue was a bilateral one and involvement of any third party, including the UN would only complicate the situation and possibly worsen relations between the two countries (*Bangladesh Observer*, 27 August, 1976 in Bindra 1982: 90). In fact, most countries including big powers and Arab states felt that the Farakka dispute was a bilateral matter and that its internationalisation would only delay the situation (*The Hindu*, 1976 in Bindra 1982: 92). Eventually, Bangladesh decided to withdraw the dispute from the Agenda and, the consensus reached by a Special Political Committee, were welcomed in India (Bindra 1982: 92-93).

Thus it is obvious that on the water issue, Zia-ur Rahman's government pursued a twin-track policy of holding India responsible for all its problems at home and seeking international support for its cause at various foray. The absence of any agreement on water sharing during the 1976 and 1977 dry seasons provided fuel to the fire. A Bangladesh White Paper of 1976 asserted that the withdrawal of water by India threatened the survival of millions of people of Bangladesh. The media, with official encouragement, portrayed it as a 'conspiracy against the independence and sovereignty of the country' (Khosla 2005: 65-68). Bangladesh held Farakka responsible for all kinds of problems raging in the northern part of the country including the destruction of a bird sanctuary, floods and causing unemployment (Pandey 2012: 270).

3.1.c.(ii) Second Phase (1977-82)

With the defeat of Indira Gandhi's Congress Party in the Indian parliamentary elections in March 1977 and the formation of the Janata Party government under Morarji Desai, there came a new opportunity for a solution to the Farakka issue (Hossain 1998: 137). During Janata Party rule which lasted for 28 months, there was a perceptible shift in the Bangladesh policy of the previous Government. Dramatic developments took place on the Indian side of the border. The BSF began to cooperate with BDR in combating the insurgents (Bindra 1982: 53). New Delhi took strict action against direct and indirect support to the Chittagong Hill Tracts migrants into India. Number of former freedom fighters and Mujib's supporters who had taken refuge in India after Mujib's assassination and were a cause of sporadic political troubles in Bangladesh were also sent back (Dixit 1999: 241). Such initiatives from India were able to create some congenial atmosphere for the negotiations on Farakka to begin (Crow 1997: 11). Thus, the second phase of negotiations between the two countries started.

The dialogues between the two countries were held in the middle of April 1977 at Dacca. The discussions were fruitful and both the countries reached to an understanding on sharing of the Ganges water (Bindra 1982: 100). The non-Congress government in New Delhi, the first since India's independence in 1947, took a special interest in sorting out India's problems with its neighbours. Soon after the elections, Indian minister Jagjivan Ram led a mission to Dhaka in April to push forward the negotiations on Farakka. This was followed by the Desai-Zia talks in London during the Commonwealth heads of government meeting. Both leaders agreed to continue the meetings between the two countries, at the official and ministerial levels. After some forty-three meetings, finally, on November 5, 1977, a Five-Year Treaty[10] on the Ganges was signed in New Delhi. Rear Admiral M. H. Khan, the chief of the Bangladesh navy and adviser to the president on water resources, and Surjit Singh Barnala, the Indian minister of agriculture and irrigation, signed on behalf of their respective governments (Hossain 1998: 137).

There were many important components of the agreement: (1) the treaty was to remain in the force for five years but was extendable by mutual agreement; (2) it defined the lean season flow period between January 31-May 31; (3) the amount of water for Bangladesh was to be calculated from recorded flows of the Ganges at Farakka from 1948 to 1973. The agreement incorporated a guarantee clause under which during the leanest period (from April 21 to May 31) in case of exceptionally low flows (below 55,000 cusecs), Bangladesh was to be guaranteed at least 80 per cent (27,600 cusecs) of her stipulated share for the concerned 10-day period (Paragraph 11 of Article II). This provision was significant for Bangladesh (Tiwary 2006: 1689). Further, a joint committee was constituted for the implementation of these arrangements. Two reviews were built in the agreement at the end of three years and the other six months before the expiry of the treaty. The JRC was made responsible for investigating and studying schemes relating to economical and feasible long-term ways for augmentation of the dry season flows within a time-frame of three years (Pandey 2012: 271).

The Treaty was politically significant on many accounts. Firstly, Bangladesh after unsuccessful attempts of internationalisation of the Ganges dispute resolved to go back to bilateralism. The agreement firmly established bilateralism as the basic tenet of India's south Asian international water diplomacy. However, the treaty invited criticism in India. The Desai government was condemned for having compromised India's national interest to Bangladesh's advantage. It was cited as a case of poor diplomacy shown by the newly elected Janata Party government. Many experts thought India conceded more than it should have. The Communist Party of West Bengal was critical against the centre for ignoring the state's interest and lack of prior consultation with the state government (Tiwary 2006: 1689). It was also argued that it would affect Uttar Pradesh and Bihar in the long run and also the Calcutta Port and certain smaller towns along the banks of the river (Alva 1979: 14). The treaty was also criticized in Bangladesh for its temporary nature. It was argued that negotiators from Bangladesh were anxious for a treaty but had failed to take advantage from India's liability for a reasonable solution of the bilateral negotiation (Tiwary 2006: 1689).

The Indian Prime Minister Morarji Desai defended the Agreement in the Lok Sabha on November 14, 1977. In a statement in the house he said that the historic nature of the agreement and its extraordinary significance for relations between India and Bangladesh. Desai's statement also reflected that India had made a large number of concessions in reaching the agreement with Bangladesh. In this regard, Bindra contends that the treaty seems to have been concluded by the Janata Government mainly because of its determination to maintain friendly relations with its neighbours (in similar lines that Gujaral Doctrine would profess years later). In fact, the process of strengthening relations with the neighbouring countries started soon after the Janata Government assumed office. This can be substantiated from the fact that in the years between 1977 and 1978, the Minister of External Affairs, A. B. Vajpayee paid official visits to Nepal, Burma, Afghanistan, Japan, Yugoslavia, Bhutan, Pakistan and China (Bindra 1982: 113).

Nevertheless, Bangladesh was the clear benefactor of the Treaty. The Treaty firmly established Bangladesh's right over Ganges water, as a downstream country. The amount of water allotted to Bangladesh was much beyond the expectations of negotiators from Bangladesh. Further, the inclusion of the guarantee clause meant that at least for the next five years India could not unilaterally withdraw water from the Ganges. The agreement also demonstrated India's willingness to come to terms with its neighbors in a manner that is beneficial to them. There was also commitment on the part of New Delhi for finding a long-term solution of problem of Ganges water (Tiwary 2006: 1689).

However, with the return of the Congress to power in New Delhi in 1980, the cordial atmosphere once again turned sour. At the end of the five-year period, both parties concluded that water-sharing arrangement for the lean season had worked according to plan, though they could not reach any agreement on the augmentation issue. The final review of the 1977 Agreement concluded that the matter of augmentation would be taken up at the higher political level. But just before that Bangladesh witnessed another coup and General Ershad came to power in Dhaka (Pandey 2012: 272). Negotiations between the two countries over the Ganges water continued, and as the expiry of date of the 1977 treaty loomed, Bangladesh urgently needed to find another agreement on the sharing of Ganges water.

But agreement proved elusive because Indian and Bangladeshi officials now differed substantially on the augmentation of water for distribution during the dry season. Dhaka officials once again attempted to bring Nepal into the picture by arguing that water reservoirs could be built there and their water used during the dry season. New Delhi viewed it as an attempt by Dhaka to pressure India by regionalizing the dispute; Indira Gandhi was vehemently opposed. The 1977 Ganges Water Agreement was thus allowed to lapse on November 4, 1982, (Hossain 1998: 138-139) thus marking the end of the second phase of the negotiations.

3.1.c.(iii) Third Phase (1982-90)

There was a change in government in Bangladesh with General H. M. Ershad coming to power in a bloodless military coup on March 26, 1982. Naturally he could not avoid the Farakka issue. During President H. M. Ershad's visit to India, the two sides agreed to an interim Memorandum of Understanding (MOU) on the Ganges water issue. It was signed on October 7, 1982 by the foreign ministers of India and Bangladesh, P. V. Narashima Rao and A. R. S. Doha, respectively. Valid for the next two dry seasons, the interim agreement essentially was a renewal of clauses of the 1977 agreement. But 80 percent guarantee of the clause was not retained. The agreement directed the Joint Rivers Commission to suggest means to increase the flow of the Ganges water over the following one and a half years (Hossain 1998: 139). The MOU had two critical components: the allocation of water and strategies for its augmentation. Discussions on augmentation once again proceeded along the well-treaded, traditional positions (Pandey 2012: 272).

The Assassination of Indira Gandhi and its Aftermath

The assassination of Mrs. Gandhi in 1984 provided a short respite to Bangladesh as Rajiv Gandhi, after becoming the Prime Minister, exhibited desire to mend fences and improve ties with Bangladesh, (Zafar 1993: 96). Rajiv Gandhi directed the top government officials to restart the negotiation process. Rajiv met President Ershad at the Commonwealth Heads of Government Conference at Nassau (Bahamas) in October 1985 and signed a MOU for a three-year period. The MOU was modelled after the 1982 understanding and decided to start afresh. A new Joint Committee of Experts (JCE) alongside the JRC was created. The JCE was headed by their irrigation secretaries for a 12-month period. Meanwhile, India agreed to approach Nepal for eliciting data on the feasibility of augmenting lean season flows at Farakka from the waters stored in Nepal (Verghese 2007: 366). Both countries' respective water resources secretaries visited Kathmandu in November 1986 to meet their Nepalese counterpart who was keen to find out Nepal's potential gain from such a deal (Pandey 2012: 272). But the water sharing issue had no meaningful success under Rajiv Gandhi as no progress could be made, apart from extension of the interim agreement on Farakka by two years (Zafar 1993: 96). In fact, between the period of the expiry of the second MOU in 1985 and President Ershad's resignation in 1990, India and Bangladesh had held about twenty meetings, at both officials and ministerial levels, without success, to reach a long-term agreement on the sharing of the Ganges water (Hossain 1998: 139).

It is argued that the rigid positions taken by the two governments made the negotiations difficult enough, and the difficulty was compounded by the political dimensions of the dispute. The deteriorating political relationship between the two countries rendered this problem an intractable one, particularly because it had become (or had been made into) a major issue in domestic politics in Bangladesh. After the MOU on Ganges Water issue (1985) lapsed in 1988, a void was created and there was no agreement or understanding between the two countries for several years. There was also no serious effort to enter into discussions with a view to finding a lasting solution to the problem (Iyer 1999: 1513). In the absence of any agreement, Bangladesh alleged that India continued withdrawing water from the Ganges. Bangladesh protested this 'unilateral' withdrawal and the harmful effects of the Ganges diversion. A vast amount of literature appeared on the claimed harmful effects of the Farakka diversion particularly during the 1988-96 period. These claimed harmful effects were used to pressurise India as well as to internationalise the Farakka dispute for more beneficial agreements (Tiwary 2006: 1689).

In 1988, Bangladesh witnessed massive floods, resulting in submergence of almost two-thirds of Bangladesh's territory. The top leaders of Bangladesh cutting across the political spectrum held Farakka responsible for the deluge. President Ershad reiterated in numerous public speeches that the waters causing so much death and destruction in the country had flowed from beyond the borders and the damage might have been mitigated if there had been the right mix of concern and commitment shown by India (Hasan 1991: 35). The Indian Air Force helicopter rescue and relief mission in Dhaka was suddenly told that it was no longer required. In Bangladesh, different political parties were engaged in competitive politics in accusing India for causing such devastation. The Acting Ameer of *Jamaat-e-Islami*, Abbas Ali Khan, for instance, blamed the subservient foreign policy of the

Ershad regime and demanded his resignation for its failure to find a way for permanent solution of the Farakka problem (*POT* 13 September, 1988 in Pandey 2012: 273). The Bangladesh Nationalist Party (BNP) Chairman, Begum Khaleda Zia, observed that the devastating floods were mainly due to construction of different barrages including the Farakka barrage in the upstream parts of various rivers for which India was responsible (*The New Nation*, 22 September 1988 in Pandey 2012: 273). Thus, what is obvious is that India and Bangladesh were basically embarking hard power strategies and traditional diplomacy to resolve the Ganges water issue with little success.

3.1.c.(iv) Fourth Phase (1990-96)

In November 1990, President H. M. Ershad resigned as President of Bangladesh amidst a popular uprising spearheaded by the students and a coalition of opposition political parties led by the Awami League and the BNP. The BNP, under the leadership of Khaleda Zia, won the parliamentary election of February 1991. Under Khaleda Zia a score of meetings took place between India and Bangladesh on the Ganges water issue. There were three prime ministerial, six ministerial, and eight secretaries-level meetings. The JRC, too, met a number of times. Yet no agreement could be reached because the governments had widely divergent views on the augmentation of the Ganges water for use during the dry season. Dhaka stuck to its previous opinion that reservoirs needed to be built in Nepal. That was not acceptable to India, which saw it as another attempt to regionalize the Farakka issue. Bangladesh vehemently opposed India's old proposal for constructing a link canal through Bangladeshi territory to connect the Brahamaputra with the Ganges. India argued that the link canal would give Bangladesh better access to water during the dry season. But the BNP government rejected that plan, on the ground that it will destroy the fertile agricultural land in Bangladesh (Hossain 1998: 139-40).

BNP in fact, like Zia-ur Rahman, adopted a twin-track strategy with regard to the Farakka issue. First, as explained earlier, it explored the bilateral track of negotiations with New Delhi to find a mutually acceptable settlement, and second, it sought to internationalise the issue in various international foray. The first did not make much headway partly due to technical constraints emanating from the lack of availability of sufficient water to satisfy demands made by both sides. For the second, there seems to be a consensus—a mistaken one—among Bangladesh's ruling regimes and different political parties that India was forced to agree for water sharing negotiations in 1977 because Bangladesh had gone to the UN in 1976 and that international pressure on India had paid rich dividends. The Bangladesh Prime Minister Khaleda Zia in her address to the UN pointed out that 'the pledges made by India at the time of commissioning the Farakka Barrage remained unfulfilled' (*Daily Star*, 19 October 1993).

Later, Dhaka raised the water-sharing issue in the Commonwealth meeting in October 1993 which according to it had become a 'life and death question for the people of the country' (*The Bangladesh Times*, 22 October 1993). Even during the visit of foreign dignitaries to the country, the Bangladesh ministers would raise the Farakka issue (Pandey 2012: 274). In such circumstances, it became well-nigh impossible to expect a long-term water-sharing negotiation. Leave aside a long-term water-sharing treaty, even an MOU could not be signed between the two countries. The Indian Prime Minister Narasimha Rao's visit did not take place because of tension in the aftermath of the Babri mosque demolition that led to the cancellation of his visit for the SAARC summit citing security reasons (*Ibid.*).

In 1996, new governments came to power in both New Delhi and Dhaka. In Bangladesh, the Awami League headed by Sheikh Hasina won the elections, while in India a non-Congress coalition government led by Deve Gowda came to power. One of its important constituents was the Left Front, which was in power in West Bengal at that time. Mr. I. K. Gujral became the Foreign Minister of India (Pandey 2012: 275). A non-Congress regime in New Delhi and the Awami League in Dhaka, as explained earlier, offered a rare window of opportunity to negotiate a mutually acceptable deal. The Awami League had returned to power after a 20-year long gap and New Delhi was keen to strengthen this regime in Dhaka. Both realised the need to overcome the impasse over the Ganges waters issue and the urgency to arrive at an agreement before the onset of the next dry season. Farooq Sobhan, the then foreign Secretary of Bangladesh in 1996, shared this assessment and noted that the "Awami League had stronger commitment towards having a treaty. India also reciprocated in the same manner (*Ibid.*)." This, in fact, marked the beginning of the last phase of negotiations.

The discussion for sharing water started at the Foreign Secretary level. The Bangladesh Foreign Secretary visited India during August 6-10, 1996 to prepare the ground work. During this visit, the Foreign Secretary also held a meeting, at the suggestion of the Indian External Affairs Minister I.K. Gujral, with the West Bengal Chief Minister Jyoti Basu to seek his help and support in finding a permanent solution to the problem of distribution of the Ganges waters. Basu assured him that he would do everything possible on his part to bring the matter to an amicable resolution. In fact, Basu's visit to Bangladesh from November 27- December 2, 1996 proved to be very crucial because it helped in significantly narrowing the differences between the two sides. Basu had wide-ranging discussions with both the Bangladesh's Prime Minister and the Foreign Minister (Pandey 2012: 276).

During September 1996, the Indian External Affairs Minister visited Bangladesh and the two sides agreed to convene a Joint Committee involving members of their respective foreign ministries who were tasked to bring water experts from both sides to work towards finalization of an agreement on water sharing. The formation of such a committee was another major departure from the past where such committees had always been under the jurisdiction of the Water Resources Ministry. By bringing the technical experts under the supervision of the political leadership, the discussions were 'moderated in a manner so as to lend flexibility and give pre-eminence to the political agenda over the obfuscation of engineering technicalities' (Karim 1998: 228).

The visit of the Bangladesh Minister for Water Resources to India from October 28- November 1, 1996 to hold further talks with his Indian counterpart was quickly followed by that of the Foreign Minister's visit and the meeting between the Joint Committee of Experts. During November 9-13, 1996, both sides reaffirmed their commitment of arriving at an agreement on a fair and equitable sharing of the Ganges waters before the onset of the next dry season (Pandey 2012: 276). While the negotiations were underway at the political level, the Joint Committee met several times to re-examine the technicalities involved and worked towards arriving at an agreed draft agreement to be placed before the two governments. This culminated in the last marathon session of the Committee from December 5-10, 1996 in New Delhi at the foreign secretaries' level (*Ibid.*). The final product, the treaty on the sharing of the Ganges waters entered into by India and Bangladesh on December 12, 1996[11] was 'a more significant document than most people had considered possible' (Iyer 2003: 230-54). The treaty was signed by the prime ministers of India and Bangladesh in New Delhi during Sheikh Hasina's three-day state visit to India (Tiwary 2006: 1690).

Various factors and circumstances were responsible for the culmination of the historic treaty. First of all, Sheikh Hasina personal commitment to finding an acceptable solution to the Farakka issue and her determination to improve relations with India played a major role. Once in power, she made improvement of relations with India, a major foreign policy goal of her administration and directed her close advisers to try to break the deadlock on the Ganges water (Hossain 1998: 140). India too reciprocated equally. Secondly, the successful conclusion of the treaty may also be attributed to the involvement of the chief minister of West Bengal, Jyoti Basu, in the negotiations. Since the Indian state of West Bengal was bound to be affected by any agreement, it was imperative that West Bengal be brought into confidence before agreement on Ganges could be reached. It is to be remembered that the Communist Party of India was a supporter of Deve Gowda's United Front government in New Delhi. Sheikh Hasina's efforts were in turn facilitated by the Indian prime minister's acceptance of Jyoti Basu's involvement in the negotiations. Gowda's rationale for doing so seemed quite simple: As long as West Bengal remained part of the negotiations with Dhaka and was ready to accept an agreement, the Indian prime minister was willing to go along with it (Hossain 1998: 140-141). In fact, Jyoti Basu became the chief negotiator from the Indian side. It was in his 'six-day' visit to Bangladesh that the draft of the Ganges Water-Sharing Treaty was finalized (Rashid 2010: 155).

Thirdly, Sheikh Hasina's decision not to internationalise the issue pleased India. Bangladesh took a major strategic risk by avoiding internationalisation of the issue. Fourthly, I K Gujral's attitude towards India's neighbours had already been soft. The Gujral doctrine,[12] a form of soft power, which focuses on non-reciprocity, that India should be prepared to give more and take less, is evidently seen to be working in forging the Ganges Treaty. Under Deve Gowda's prime ministership, I. K. Gujral enjoyed vast freedom on foreign affairs issues. Fifthly, India also stopped linking the water issue with that of the transit. This was a major departure from Congress government's longstanding policy to link water with a transit facility for Indian goods, which Bangladesh opposed vehemently (Tiwary 2006: 1690).

Nevertheless, the signing of the Ganges Water Treaty (GWT) in December 1996 was an important demonstration of the willingness of the two countries to find a mutually acceptable solution to the impasse in which they had become locked. It also provides a useful insight into what both sides found acceptable as a compromise. The Treaty is scheduled to last for 30 years, and Bangladesh will receive at least 90% of the flows agreed upon after that period, until a new agreement is made (Colombi and Bradnock 2003: 50-51). The 1996 Treaty has three parts: the preamble, the operative part containing 12 Articles and the Annexures. Articles I to XI set forth the provisions for sharing of the Ganges flow and related matters. Though the 1977 agreement contained a 'guarantee clause' and the 1985 deal had a 'burden sharing' formula, the 1996 Treaty did not include any compulsory in-built safeguards for Bangladesh. There are, however, various provisions which provided a modicum of security. For instance, there is a provision of 35,000 cusecs to either side in the alternate 10-day segments in the period from 11 March to 10 May. Another important aspect of the Treaty is that when the flow goes below 50,000 cusecs, the Treaty recognises an emergency situation and provides for immediate consultations by the two governments. The treaty also provides for a conflict resolution mechanism by prescribing a joint monitoring of flows, which should eliminate or minimise the possibility of disagreements over the data (Pandey 2012: 276).

The terms of the treaty have many beneficial features for both the countries. It has various outstanding features favourable to Bangladesh - long duration validity which will help Bangladesh in long-term water resource planning and management; water sharing provision has been delinked from augmentation; the fail-safe arrangement safeguards Bangladesh's interest in case the two sides fail to arrive at an arrangement at the end of the review period. In simple words, the 1996 GWT is a better deal in the term of amount of water for Bangladesh in comparison to previous treaties. As far as the Indian benefits are concerned, the sharing between the two countries when the total flow reaching Farakka is 70,000 cusecs or below will be in the proportion of 50:50 and not 62.7:37.3 as provided in 1977 agreement. There is an arrangement for the diversion of 35,000 cusecs during the three 10-day period of the lean season. These provisions will have a cumulative effect of better protecting the Calcutta port than was possible under the 1977 agreement. Another advantage for India is that it can undertake projects for upstream utilisation, but justice and fairplay would warrant that India should not unilaterally reduce the total flows reaching Farakka (Tiwary 2006: 1690).

The Ganges treaty of 1996 resolved the dispute over Ganges water sharing during the dry season. However, by then, years of disagreements over sharing of Ganges water had contributed to the deep-seated mistrust and aversion against India among the people of Bangladesh. Even after the Ganges Treaty, on many occasions, there have been claims by Bangladesh that the flow in the River Padma drops below the benchmark agreed in the treaty. Therefore, the perception of 'lack of trustworthiness' created by the Farakka Barrage still continues in the minds of the people (Rahman 2015:

103). It is also important to note that – though many considered the Ganges Water Treaty of 1996 to be a success story, many others claim that the treaty lacks the flexibility of the 1977 agreement, which assured a minimum guarantee or an alternative water agreement in case of reduced water flows. Also it is claimed that the treaty does not offer remedies for a long term solution in the event of potential water scarcity (Bisht 2012: 165). Some even claim that the 1996 Ganges Waters Treaty is not being honoured either in letter or spirit (Mukharji 2007: 558). In particular, one of the main concerns of Bangladesh is that the treaty does not explore means to engage other co-riparians. This is considered to be a major shortcoming of the treaty (Rahman 2006: 165).

Although the 1996 Ganges Water Treaty resolved the Farakka dispute, agreements on the sharing of other major rivers are yet to be concluded (Chakma 2012: 14). Apart from the management of the Ganges, the sharing of the water of 53 other rivers has remained unresolved for years. Bangladesh contends that it is necessary to settle disputes over the water sharing of at least seven of the rivers – Teesta, Dharla, Dudhkumar, Manu, Muhuri, Khowai and Gomti, on a priority basis with Teesta having a top priority (Hossain 1998: 155). In fact, for the last few years, especially since September 2011, the Teesta River water sharing issue has emerged as a dominant discourse leading to bitterness between Bangladesh and India (Rahman 2015: 103).

Table 1:Timeline of Farakka Negotiations[13]

29 Oct 1951	Pakistan first calls Indian attention to reports of Indian plans to build a barrage at Farakka to divert Ganges water to Calcutta Bay. India responds that the project was only under preliminary investigation.
28 June 1960	Meetings commence at level of 'expert' between Pakistan and India to exchange data on regional projects.
1960-1968	Expert's level meetings continue; there are five in all, most focusing on data issues.
30 Jan 1961	India informs Pakistan that construction had begun on the Farakka Barrage.
1968-1970	Five meetings continue at the level of secretary. Fundamental disagreements over approaches to Ganges development and the data required to make policy decisions.
1970	India completes construction of Farakka Barrage.
1971	Bangladesh gains independence.
Mar 1972	India and Bangladesh establish Indo-Bangladesh Joint Rivers Commission, to look into the water sharing issue.
16 May 1974	Prime ministers of India and Bangladesh sign a declaration agreeing to find a mutually acceptable solution to Ganges development, and to turn the question of the best way of supplementing Ganges flow over to the Joint Rivers Commission.

(Contd...)

16 Apr 1975	The two sides agree to a limited trial operation of the Farakka Barrage. India continues to divert Ganges water after the trial run, without renewing or negotiating a new agreement with Bangladesh.
June 1975-June 1976	Meetings continue, with little result.
Jan 1976	Bangladesh lodges a formal protest against India with the United Nations, which adopts a consensus statement encouraging the parties to meet urgently, at the level of minister, to arrive at a settlement.
5 Nov 1977	Ganges Waters Agreement signed, covering allocation of Ganges water between the two riparians for a period of five years. No long-term solution was found within that time frame.
Oct 1982	Joint communiqué issued, pledging to resolve Ganges issues within 18 months, a task not accomplished.
22 Nov 1985	Memorandum of understanding issued, on the sharing of Ganges dry season flow through 1988. When accord lapses, no new agreement is signed.
29 Sep 1988	Summit in New Delhi between heads of government. Bangladesh Secretary of Irrigation and India's Secretary of Water Resources were given the task to work on an integrated formula for the sharing of common rivers between India and Bangladesh.
April 1990-Feb 1992	Secretaries' Committee met six times alternatively between Dhaka and NewDelhi.
12 Dec 1996 1996-2004	Ganges Water Treaty signed by the Prime Ministers of India and Bangladesh Bangladesh's attempts to talk with India over agreements concerning seven rivers are met with non-interest.
Dec 2002	India announces plans for river linking project connecting rivers from north to those in the south and east.

Section- II

3.3 Teesta Water Sharing Issue

The sharing of the Teesta water has become one of the most contested issues in India-Bangladesh relations of late. The Teesta River flows through the state of Sikkim and West Bengal to Bangladesh. India has built the Gajoldoba barrage on the Teesta, 60 Km north of Bangladesh to divert water for irrigation purposes in West Bengal. Bangladesh has been complaining that India diverts water to the Gajoldoba barrage at the cost of Bangladesh's lower riparian needs (Bisht 2012: 165). According to the JRC, Bangladesh was supposed to get 2700 cusec of water. However, Bangladesh contends that it is receiving a very small amount during the dry season. In fact, Bangladesh has been claiming an equal share of the water of Teesta for long because it is anticipated that if the water is not shared proportionately and if India is not generous in sharing Teesta water, a number of districts (Nilphamari, Rangpur and Dinajpur, etc.) of Bangladesh might turn into deserts (*The New Age*, May 13, 2009).

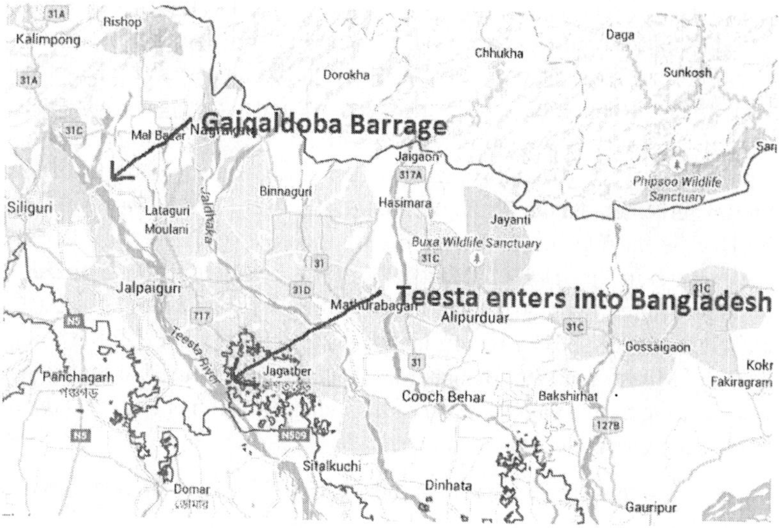

Source: https://www.quora.com/What-are-the-disputes-over-India-Bangladesh-Teesta-deal

Map 5: flow of Teesta River and the Location of Gajaldoba Barrage

With regard to Teesta, both countries have come to an *adhoc* understanding since 1983, whereby during the lean period, Bangladesh is allocated 36 percent of water and India 39 percent, leaving the remaining 25 percent to be decided on later. But water sharing has been impeded by implementation issues – primarily stemming from the divergence in data interpretation (Parsi 2011: 175). It was in 2010, particularly at the 37th meeting of the JRC in Delhi that the Bangladesh water resource minister, Ramesh Chandra Sen demanded the 50-50 distribution of the Teesta water at Gajaldoba point (Haque 2011: 170). At present the main point of contention relating to the Teesta water is the sharing of water on a '50:50' basis and Bangladesh's demand for a minimum guarantee clause, which is fixed at 3500 cusecs of water for Bangladesh. This is an issue because according to Kalyan Rudra, (appointed by Mamata Banerjee to coordinate an expert committee on Teesta waters); in the lean season the total water availability is 3000-4000 cusecs. This means that even after applying the distribution formula Bangladesh would not get more than 2000 cusecs, (Haque 2011: 175) a figure which is unacceptable to Bangladesh (Bisht 2012: 175).

A Joint Technical Group (JTG) was formed to look into water availability in both countries and to work out interim India and Bangladesh shares. There were some progress on this issue when the two countries agreed to sign a 15 year interim accord on sharing the waters of the common rivers Feni and Teesta at a secretary-level meeting in January 2011 (Pattanaik 2011: 155). The agreement was expected to be signed during the scheduled visit of the then Prime Minister Manmohan Singh to Bangladesh on September 2011. India and Bangladesh even had exchanged drafts of the interim agreement on the 'Principles of the Sharing of Teesta Waters during the Dry Season' at the 37th meeting of India-Bangladesh Joint Rivers Commission in New Delhi in March 2011 (Hossain 1998: 155). Both sides reportedly agreed to a 50-50 sharing of water of Teesta River (*The Daily Star*, September 8, 2011). Unfortunately all the efforts went in futile when the Chief Minister of West Bengal, Mamata Banerjee, refused to accept the water sharing formula agreed upon by the Indian Government on the ground that it would harm her state's interests (*Ibid*., pp. 155-56).

However, the 2015 June visit of Indian Prime Minister Narendra Modi's to Bangladesh has opened a new vista as far as Indo-Bangladesh relations is concerned. With an amicable resolution of the land and maritime boundary issues, one can hope that the Teesta water issue will also be dealt in a similar manner. Modi said the following about the Teesta issue: "I am confident that with the support of state governments in India, we can reach a fair solution on the Teesta and Feni rivers."[14] In fact, the delegates of the two countries met in June 2016 to propel the issue forward and satisfactory results have been expected in the said meeting.

The domestic imperatives are important in this regard. This is evident in Modi's stance. In fact, from what Modi said, it is clear that Mamata Banerjee's opinion on the matter will be of prime importance while taking any decision on the issue. Equally important it is to note here that while Teesta water-sharing may not been as significant as the Land Border Agreement in Modi's scheme of things and India-Bangladesh diplomacy, it is an issue that is very close to Banerjee's heart. Therefore, by letting Banerjee lead the Teesta issue, Modi is actually trying to deal with the imperatives of domestic politics. It is further a convenient way to take a first step towards winning Banerjee's confidence without which the resolution of Teesta issue is hard to imagine.[15] Consequently, West Bengal Chief Minister who had previously opposed the Teesta Water Agreement too has given positive indications with regard to the resolution of the Teesta issue. Over the past couple of months, Mamata Banerjee has reassured Bangladesh that it will not get an unfair deal on water sharing.

Nevertheless, the failure to conclude the Teesta Agreement till now has generated enormous resentment and frustration among the people of Bangladesh. Since then Teesta water sharing issue has emerged as one of the key drivers of perception formation in Bangladesh vis-à-vis India. It contributed enormously to the negative perceptions of 'suspicion and mistrust' towards India and also a perception that there was 'lack of seriousness' on the part of India (Rahman 2015: 103).

3.4 Tipaimukh Dam Controversy

Indo-Bangladesh relations are also strained over the issue of Tipaimukh dam which is proposed to be built in the state of Manipur on the Barak River in order to generate 1500 MW of hydropower (Rizvi 2011: 166). The proposed Tipaimukh dam is to be located 500 meters downstream from the confluence of Barak and Tuivai rivers at the south western corner of Manipur. The dam was originally conceived for containing only the flood waters of the Cachar plains of Assam but later on, the focus shifted to hydroelectric power generation. A high capacity dam with a height of 162.8 meters would thus be built in Tipaimukh (Hossain 1998: 151-52).

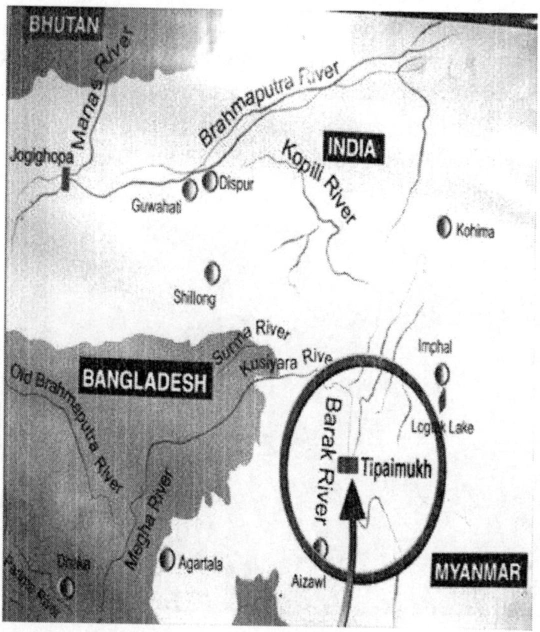

Source: Google Image

Map 6: Location of Tapaimukh Dam

While New Delhi contends that Tipaimukh is run on the river project, some in Dhaka have challenged this (Rizvi 2011: 166). Bangladesh contends that the construction of the Tipaimukh dam will inflict huge damage on Bangladesh's economy, ecology and will mean disaster for its population. Experts argue that the completion of the project will hit Bangladesh fatally, and with no less a magnitude than the Farakka Barrage (Hossain 1998: 154). It is believed that it would diminish water flow in three major rivers of Bangladesh – the Meghna, Surma and the Kushiyara, would lead to the increase in the rate of sedimentation, which in turn would gradually decrease the water carrying capacity of these rivers. All these effects will be seen in the Northeastern region and especially in the Hoor area of the country which would totally change the existing scenario in this area. The fertile land of Hoor would turn to desert. Agriculture would be destroyed. Rice varieties like, Boro, Shail and Aman would be lost as well as the regional biodiversity (*Ibid.*, p. 152).

Further, Bangladesh also contends that the dam will result in lower levels of flow, impacting availability of under-ground water through tube wells, used extensively for agricultures (Zakzaman 2006: 123). Consequently, the economy of Bangladesh and the normal life of its people would be seriously impaired (Hossain 1998: 154). These controversies for long have stalled any decision on the subject and progress has slowed down since March 2007 due to the environmental reasons and protest from the locals. Though the issue grabbed attention in late 2011, there has been growing oppositions from some sections within Bangladesh demanding more openness and transparency from India (Bisht 2012: 167).

Source: Google Image

Map 7: Tapaimukh Dam

3.5 India's River Linking Project (RLP)

India's river linking project (RLP) includes both the Himalayan and peninsular rivers of India. It is proposed that the Brahmaputra would be linked with the Ganges to carry waters to Orissa and eventually to South India. The project will divert waters from the Brahmaputra towards the Ganges, thereafter driving it into the Mahanadi and Godavari. The Godavari will be linked to the Krishna and then to the Pennar and Cauvery. The Narmada will flow into the Tapti and the Yamuna into the Sabarmati (Azam and Karim 2003: 151). The left tributaries of the Ganges would also be linked at several places and the increased volume of water in the Ganges would then be channeled to Rajasthan, Gujarat and Maharashtra. The eastern peninsular rivers would be linked with western peninsular ones and water would also be transferred to southern Karnataka and Kerala (Pattanaik 2004: 151).

The project also envisages the construction of water reservoirs at many places throughout the length and breadth of India. The RLP is envisaged to connect 38 rivers through 30 links, 9000 km long canals, 74 reservoirs and several embankments by 2016. The project is estimated to cost between $ 112 billion to $ 200 billion (Kabir and Khanom 2008: 177-209). If the project is implemented, it is argued that the Brahmaputra's flow will be reduced to 40,000 cusecs from its normal flow of 1, 40,000 cusecs while the combined flow of Padma and Brahmaputra at Maowa point will also be reduced to 30,000 - 40,000 cusecs from the normal flow of 2, 00,000 cusecs. There will be no flow in the Dharla, Dhudhkumar, Teesta and Mahananda rivers even during a normal monsoon. Flows in Madhumati, Naba Ganges, Ichamati, Mathabhanga, Kapotakhya and Betna will also be reduced substantially (Hossain 1998: 151).

According to Harun ur Rashid – the RLP has caused grave concerns for Bangladesh mainly for four reasons: (a) Bangladesh has been officially kept in the dark; (b) the size of the dam is massive; (c) it will cause devastation in Bangladesh because all major sources of river will be subject to unilateral diversion by India and; (d) the project goes against Article 9 of the 1996 Ganges Water Treaty that explicitly provides that both sides "agreed to conclude water sharing treaties/agreements with regard to other common rivers (Rashid 2010: 189-90)."

Bangladesh argues that India's river linking project is a tremendous security threat to Bangladesh, both in the traditional and the non-traditional sense. The proposed RLP would further reduce the inflow of freshwater from upstream which would gradually lead to a reduction of ground water

(Kabir and Khanom 2008: 177-209). The decreased water flow in the river will increase sedimentation as well as salinity intrusion in the rivers. The impact of the Indian river-linking project on Bangladesh will be multi-dimensional affecting agriculture, fisheries, navigation, environment, geomorphology, etc. (Hossain 1998: 154). Furthermore; the risk of dam failure is a significant issue. A dam-break is a catastrophic failure which results in the sudden draining of the reservoir and a severe flood wave that may cause destruction and deaths downstream in Bangladesh. In 2004 Bangladesh protested to the proposed dam and thereafter India kept quiet on the dam. It was again revived in 2007 and India seems to be determined to proceed with the project (Rashid 2010: 184).

As such, Bangladesh has vociferously protested the plan. Different avenues/routes of protest are being utilised. Already there is a lot of media focus in Bangladesh on India's plan to interlink rivers. Some Bangladeshi professionals have written to the Supreme Court of India to scrap the interlinking programme. The plan has already entered the domestic politics lexicon where the specter of Farakka is being re-invoked (Tiwary 2006: 1692). The diplomatic channels are following the state positions. The Bangladesh government is reported to have taken up the issue with the Indian government and has been assured that international laws on water sharing would be adhered to in the interlinking programme. The senior officials in the Indian ministry of water resources said none of the projects were likely to affect Bangladesh in a manner that was being projected in the media (*Ibid.*).

Conclusion

It is obvious that even after the conclusion on the 1996 Ganges Water Treaty the sharing of trans-boundary water resources remain at the core of India-Bangladesh relations. Hence, the question of sharing of water resources between the two acquires utmost significance. As the chapter demonstrates, the negotiations on Farakka went through four phases. It is interesting to note that during the first phase (1971-1977), we find enough soft power inferences which India employed in its relations with Bangladesh. India's assistance during the process of rehabilitation and reconstruction of Bangladesh can be seen from a soft power perspective. Consequently, progress was made in the water sharing issue with the formation of JRC in 1972. However, the assassination of Bangladesh' Prime Minister Sheikh Mujib proved to be a serious blow to the India-Bangladesh relations. It obviously also had a detrimental impact on the Farakka issue.

India-Bangladesh relations improved considerably with the coming of the Janata Party led government at New Delhi. Thus, dramatic progress was witnessed in the second phase (1977-82) as far as cooperation on the Farakka issue is concerned. India and Bangladesh signed a five year treaty on the sharing of the Ganges water. However, the most significant achievement with regard to the Ganges water sharing issue came in the fourth phase in 1996, with the signing of the Ganges Water treaty. Interestingly, we find plentitude of soft power inferences in it. The 1996 Ganges Water Treaty aptly demonstrates how soft power can be employed with effect to resolve even the contentious bilateral issues. Undoubtedly, Sheikh Hasina should be credited for her pro-India policy, which brought Dhaka closer to New Delhi. However, at another level, it is evident that Jyoti Basu the Chief Minister of West Bengal played a pivotal role in the resolution of the Ganges Water dispute. The move to include Jyoti Basu proved to be very significant as Basu helped in significantly narrowing the differences between the two sides. In other words, India and Bangladesh were actually using their cultural affinity or soft power to resolve one of the major irritant in their bilateral relations. Needless to say that West Bengal will always play an important role not only when it comes to solving bilateral disputes between India-Bangladesh, but also to build their bilateral relationship in general.

Gujral's attitude towards India's neighbours had already been soft. His doctrine popularly called 'the Gujral Doctrine' exemplifying the ethos of generosity and non-reciprocity has soft power connotations and is evidently seen to be working in forging the Ganges Water Treaty. The conclusion of the Ganges Water Treaty also shows how the 'regime compatibility' plays a critical role in India-Bangladesh bilateral ties. As the negotiations on Farakka have shown, and which will be substantiated by the succeeding chapter, India and Bangladesh tend to reach to negotiations when Awami League is in power in Bangladesh. In fact, as the chapter shows, both India and Bangladesh's approach towards the issue of river water sharing have 'not' been shaped so much by the technical but by the 'regime compatibility' factor.

When Sheikh Hasina came to power chose to be follow policies that was India-friendly. This defiantly earned some leverages when the negotiations on Farakka was made. Historically too Awami League has always been considered pro-Indian, especially with its secular orientations which makes it easy for the exploration of the Bengali connections. Moreover, the AL Government had come to power after a long gap of twenty years and obviously India didn't want to lose an opportunity to improve its relations with Bangladesh which becomes easier when AL comes to power. Also it is in the Indian interest that AL retains power in Bangladesh. Obviously the solution to Farakka would give AL a better cushion for the next term and also for the LBA issue. Lastly, meaningful negotiations can only take place in favourable environment. The important take away from the chapter, which will be illustrated in the succeeding chapters, is that, we can use soft power to create favourable conditions for negotiations to take place.

Notes

1. http://www.sos-arsenic.net/english/groundwater/waterbattle.html
2. http://www1.american.edu/ted/ice/indobang.htm November, 1997 Robie I. Samanta Roy
3. http://udayindia.in/2015/05/02/policy-on-sharing-river-water-between-india-and-bangladesh/
4. http://www.transboundarywaters.orst.edu/research/case_studies/ anges_New.htm
5. http://www.transboundarywaters.orst.edu/research/case_studies/ anges_New.htm
6. http://www.transboundarywaters.orst.edu/research/case_studies/ anges_New.htm
7. First, he desired Indian personnel with experience in district administration to come and serve in Bangladesh on deputation for a period of three to six months till Bangladesh civil servants could replace them. Second, he wanted a part of the Indian armed forces to remain in Bangladesh for about a year more to neutralize pockets on anti-Bangladesh resistance within the country. Third, that India should render across the broad economic assistance and help create a Bangladeshi national airlines and shipping. He desired that India undertake the repair of main roads, bridges and railway communications. India was prompt in responding to these requirements.
8. Refer to Appendix I Indo-Bangladesh Friendship Treaty, Article VI of the treaty stated that "the high contracting parties further agree to make a joint study and take a joint action in the fields of flood control, river basin development and the development of hydro-electric power and irrigation."
9. This agreement was replaced on July 5, 1973 by a new Three-year Trade greement
10. Appendix II
11. Refer to Appendix
12. Former Prime Minister, Late Mr. I.K. Gujral propounded the Gujral Doctrine when he was the Union Minister of External Affairs in 1996-1997 in the H.D. Deve Gowda Government. The Gujral doctrine was a five-point roadmap which sought to build trust between India and neighbours, of solution to bilateral issues through bilateral talks and to remove immediate quid pro quos in diplomatic relationship between India and her neighbours. The 'Doctrine' emphasized on the importance of unilateral accommodation for friendly and warm relations with India's neighbours. The five principles are: **1.**With neighbours like Bangladesh, Bhutan, Maldives, Nepal and Sri Lanka, India does not ask for reciprocity, but gives and accommodates what it can in good faith and trust. **2.**

No South Asian country should allow its territory to be used against the interest of another country of the region. **3.** No country should interfere in the internal affairs of another. **4.** All South Asian countries must respect each other's territorial integrity and sovereignty. **5.** They should settle all their disputes through peaceful bilateral negotiations. Cited from http://byjus.com/free-ias-prep/gujral-doctrine

13. Aaron T. Wolf and Joshua T. Newton (not dated) Case Study of Transboundary Dispute Resolution: The Ganges River controversy available at http://www.transboundarywaters.orst.edu/research/case_studies/Ganges_New.htm
14. http://www.ndtv.com/india-news/efforts-underway-to-resolve-teesta-isue-with-bangladesh-indian-envoy-pankaj-saran-1217511
15. http://www.firstpost.com/politics/modi-sings-mamatas-tunes-on-teesta-issue-was-bangladesh-the-ice-breaker-they-needed-2283612.html

Chapter - IV

Border Issues and the Enclaves: A Contestation

The chapter deals with the border dispute between India and Bangladesh which is one of the most contentious issues between the two countries. The border dispute, however, has twin dimensions. The first pertains to the dispute emanating from the land boundary and the other, the maritime boundary dispute. The study will, however, primarily focus on the land boundary, though the maritime boundary dispute will also be dealt briefly. The land boundary problem drew importance immediately after the partition of the sub-continent in 1947. The 'Bagge Award' (1950) and the 'Nehru-Noon Accord' (1958) attempted to resolve the border problems, but were unsuccessful. After the independence of Bangladesh, the land boundary agreement (LBA) 1974 tried revisit the border problems. Unfortunately the 1974 Land Boundary Agreement was not ratified by the Indian Parliament. Consequently, India-Bangladesh border problems remained unresolved. Efforts were also made in 2011 but in vain. Finally, with the visit of the Indian Prime Minister Narendra Modi to Bangladesh on June 2015, the LBA was signed, thus ending the age old bilateral irritant between India and Bangladesh.

This chapter is structured in two major sections. The first section deals with the historiography of the land boundary problems. The section further divides the negotiations on Land Boundary into phases starting from the Bagge Award of 1950 (Indo-Pakistan Boundary Disputes Tribunal) to the conclusion of the LBA in 2015. As we shall see, the negotiations on the land boundary went into three main phases; the first phase (1971-1996), the second phase (1996-2015) and the third phase (2015 onwards). The main thrust of the section, however, is to demonstrate the employability of soft power in the conclusion of the LBA in 2015. The second section of the chapter deals with the other major problems pertaining to the border which the LBA 2015 fails to address. In this regard, the section deals with the four major challenges related to territorial border—illegal migration, security concerns, maritime boundary dispute and the problems associated with the fencing of the border.

4.1 Section-I

It is ironic that the border which was drawn by the British in 1947 to rationally re-organise the political space in the region has eventually not only generated its own irrationality, but has also created many new problems for the region (Banerjee *et al.,* 1999: 2549). Cyril Radcliffe, who headed the Boundary Commission to partition India in 1947, spoiled the job in the eastern side of the border by drawing a straight line through villages and rivers, houses and market-places. Neither did the Indian members of the commission at that time, nor did their successors who came to rule the country later, cared to undo the damage by rationally demarcating the border. As a result, border conflicts continued to plague India-Bangladesh relations (Banerjee 2001: 1505). As such, one of the most pressing concerns between India-Bangladesh relates to the problem of border management.

India and Bangladesh share almost 4096 kms of land border. Official records suggest that only 6.1 kms of land, at three sectors viz. Daikhata-56 (West Bengal), Muhuri River-Belonia (Tripura) and Lathitila-Dumabari (Assam), is considered as officially disputed by the governments of both countries. But the border disputes between India and Bangladesh are by no means confined to delineation problems. It is further linked with problems like illegal migration, border killings, smuggling, trafficking and other cross border criminal and terror activities (Dutta 2010: 7). The porous border also makes it easy for terrorists to move at will (Mukharji 2007: 559). Notwithstanding the presence of a sizeable border security force on both sides, as well as over 3,000 km of barbed wire fencing on the Indian side, the number of persons killed on the border, for the most part Bangladeshis, is among the highest in the world.[1] Other problems pertaining to the border relates to the exchanges of the enclaves[2] and the question of adverse possessions. The three problems attached to the LBA have, however, been resolved first, with the historic passing of the LBA in the Indian Parliament in May 2015 and the subsequent conclusion of Land Boundary Agreement (LBA) in June 2015. Yet the other problems pertaining to the boundary persists.

4.1.a The origin of the Land Boundary Problem

The Indo-Bangladesh border, determined as per the Radcliffe Award of 1947, brought into fore host of complexities. Although the demarcation of the border between India and the then Pakistan started soon after the partition of the subcontinent, progress was slower than expected, partly due to the difficulties in determining precisely where the border ran. Even after the creation of Bangladesh, the boundary dispute between the two countries inherited the legacy of history and fractured politics.[3] The first effort to resolve the border complexities came in the form of the Bagge Award of 1950.[4] The Indo-Pakistan Boundary Disputes Tribunal was set up in December 1949 under the Chairmanship of Algot Bagge, former member of the Supreme Court of Sweden with a member each from India and East Pakistan for the adjudication and final settlement of the arising out of the interpretation of the Radcliffe Award and for demarcating the boundary (Jamwal 2004: 5).

The Bagge Award, though, was unable to resolve India's border issue with East Pakistan. Consequently another effort in this regard was made in 1958, with the visit of the then Prime Minister of Pakistan Firoze Khan Noon to New Delhi at the invitation of Pandit Jawaharlal Nehru. Both the Prime Ministers discussed Indo-Pakistan (including East Pakistan) border problems and sought to reduce tension and establish peaceful conditions along the Indo-Pakistan border. The Nehru-Noon Agreement[5] on India-East Pakistan Border was signed in New Delhi on September 10, 1958, which aimed to address the border disputes related to West Bengal, Assam, and Tripura. The agreements covered the Bagge Awards, Hilli, Berubari Union No 12, 24-Parganas-Khulna and 24-Parganas-Jessore boundary, Bholaganj, Piyain and Surma rivers, Feni river and Cooch-Behar enclaves (*Ibid*, p.7).

The Nehru-Noon Agreement of 1958, in so far as the mutual exchange of the enclaves and the transfer of the southern half of South Berubari Union No.12 to East Pakistan by India was concerned, could not be implemented due to litigation filed by Indian nationals, claiming that the entire union of South Berubari, was Indian territory at the time of coming into force of the Indian Constitution and the enclaves belonging to Cochbehar state were also parts of India. Therefore, neither the southern half of the Union nor the enclaves could be ceded to a foreign country. In due course the case reached Supreme Court of India. The Court ruled that Constitution of India had to be amended so as to facilitate the transfer. The Indian Constitution was accordingly amended in 1960 (9th Amendment). However, the stipulated exchanges did not take place.[6]

4.1.b Negotiations on Land Boundary Issue

4.1.b.(i) First Phase of Negotiations (1971-1996)

Soon after the creation of Bangladesh, issues of un-demarcated borders, exchange of enclaves, and the adversely possessed lands were thought to be resolved through the 1974 LBA between India and Bangladesh (Rahman 2015: 105). Under this agreement, India was allowed to retain Southern Berubari (which lies within Jalpaiguri *thana*) along with the adjacent Muslim enclaves. In exchange Bangladesh was given the enclaves of Dahagram and Angarpota. Since, the two enclaves were not contiguous to the Bangladesh mainland, a bilateral agreement was required for a perpetual lease of area measuring 178 mt. x 185 mt. (Tin Bigha) to Bangladesh (Jamwal 2004: 7). Bangladesh ratified the Agreement in 1974, but India held back the process on the ground that it would require a constitutional amendment to implement the Agreement (*The Daily Star*, May 11, 2015). In fact, the border complexities were many. Even apart from the swathes of un-demarcated borderland (6.1km), the terrain made it difficult to draw and maintain boundary lines in the delineated border sections. Most importantly, the borders were uneven, overlapping and easily permeable, making them source of continuous bilateral tension (Datta 2016: 3). The border problems could not be resolved during the Mujib era. Consequently, three outstanding issues remained unresolved – (i) an un-demarcated land boundary of 6.1 km in three sectors; (ii) adverse possessions;[7] and (iii) an exchange of enclaves[8] (*The Diplomat*, May 25, 2015).

After the assassination of Mujib, India-Bangladesh relations became entangled into various other complexities making its resolution all the more difficult. Progress on border issues was delayed for a long time and subsequent governments failed to address the issue (*The Daily Star*, June 06, 2015). However, the only breakthrough with regard to border was achieved in June 26, 1992 when the perpetual lease of the Tin Bigha to Bangladesh finally granted by India. The lease was perpetuated after protracted negotiations and exchanges of letters of understanding between the two Governments, first in October 1982 and then in March 1992. The lease provided connection between the enclaves of Dahagram and Angarpota and mainland Bangladesh in a somewhat limited fashion, that is, at alternate hours during daylight. Later, however, at the intervention of the Indian Union Home Ministry this was further eased to cover the entire day light period.[9]

4.1.b.(ii) Second Phase (1996-2015)

Though the LBA remained important for different regimes in the post-Mujib era, it was only in 1996, when Sheikh Hasina became Prime Minister, that the LBA issues were revisited (Bhardwaj 2015: 97). With the Awami League (AL) government coming to power in Bangladesh, after a gap of 21 years, the relationship started to improve as both Dhaka and New Delhi began to pursue affirmative approaches towards each other. The conclusion of the Ganges water sharing agreement (1996) laid a strong base and it demonstrated the inclination for gradually improving relationship (Rahman 2015: 97). In addition, the Peace Accord 1997 signed between the government of Bangladesh and the representatives of Chakma people in the Chittagong Hill Tracts facilitated the return of the Chakma refugees from India to Bangladesh (Rashid 2010: 152). However, there were limits to this improvement due to two basic reasons. First, the Awami League (AL) had a thin majority in the Bangladesh parliament, which meant that the government had little room to maneuver against strong opposition, such as, the Bangladesh Nationalist Party (BNP) and the *Jamat-e-Islami*. Second, following the ascendency of Bharatiya Janata Party (BJP) in 1998, the steady improvement of India-Bangladesh relations were stymied as the BJP government strongly raised the controversial issue of 'Illegal Muslim Immigrants' from Bangladesh to northeast India (Wright 2007: 10).

Nevertheless, the relations between the two countries improved considerably when the AL government came to power in Bangladesh. This trend in fact remains strong even today. In this regard Sreeradha Datta contends that, given the history of the Bangladesh War of Liberation, the Awami League party in Bangladesh and the Congress party in India has always shared close ties, with the bilateral relations always reflecting this in the last four decades. However, an important aspect which needs special mention is that, while typically a non-Congress government in Delhi has not substantially affected these bilateral relations, non-Awami League governments in Dhaka have (Datta 2016: 227). With regard to the boundary issues too some progress was witnessed. In April 1997, the list of enclaves, along with maps, was jointly reconciled, signed and exchanged between the two governments. Some progress was also made in December 2000, when the two countries established the Joint Boundary Working Group (JBWG), a bilateral mechanism which was entrusted to make recommendations to settle the border problems (Bhardwaj 2015: 97). The initial three meetings of the JBWG took place in July 2001, March 2002, and July 2006 (Arora 2010:43).

The India-Bangladesh relations deteriorated again with the return of BNP to power in Bangladesh in 2001. The policies of the two countries once again divulged discrepancies as they developed differences at various levels. India was concerned with the continuous rise of Islamic fundamentalism in Bangladesh, harbouring of Indian terrorists within Bangladesh, non-cooperation in export of gas to India and the presence of huge number of illegal Bangladeshi immigrants in India. On the other hand, Bangladesh contended that the BJP led government was not enthusiastic to resolve bilateral issues with Bangladesh's new government. As a result, unfriendly relation existed between the two countries. Although India's Foreign Minister visited Bangladesh in August 2002 and spoke of determination in resolving all pending disputes, no positive outcome was visible during BJP-led Vajpayee government (Rashid 2010: 164). Hence, the border issues could not be resolved during the BNP tenure. BNP's rule ended in 2006 giving way to the Bangladesh military rule, *albeit* indirectly under the caretaker government, from 2006 to 2008. Territorial disputes remained unresolved, under the caretaker government too. As outside and inside pressures mounted to return to democracy, the military eventually relented and general elections were held on December 29, 2008. In the elections the 14-party coalition led by the Awami League accomplished a landslide victory and formed a new government in early January 2009 (Chakma 2012: 11).

Substantial changes took place in Indo-Bangladesh relations with the advent of AL government in Bangladesh in 2009. Prime Minister, Sheikh Hasina was prompt in reassessing Bangladesh's foreign policy orientation, particularly its India policy. The developments of the subsequent three years are a clear testimony that the Hasina government reversed the policies of its predecessors and adopted a pro-India approach. Theoretically, there were alternative choices for Dhaka vis-à-vis New Delhi. For example, it could have continued with the policy of its predecessors and maintained closer ties with China and Pakistan at the expense of India; or it could have opted for a 'neutral' or 'balanced' approach, engaging India, China and Pakistan/ Islamic countries on an equal footing. The Hasina government chose to draw closer to India (Chakma 2012: 11).

After coming to power, Sheikh Hasina government adopted certain policies and strategies that pleased India. First among them was to extend security cooperation to India and pay heed to the longstanding Indian complaint that terrorists and insurgents were using Bangladeshi territory. Accordingly, it reopened the Chittagong arms haul case (2004)[10] and arrested the former National Security Intelligence Chief Major General (Retd.) Rezaqul Haider Chowdhury and Brigadier General (Retd.) Abdur Rahim who were involved in the case (Datta 2016: 228). Dhaka, in due course of time also took action against Harkatul Jihad al Islam (HuJI) and Jamaatul-Mujahideen Bangladesh (JMB), and handed over two Laskar-e-Toiba (LeT) members of Indian origin who had been operating from Bangladesh. Such actions by Dhaka proved helpful for New Delhi to combat terrorism within India (Chakma 2012:12-13).

The Hasina government also took actions against the Indian insurgents using Bangladeshi territory. In November 2009, Dhaka caught and handed over the foreign secretary of United Liberation Front of Assam (ULFA), Sashadhar Choudhury, and finance secretary Chitraban Hazarika, to the Indian security forces. Dhaka also captured and handed over the ULFA chairman, Arabinda Rajkhowa, together with his bodyguard, Palash Phukan, and the Deputy Commander-in-Chief of ULFA, Hitesh Kalita, to Assam Police (*Deccan Chronicle,* December 4, 2009). The Bangladeshi authorities acted in a similar manner against other Indian insurgent groups. Indeed, Dhaka's willingness and the help it rendered to address India's security concern was of critical importance to India. It contributed profoundly in bringing the insurgency problem in its northeast region under control (Chakma 2012: 13). Such initiatives by Dhaka actually generated 'pull-factor' for Bangladesh and as such earned Bangladesh, soft power.

While reciprocating, India also extended its cooperation to Bangladesh on security and intelligence matters. In January 2012, Dhaka unearthed a coup plot by some *Jihadi*-leaning military officers against the government. The tip-off, it was afterwards revealed, came from Indian intelligence agencies (*The Telegraph*, January 21, 2012). This in fact, was a testimony to the intelligence cooperation that existed between the two countries. It also in a way exhibited Hasina's pro-India foreign policy orientation (Chakma 2012: 13). Another important step that the AL government after it assumed power in January 2009 was that it took further steps to recognise all those who contributed to the liberation of Bangladesh.[11] Both countries now jointly celebrate Victory day in Dhaka and Kolkata. In fact, initially the military backed caretaker regime that assumed power in January 2007 took steps to publicly recognise India's contribution to the liberation of Bangladesh and decided to felicitate Indian soldiers by inviting them to participate in the victory day celebration in Dhaka in 2007, which was first of its kind (Pattanaik 2016: 219-220).

It was following Prime Minister Sheikh Hasina's visit to India in January 2010 that the Congress-led UPA made a sincere effort to resolve the land boundary issues (*The Daily Star*, May 20, 2015). In fact, the template for the improvement of bilateral ties between neighbours was really laid with the Joint Communiqué of 2010 which paved the way forward for the two neighbours in a way quite un-heralded in the past. The 51 point MOU that was agreed upon during Hasina's 2010 India visit exemplified the growing partnership and provided a road map of future cooperation. Consequently, progress was made in border issues as both the countries agreed to take steps at the earliest to demarcate the boundary, exchange the enclaves and settle the land that were in 'adverse possession' (Pattanaik 2016: 220).

Further, India and Bangladesh agreed to convene the JBWG to take the process forward.[12] As the result, experts and political aides of both countries met several times to find a solution to demarcate the border (Rahman 2015: 105). In the fourth JBWG meeting, in New Delhi on November 10-11, 2010, both sides expressed satisfaction at the electrification of Dahagram and Angarpota. India and Bangladesh also implemented 24-hour unfettered access through the Tin Bigha Corridor, and put in place all the necessary arrangements, including infrastructure and security, expeditiously in the later years (Bhardwaj 2015: 97). Consequently, during Manmohan Singh's September 2011 visit to Bangladesh, India agreed to keep the Tin Bigha corridor open for 24 hours, thereby removing a longstanding impediment in India-Bangladesh relations (Chakma 2012: 16). Following this, detailed negotiations, joint visits to the concerned areas and land surveys were also undertaken.[13]

It was under the aegis of the Joint Boundary Working Group (JBWG) that the crucial decision on joint visits to all disputed border areas and territories, including enclaves and adverse possessions, was taken. These joint visits began in 2007, but picked up pace and momentum only in 2009, after the ninth parliamentary elections in Bangladesh. In May 2007, the India–Bangladesh delegation carried out an elaborate process of consultation with people in the areas involved (Bhardwaj 2015: 98). From the feedback that was received, it was clear that the people residing in the areas involved did not want to leave their land and preferred to remain in the country where they had resided all their lives. As a result, both sides decided to avoid large scale uprooting and displacement of populations against their wishes, though this was contrary to the 1974 LBA. The 2011 Protocol thus, departs from the 1974 LBA in this regard (Bhardwaj 2015:98). Apart from it, the views of the concerned State Governments in favour of realigning the boundary to maintain status quo in respect of territories in adverse possession were also taken into account (Bhardwaj 2015:98).

4.1.c.(i) The LBA 2011

The years of painstaking negotiations paid off by August 2011, when India and Bangladesh were able to agree upon, joint border maps, settling decades of differences relating to the LBA issues. While the strip maps were signed in July 2011, the then Prime Minister Manmohan Singh signed the protocol to the 1974 LBA during his visit in September 2011 (Pattanaik 2016: 220). Once again, the Bangladesh Parliament ratified the protocol (Bhardwaj 2015: 98). Unfortunately, UPA lacked the numerical strength in the Lok Sabha. When it planned to place the Bill in the Parliament, the BJP, then in opposition, stiffly opposed the move (*The Daily Star*, May 20, 2015). Opposition to the bill also came from the Trinamool Congress (TMC) and Asom Gana Parishad (AGP) (Rahman 2015: 105).

Though the LBA 2011 could not materialise, yet there are few critical points that need mention. The very fact that the LBA came so near to being concluded is indeed commendable. The advent of AL in Bangladesh, and Hasina's decision to adopt pro-India approach over all other options laid the necessary platform for India-Bangladesh relations to foster. The joint communiqué 2010 just strengthened it. Moreover, Bangladesh' initiative to address India's security concern created an atmosphere of trust and friendship. It is evident that with the coming of AL to power in Bangladesh, the Indo-Bangladesh relations tend to improve and India is willing to concede more. In short, as mentioned in previous chapter, the 'regime compatibility' factor holds utmost importance to India-Bangladesh bilateral ties, which the chapter also substantiates. This, when seen from the 'power of attraction' perspective definitely qualifies as a soft power. In fact, a critical observation would reveal that the employability of soft power becomes all the more vivid in and after 2010.

One of the most prominent soft power strategies that has constantly been used in the past pertains to trade, economic inducements and investments. The 2010 communiqué also exemplifies it. The trajectory of India-Bangladesh trade witnessed an upward swing following the New Delhi joint communiqué of 2010. A number of important developments took place on April 2011 when India's Commerce and Industry Minister Anand Sharma visited Bangladesh. India offered a tariff-free quota of 10 million pieces of apparel from Bangladesh, marking an increase of 25 percent over previous years, while countervailing duties were lifted on all jute exports from

Bangladesh (Kumar 2012: 120-121). Bangladesh exports received a major boost when the Indian Prime Minister, Manmohan Singh, visited Dhaka in September 2011. Manmohan Singh announced duty-free access to 46 textile items from the country. Bangladesh had been pressing to get a duty waiver on 61 products. This decision was a major milestone in bilateral relations (Kumar 2012: 121). In fact, as per official estimates exports from Bangladesh to India increased by 56 per cent in the first 10 months of 2010-11 (*Task Force Report*, September 2011: 48).

India's direct investment also witnessed an upward swing. From a meagre amount of $ 2.73 million in end-June 2000, the stock of India's Foreign Direct Investment (FDI) reached $ 114.46 million by end-June 2010 (Kabir 2012: 126). It was during India's External Affairs Minister S. M. Krishna's visit in July 2011 that the high commissioners of the two countries signed an agreement for the protection and promotion of investments. This agreement pertained to exchange of instruments of ratification in respect to the Bilateral Investment Promotion and Protection Agreement (BIPPA). Another agreement concerning Standard Operating Procedure (SOP) for entry of trucks from Bhutan into territories of the two countries near the border was also signed during the External Affairs Minister's visit. BIPPA was received well by the business community in Bangladesh. While it was expected to encourage substantial Indian investment in Bangladesh, it could also lead to Bangladeshi investments in Northeast India (Habib 2011: 49). So far, the interaction between the two business communities has been quite encouraging. It has resulted in several joint venture agreements for export-oriented manufacturing activities in Bangladesh (*Task Force Report*, September 2011: 49).

That India was using its soft power is also evident in its grant of soft loans. India announced a credit line of $ 1 billion during Prime Minister Singh's visit, out of which $ 200 Million were converted to grant, to build railways, communications, and infrastructure. (Pattanaik 2016: 220). The credit line was noteworthy in the sense that it was at that point of time, the largest credit line offer by India to any single country (Chakma 2012: 16-17). In the particular visit, efforts were also made to connect their energy grids and build transmission lines thereby instituting energy trade. Consequently, India supplied 500 MW power to Bangladesh out of which 250 MW is provided at a commercial rate (Pattanaik 2016: 220). In return, Dhaka allowed India to transport Over Dimensional Cargoes for the Palatana project in Tripura through its territory, even though it could not conclude a transit agreement with India due to political difficulties falling out of India's inability to sign the agreement on Teesta (*Ibid.*).

The use of soft power is also evident with the initiation of the *border haats* (markets). As per the joint communiqué of January 2010, *border haats* was initiated on July 23, 2011, along the Kalaichar border (West Garo Hills district of Meghalaya) and Baliamari border (in Roumari and Rajibpur upazilas of Kurigram) in Bangladesh. Others locations for such *haats* were also identified in Sonarhat-Lyngkhat border (Sylhet-East Khasi Hills), and Narayantala-Balat border (Sunamganj-East Khasi Hills). The *haats* were aimed to provide the locals a platform to sell locally produced vegetables, fruits, spices, fish, poultry, minor forest produce, produce of local cottage industry, small agricultural household implements, second hand garments, melamine products and processed food items (*Task Force Report*, September 2011: 47-48). Both nations subsequently strengthened the infrastructure at the borders, including construction of land customs stations and integrated check posts, particularly at Petrapole and Agartala, to facilitate trade. India has offered assistance for the construction of the bridge over river Feni, and the construction of the connecting road on the Bangladesh side (Kumar 2012: 120-121).

Besides, efforts were also made to boost Indo-Bangladesh ties through media and cultural cooperation. The 2010 communiqué gave a greater fillip to Indo-Bangladesh cultural ties. Special emphasis was given on the promotion of exchanges in the fields of music, theatre and arts. A bilateral Cultural Exchange Programme (CEP) 2009-2012 instituted the framework for such exchanges. To promote bilateral cultural exchanges, the Indira Gandhi Cultural Centre (IGCC) of Indian Council for Cultural Relations was inaugurated at Dhaka on March 11, 2010. The joint inaugural ceremonies of 150th anniversary of Rabindranath Tagore were held in Dhaka on May 6 and New Delhi on May 7, 2011 and year-long celebrations were carried out and concluded.[14]

India-Bangladesh cultural cooperation, sustained by the efforts of the Indian Council for Cultural Relations (ICCR) has been playing a pivotal role by sponsoring visits of artists from India and Bangladesh. Further, in order to promote people to people exchanges, hundred scholarships are being granted by ICCR every year to the Bangladeshi students for pursuing general courses in arts, sciences, engineering and also specialised courses for culture, drama, music, fine arts and sports, and so on.[15] Even during Bangladesh Prime Minister Sheikh Hasina's visit in January 2010, India offered 300 more scholarships annually for five years to students from Bangladesh for studying and training in Universities and training institutions in India (*India-Bangladesh Joint Communiqué* 2010)

Further, as part of the Track II initiative a delegation of researchers and experts from Institute for Defence Studies and Analyses (IDSA) and Bangladesh Heritage Foundation (BHF) visited Tripura in 2010. The high point of this visit was the joint tour of the Bharat-Bangladesh Maitree Udyan Park, Chottakhola, Belonia. Chottakhola, a border town 130 kms from Agartala, was one of the base camps of the Muktijuddhas (Bangladeshi freedom fighters) from where they launched their war against Pakistani troops in Noakhali, Feni and parts of Comilla districts. The Bangladeshi foreign minister Dipu Moni had laid the foundation stone of the Bharat-Bangladesh Maitree Udyan in 2010. This park was to be built over 20 hectares and having an entrance that would represent the region's rich cultural heritage and the links that exist between India and Bangladesh. It was also agreed that IDSA and BHF would initiate a joint project on India's role in Bangladesh's Liberation War which will specially record the role of Tripura in the Bangladesh freedom movement. Apart from a documentation section, this project aimed to chronicle oral history and tap available local narratives on the subject, both in India and Bangladesh (*Task Force Report*, September 2011: 55).

India can get enough soft power leverage by investing in the energy sector in Bangladesh and by providing technical cooperation to it. The UPA seemed keen on these aspects. Thus, India and Bangladesh signed an MOU during Sheikh Hasina's visit to New Delhi in January 2010. Under this agreement, Bangladesh could import 250 MW of electricity in the first year from India from late 2012, and could buy another 250 MW through competitive bidding. Emphasis was also given to expedite inter-grid connectivity. The 250 MW grid interconnection required an investment of Rs 869.21 crore ($ 193.62 million), of which Rs 160.33 crore ($ 35.72 million) was to be used for building infrastructure on the Indian side. Bangladesh has a dire need to bridge its demand and supply gap and Indian help in this sector will help build trust and popular goodwill and in short will earn India soft power leverage. Further, India and Bangladesh also agreed to cooperate in the development and exchange of electricity, including generation from renewable sources. As a result, Bangladesh Power Development Board (PDB) and Power Grid Corporation of India Ltd (PGCIL) signed a 35-year power transmission agreement in July 26, 2010 (*Task Force Report*, September 2011: 51). In addition, through a formal agreement was signed in March 2012, India has offered its assistance to build a 1,320 MW electricity production plant in Khulna as a joint venture. Given Bangladesh's severe power shortage, India's assistance, on one hand, can play a vital role in meeting domestic power demand and propelling economic growth and on the other, earn India soft power leverage (Chakma 2012: 17).

4.1.b.(iii) Third Phase (2015 onwards)

The passing of the LBA on May 7, 2015 in the Indian Parliament and its subsequent conclusion on June 6, 2015 during Indian Prime Minister's two-day visit to Bangladesh encrypts a momentous chapter in India-Bangladesh relations. A genuine effort has thus been made to remove one of the most pertinent irritant which has proved to be detrimental in the relationship between the two countries over the years. Interestingly, we can decipher elements of soft power which the Indian government under Modi seems to be relying on to deal with at least its neighbours of late. India's neighbourhood policy under Modi is worth contemplating. In the words of Smruti Pattanaik:

> Prime Minister Modi himself has taken keen interest to see that top priority is accorded to India's immediate neighbours to reinvigorate India's historical and socio-cultural ties and to restore the economic and trade linkages that existed before partition. The invitation to the heads of the governments of the SAARC countries for the swearing-in ceremony in May 2014 provided a glimpse into the NDA government's vision for the neighbourhood (Pattanaik 2016: 219).

However, it was important to deal with the domestic imperatives which have often impinged Indo-Bangladesh relations in the past. When the BJP-led NDA swept to power in 2014 with two-third majority, Narendra Modi government was faced with the daunting task of bringing all the stakeholders on board for the ratification of the LBA Bill in Parliament (*The Daily Star*, May 20, 2015). Support of the opposition was crucial in this regard (Pattanaik 2016: 221). Apart from it, the BJP leaders in Assam, which is one of the four states involved with the Agreement, opposed the bill stating that it would erode its chances in the state elections in 2016. At that point Delhi tinkered with the idea of leaving out Assam and passing the Bill. The Congress-led Assam government, however, strongly opposed BJP's move. Congress, the main opposition party in the Lok Sabha, also opposed against Assam's exclusion. Thus, after bickering for weeks, a compromise was achieved between the BJP and Congress and finally the Bill went through unopposed in both the Rajya Sabha and Lok Sabha (*The Daily Star*, May 20, 2015).

It was interesting what Sushma Swaraj, Indian External Affairs Minister, said while presenting the Bill in the Lok Sabha. She said that it would be beneficial for both countries. Though India seems to be ceding land to Bangladesh, it was 'notional' as these territories were deep inside Bangladesh. She further contended that the Agreement, apart from demarcating the boundaries, would also help check 'illegal immigration' (*Ibid.*). Thus, after dillydallying for 41 years, the Indian Parliament finally passed the Land Boundary Agreement (LBA) Bill on May 7, 2015 (*The Daily Star*, May 20, 2015). With it a new chapter was written in the history of India-Bangladesh relations.

The LBA[16] was thus signed on June 6, 2015 during Narendra Modi's two-day visit to Bangladesh. PM Modi described the land deal as "an agreement to join hearts" and "no less significant than the fall of the Berlin Wall."[17] After the conclusion of LBA he remarked in a joint news conference- "We have shown political consolidation and goodwill with the signing of this deal." His counterpart Sheikh Hasina said- "I salute all the citizens of India for supporting this bill in parliament (*The Daily Star*, June 6, 2015)." Dhaka's Foreign Minister Abul Hassan Mahmood Ali described the deal, as "a historic milestone in the relationship between the two neighboring south Asian countries."[18]

Source: http://www.newsbangladesh.com/english/details/5397

Map 8: Location of the Enclaves

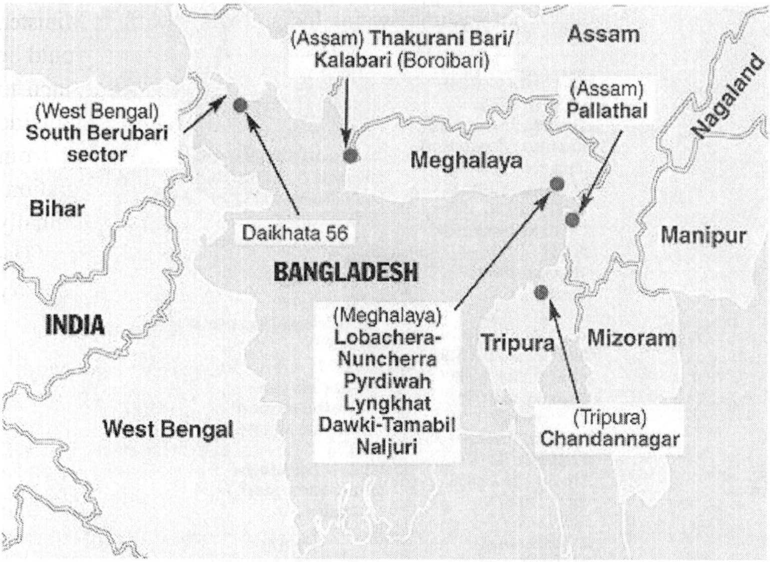

Source: http://www.jobtodayinfo.com/2015/05/daily-gk-update-5th-may-2015-current.html 122

Map 9: Adverse Possesions & Pending Segments Along the India-Bangladesh Border

Accordingly, after the exchange of instrument of ratification, 75 teams and 30 observers from the two countries worked round the clock from 6 to 16 July to ascertain the view of exchange dwellers regarding their choice of citizenship. On the mid-night of July 31, 2015 the exchange of enclaves was concluded nearly 70 years after partition. Interim strip maps were prepared by both the sides on land under adverse possession as well as demarcation of the border were exchanged in June 2016 and the demarcation of the 6.1 kilometers of border on the ground was scheduled to be completed July 2016 (Pattanaik 2016: 221).

According to the agreement, Bangladesh was handed over 111 enclaves (17160 acres of land) from India's possession (in the districts of Panchagarh, Lalmonirhat, Kurigram and Nilphamari in Rangpur division) and India received 51 enclaves (7110 acres of land) from Bangladesh in West Bengal's Cooch Behar.[19] With the signing of the LBA, the un-demarcated land boundary (6.1 km) in three sectors, viz. Daikhata-56 (West Bengal), Muhuri River-Belonia (Tripura) and Dumabari (Assam), has been delineated. An estimated total of 51,549 people (37,334 in Indian enclaves within Bangladesh and 14,215 in Bangladesh enclaves within India), can now look forward to an existence free from the uncertainties and fears that had plagued

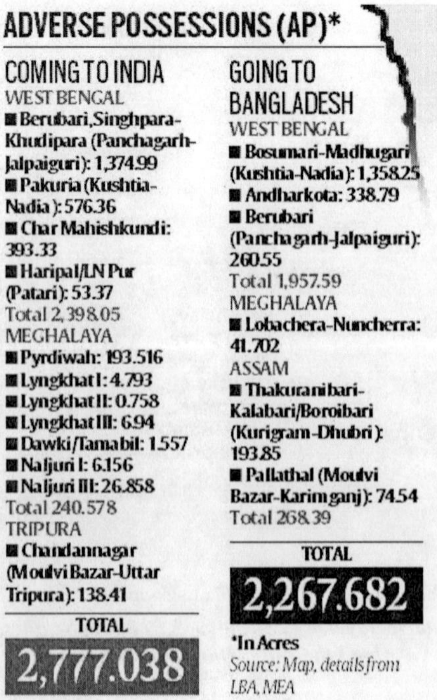

Source: http://images.indianexpress.com/2015/05/graph.jpg

Figure 1: Total Area Under Adverse Possessions

the enclave residents for decades (Datta 2016: 4-5). As it stands on the ground, India lost around 40 sq km/10,000 acres to Bangladesh. However, with the adjustment of adverse possessions India will receive 2777.038 acres of land and would transfer 2267.682 acres of land to Bangladesh.[20]

4.1.d LBA 2015: Soft Power Implications

The visit of Indian Prime Minister Narendra Modi also resulted in the signing of 22 Agreements, including one each on curbing of human trafficking, smuggling of fake currency, and setting up an Indian Economic Zone (Datta 2016: 226). Besides, plethora of agreements concerning trade, investment, power, cultural relations, border management, *people-to-people* contacts were also reached upon.[21] India took a leap forward and promised Bangladesh a New Line of Credit (LOC) of US $ 2 billon – doubling the previous $ 1 billion credit line, offered in 2010. This indeed is a largest credit loan that India has offered to any state in the neighbourhood, or elsewhere (Datta 2016: 226). As mentioned earlier, India can garner enough soft power leverages by inducements and investments. In this regard, the credit line offered to Bangladesh is important from soft power perspective as it will prove to be instrumental to improve its infrastructure, IT, education and health segments in Bangladesh.[22] More importantly, the credit line will give a boost to further economic engagement (Pattanaik 2016: 221). The two Prime Ministers also welcomed the signing of the MOU to implement the grant assistance of INR 5 crores (US $ 730000) from the India endowment for Climate Change for installation of 70,000 improved cook stoves in Bangladesh.[23] Moreover, a string of trade and investment agreements accompanied the land deal, with $ 4.5 billion of investments in power.[24] This again can be seen as a soft power strategy employed by India to improve its relations with Bangladesh.

Any effort by India to help Bangladesh in boosting its energy sector will earn India soft power. As such during Modi's visit, steps were taken to engage Indian private sectors in generating power to help Bangladesh achieve its 2021 target of electricity generation (Pattanaik 2016: 224). In this regard, Adani Power Limited and Reliance Power Limited of India signed deals worth over $ 4.5 billion with state-run Bangladesh Power Development Board (BPDB) to develop six units of power plants to produce 4,600 MW of electricity. Reliance is supposed to invest $ 3 billion to produce 3,000 MW power, while Adani will set up two coal-fired plants with a total capacity of 1,600 MW, costing more than $1.5 billion. "Bangladesh will be able to more than double power imports from India to 1,100 MW from 500 MW at present," Modi said.[25]

Another soft power aspect which is evident in the current agreements between the two countries lies in their recognition to establish *people-to-people* contact and to extend cultural ties between the people of two countries. Consequently, during Modi's visit to Bangladesh, focus was made in enhancing exchanges between the people of the two countries so as to foster greater understanding and goodwill between the two countries. In this context, it was agreed by India and Bangladesh that Doordarshan and Bangladesh Television (BTV) will enter into agreement to allow BTV to join Prashar Bharati's DTH platform.[26] Apart from it, Modi's announcement of buses and new trains invigorated the connectivity networks that India is trying to build (Pattanaik 2016: 220).

The Kolkata-Dhaka-Agartala bus will provide link not just between Dhaka and other two Indian cities but would help the people from Kolkata to reach Agartala through a shorter route in less time. Similarly, Dhaka-Shillong-Guwahati will link Bangladesh with Meghalaya and Assam, the two states which share borders with Bangladesh. All these initiatives are a significant move to connect people of the two countries and, as such, can be viewed from soft power prism.[27] In addition, Bangladesh has decided to provide access to Chittagong and Mongla port, which in turn, will help India access its Northeast. It is beneficial for Bangladesh too as it is also an outlet for these Bangladesh locked region to outside world, including India. Apart from the establishing close connections among the people of the region, it has connectivity advantage too as it shortens the transit time to reach the India's northeast. These ports are significant for India for economic reasons.[28]

Education cooperation which is an instrument of soft power is also clearly evident in the current bilateral relation between India and Bangladesh. During Narendra Modi's June visit to Bangladesh the two countries reaffirmed their commitment to widen cooperation on education sector for mutual benefit. In this connection, they were appreciative of the various collaborative arrangements between the universities and educational institutes of the two countries. The two Prime Ministers also welcomed the Bangladesh-India Education Initiative and expressed confidence that the framework provided by the initiative will enable relationships to prosper between institutions of the two countries (*Notun Projonmo – Nayi Disha*, June 07, 2015). It is to be noted that India has been providing the capacity building programme for Bangladesh under the ITEC programme, especially the custom designed courses such as the mid-career training programme for Bangladesh civil servants. The Bangladesh Prime Minister Sheikh Hasina sought continued support of India in training of Bangladesh officials, to which India responded positively (*Ibid.*).

Implications of soft power can be traced in Prime Minister Modi's paying homage to at the National Martyrs' Memorial at Savar and his visit to Banghabandhu Memorial Museum, dedicated to the founder of Bangladesh Sheikh Mujibur Rahman, and paying tribute to him (*Ibid.*). As a gesture of good will and gratitude for India's help in liberation war, Prime Minister Modi received, on behalf of the former Prime Minister of India Mr. Atal Bihari Vajpayee, the prestigious 'Bangladesh Liberation War Honour'(*Ibid.*). On Sheikh Hasina's request, Modi agreed to give assistance in bringing back to Bangladesh, the mortal remains of the Bangladeshi freedom fighters who had been buried in the Indian soil during 1971 war of liberation (*Ibid.*). Besides memento of INS Vikrant, which had played an important role in the liberation war was handed over to Bangladesh's Prime Minister Sheikh Hasina by the Indian Prime Minister Modi. In addition,

Modi also handed over to Hasina the audio recording of Bangabandhu Sheikh Mujibur Rahman's historic speech on February 6, 1972 at Brigade Maidan, Kolkata during his first State visit to India after the independence of Bangladesh. Simalrly, Hasina handed Modi a photograph of the 'Signing Instrument of Surrender 1971' (*Notun Projonmo – Nayi Disha*, June 07, 2015).

Soft power implications can also be observed in India's assistance to Bangladesh under the bilateral MOU on Small Development Projects, for city improvement being undertaken in Rajshahi, Sylhet, Khulna and Narsingdi (*Ibid.*). India's assistance in bringing back Bangladeshi nationals from Yemen in April 2015 too has soft power connotations. In the joint declaration during Modi's visit to Bangladesh, Sheikh Hasina thanked Modi in this regard. Apart from it, Modi's address at the Dhaka University gave him an opportunity to connect beyond the political class to the civil society. In addition, his meeting with the BNP leader was equally significant as India continues with its effort to develop a working relationship with the entire spectrum of the political class and ideologies except for the *Jamaat Islami*, which is antithetical to India's core values of pluralism and secularism (Pattanaik 2016: 220-221). This is important as the BNP does remain a significant political force and may, at some future date, assume governance in Bangladesh. Statements recently emanating from the BNP display a positive attitude, and its chairperson, Khaleda Zia, has spoken of leaving the past behind (Mukharji 2016: 207).

Also, a favourable augury is the domestic milieu in both the countries. It may be noted that the domestic politics has impinged Indo-Bangladesh bilateral to a large extent. Surprisingly, this time around, there was a unanimity among political parties in India for strengthening bilateral ties with Bangladesh. It is also significant that, for the first time, the main opposition party in Bangladesh, the Bangladesh Nationalist Party – welcomed the Land Boundary Agreement, and expressed its appreciation to the Indian Parliament. Nor have there been any serious objection to the slew of agreements signed during Prime Minister Modi's visit. Interestingly, the media in both countries has also been supportive of the emerging ties between the two countries (Mukharji 2016: 205).

4.1.e Effects of the Land Boundary Agreement

The effects of the LBA are manifold. Firstly, the successful conclusion of the LBA will ensure national identity to over 50000 stateless people living in these enclaves. Prior to the conclusion of the LBA 2016, the people of these enclaves remained stateless without any rights that a citizenship of a country would confer. As such, neither governments could provide them with the basic rights and needs such as water, power, health and sanitation.[29] According to a joint survey (2007), the total number of people living in the enclaves is 51,549, of which 37,334 are in Indian enclaves inside Bangladesh. According to the LBA Protocol, these people will be allowed to stay and become citizens of the country in which the enclave is located or they can opt to migrate (*The Daily Star*, May 20, 2015). Thus, it has a humanitarian aspect too as it will help the people inhabiting in these areas to solve their identity crisis.

Secondly, the enclaves would cease to exist. The ratification of the LBA paved way for exchange of enclaves, which was duly accomplished on July 31, 2015. Thirdly, it will help India to fence its borders with Bangladesh. Fourthly, it will alter the physical map of India and Bangladesh.[30] Fifthly, as Smruti Pattanaik contends – "the conclusion of LBA will lead to facilitate in a better management of border which in turn is a harbinger of peace and stability. It will probably end one of the major concerns, that is, border killings. As it has been observed in the past, the land under adverse possession had led to animosity and has resulted in the killing of 16 BSF soldiers in 2001."[31] In fact, border killings are a recurring phenomenon at the India-Bangladesh border. Now with the conclusion of the LBA, it can be hoped that the border killings would cease.

Prior to the conclusion of LBA, neither India nor Bangladesh had any administrative control or access to their enclaves. India could neither establish a *modus vivendi* with Bangladesh to look after its population nor find an alternative site for their relocation. The same held true for Bangladesh. The border populations, not used to movement restrictions, were prone to running into legal and political problems with border security forces. All this led to a worsening of relations on the ground, compounding the difficulties for the border populations (Datta 2016: 3). The display of political expediency, in the face of the foreign policy, and especially the neighbourhood thrust, of the National Democratic Alliance (NDA) Government was clearly evident. Prime Minister Narendra Modi took the initiative to "reverse the BJP's position in the last years of the UPA, that the LBA was 'unconstitutional' and ... [for] building a national political consensus in favour of the boundary settlement" (*Indian Express*, June 5, 2015).

Their earlier demand about Assam being delinked from the Bill, on grounds of its 'emotive' issues with Bangladesh, was no longer a consideration, as building bridges with the neighbourhood assumed priority. The West Bengal Government, which too had serious reservations with the

Centre in the past including over its bilateral commitment to Bangladesh, too rescinded its earlier position. Possibly the prospects of fiscal support by the Modi Government has helped facilitate the process (Datta 2016: 8-9). In the years between 1972 and 2016, the two neighbours from time to time addressed several of the outstanding bilateral issues, namely water, trade, insurgency, and terrorism, but the border issue remained unsettled until just recently. Indeed, unresolved border issues led to several associated problems which assumed critical importance in the last four-and-a-half decades (Datta 2016: 3). However, it is to be remembered that though the border problems have been resolved with the conclusion of LBA, yet there are other issues related to border which needs to be addressed. Equally important is it to remember that these are the current issues which the LBA does not cover and which needs immediate attention. These issues will be espoused in the following section.

4.2 Section-II

4.2.a Border and Its Related Problems

4.2.a.(i) ***Illegal Migration*** The large influx of Bangladeshi migrants into India is one of the most important concerns for India for numerous reasons. India shares border with Bangladesh running through the Indian states of West Bengal, Assam, Meghalaya, Tripura, and Mizoram. Indian officials have alleged that continued illegal immigration from Bangladesh has altered the demography of India's border areas resulting in ethnic imbalance, electoral irregularity, and loss of employment opportunities for Indian nationals (Sengupta 2005: 240-241). The northeastern states in India are particularly vulnerable to population movement: less than 1 percent of the region's external boundaries are contiguous with the rest of India, whereas 99 percent are international boundaries (Pant 2007: 241). For instance, in the North-eastern states like Nagaland, the population of Bangladeshi, mostly Muslim immigrants, have more than tripled in the past decade, from 20,000 Bangladeshi immigrants in 1991, to more than 75,000 as of 2001 (Dutta 2010: 8). In fact, Indian source claims that the annual illegal immigrants from Bangladesh total approximately three million and the number of Bangladeshi nationals living in India is approximately 15 to 20 million (Singh 2005: 64). This is, in fact, quite a staggering figure – it is a more than two-thirds of Australia's population (Karim 2009: 8).

It is imperative to point out that India has absorbed most of the Hindu migrants from Bangladesh, and has no choice to continue to do so because they flee from persecution. The illegal Muslim migrants are, however, economic migrants, and cannot be treated at par with the Hindu migrants. Hence, India must develop a refugee policy which is in distinct from a migration policy. Bangladesh is a net exporter of people. More than 8 million Bangladeshis have migrated abroad. The push factors are many: high population density, lack of land, poverty, chronic unemployment, and a thriving human trafficking mafia that trades in poverty and human misery (Chakravarty 2016: 217).

The problem posed by the Bangladeshi migrants, however, is no longer confined to a few Border States along the Indo-Bangladesh border. These migrants are now seen in as far-off places as Delhi, Rajasthan, Madhya Pradesh and Maharashtra. These Bangladeshis have taken over most of the low-paying jobs in a number of states, thereby depriving the local Indian population of sources of livelihood. The illegal migration from Bangladesh has changed the voter composition of a number of constituencies in the adjoining states and even in the National Capital Region of Delhi (Godbole 2001: 4443). Further, the domestic politics in both the countries compounds and complicates this issue, making an amicable bilateral solution difficult (Pant 2007: 242). It is also important to note that the issue of illegal Bangladeshi migrants in India is often looked at through the political prism in India and seen to be used as vote bank politics especially in the state level politics (Bhardwaj 2014: 5).

The porous nature of land-and maritime-borders is convenient for an extensive illegal trade between the two countries. From arms and ammunition to a whole range of commodities including jute and rice, besides cattle as well human capital, are being smuggled across the Indo-Bangladesh borders. Likewise, cattle has been prominent in the informal trade, with moderate estimates of about 20,000 to 25,000 cattle heads worth US $ 81,000 from India being smuggled daily into Bangladesh (Bhattacharya 2015: 5). The cattle trade is a mafia-controlled business that poses an intractable problem for bilateral relations. With the NDA government in power in India, it seems impossible that the cattle trade can be dealt without religious sentiment in India becoming inflamed (Chakravarty 2016: 217). The residual problem of fake Indian foreign currency that is pumped in by Pakistan via Bangladesh still continues. It is a challenge that has to be faced jointly by Bangladesh and India, and so are the other problems of smuggling of banned substances (*Ibid*., p. 215).

It is obvious that such a large migrant population can pose serious security threats. This is a fertile ground for organisations like the Inter Services Intelligence (ISI) of Pakistan to penetrate and expand their activities

(Godbole 2001: 4443). Hence, New Delhi's concerns are not only about demographic changes but also about the security threat posed by anti-India radicals and insurgents who sneak in along with economically deprived Bangladeshi migrants (Pant 2007: 242).

4.2.a.(ii) ***Security Concerns*** It is widely known that India's north-eastern states are plagued by insurgency. It is estimated that there are about 175 insurgent groups operating in the states surrounding Bangladesh. Bangladesh itself has been fighting an insurgency for the last few decades in its south-eastern part called Chittagong Hill Tracts, although it has been greatly restricted ever since the signing of the peace accord with the insurgents in 1997. It is likely that there could be a spillover effect of insurgents taking shelter in each other's country or using cross-border routes for the transportation of smuggled arms. One Indian source alleges, "a new arms bazaar in the no-man's land near the Bangladesh-Myanmar border town of *Naikhangchari,* which has become home to Indian insurgent outfits such as the United Liberation Front of Assam and the National Democratic Front of Bodoland. The Harkat-ul-Jihad-al-Islami (HuJI, Movement of Islamic Holy War), a terrorist outfit in Bangladesh, is known to be imparting training to these outfits" (Khan 2009: 6). In fact, number of recent terrorist attacks in India have been traced back to Bangladeshi nationals working on behalf of Harkat-ul-Jihad-al-Islami, which is suspected of being an al-Qaeda front and also has links with the Jaish-e-Mohammed (The Army of Mohammed) and Lashkar-e-Toiba (Soldiers of the Pure) *jihadi* groups based in Pakistan (Pant 2007: 245).

It is imperative to note that even before the emergence of Bangladesh as an independent state, the Chittagong Hill Tracts were used by the Pakistani army to train and shelter Mizo and Naga insurgents fighting against India. It has been suspected that Bangladesh, and Pakistan's ISI, has been coordinating anti-India activities along with outfits like the United Liberation Front of Assam, the National Socialist Council of Nagaland, the National Liberation Front of Tripura, and the All Tripura Tiger Force (*Ibid.*, p. 243). There are also reports that Indian insurgents are procuring arms from China and Myanmar and using Bangladesh as a transit point. This was revealed in a written statement of India's minister of state for home affairs in the Rajya Sabha (Pattanaik 2012: 209). Illicit arms that find their way into each other's territory also feeds to political violence and insurgency and creates general insecurity among the citizens. The Chittagong arms haul of 2004 also revealed the transnational nature of the network. Terrorist can use Bangladesh to transfer arms given the nexus between law enforcing authorities and the arms merchants. There are also chances that pilferage may happen during the transfer of small arms which may fall into the hands of ordinary criminals (*Ibid.*, pp. 208-209). Apart from it, the lack of cooperation between the agencies of the two countries has helped the smugglers and the terrorists operating in the region. The porousness of the border has only compounded the problem and, therefore, has made it difficult to address the issue (*Ibid.*, p. 209).

The rise of Islamic fundamentalism in Bangladesh has further aggravated India's relations with its neighbour. After independence, Bangladesh not only had declared secularism to be one of its founding principles, but it had also banned religious political parties. As the military became a major political force in Bangladesh over the years, it used the country's Islamic identity to give its rule increased legitimacy, and mainstream political parties started using Islam for their own partisan purposes as well. As a result, religion has come to occupy a central place in Bangladeshi political discourse (Riaz 2007: 310-320). Militant groups have percolated into all sections of Bangladeshi society, including mosques, seminaries, educational institutions, the judiciary, mass media, and the armed forces. In fact, Islamists are being trained in over 50 camps across the country (Lakshman 2007: 243).

The rise of Jamaat-ul Mujahideen Bangladesh (JMB) in Bangladesh is a testament to the country's growing Islamic radicalization (Pant 2007: 244). The JMB is an outgrowth of the Salafi form of Islam, a strain that wants a return to Islam's puritanical roots as practiced during the first three generations of the religion. Ever since the withdrawal of the former Soviet Union from Afghanistan, there has been a gradual growth of Salafists around the globe and Bangladesh is not an exception. The Salafist ideology—nurtured in the ultra-conservative atmosphere of Saudi Arabia—has been exported to the rest of the world ever since the boom in Saudi oil revenues in the 1970s. Charities in Saudi Arabia and Pakistan are among the major donors to Bangladeshi NGOs, and a large portion of this money is quite possibly being used to fund *madrassa*s (Islamic religious seminaries) that educate willing recruits to the *jihadi* cause. As a consequence, Islam in Bangladesh, which has traditionally been tolerant and syncretic in nature, has come to be dominated by the radical strain in more recent years (Rahim 2001: 235-239). Although the JMB was finally banned by the Dhaka government in early 2005 following threats of withdrawal of aid by the West, the group still managed to set off serial bomb blasts that August in 63 out of the 64 districts of Bangladesh (*The Daily Star*, August 18, 2005).

Further, criminal activities like the smuggling of narcotics and contraband substances are also persistent along the border. Women and children are also trafficked on the border (Kumar 2012: 117-118). Bangladesh is increasingly being used as a transit point by drug dealers and the drug mafia, which dispatch heroin and opium from Burma, and other countries of the golden triangle, to different destinations. As a result, Bangladesh's Department of Narcotics Control has come under the scanner several times and invited criticism. According to the International Narcotics Control Board (INCB) 2007 annual report, Bangladesh has become the prime transit route for trafficking heroin to Europe from Southeast Asia, (Dutta 2010: 8).

Nevertheless security cooperation between India-Bangladesh has been one of the cornerstones in their bilateral relationships, which has generated soft power for both the countries, especially for Bangladesh. Such cooperation has contributed to creating goodwill, trust and the congenial atmosphere for bilateral partnership to flourish. It can be recalled that the previous BNP government sheltered leaders of Indian insurgent groups and was unwilling to acknowledge their presence. This in turn had undermined India's relations with Bangladesh to some extent. Sheikh Hasina, after assuming power in January 2009, reversed this trend. The Bangladesh Prime Minister not only handed over the leaders of the insurgent groups but also declared that her government had 'zero tolerance' for terrorism (Pattanaik 2016: 221-222). The most significant aspect of the bilateral cooperation was when Dhaka handed over the insurgents from Northeast of India who had taken shelter in Bangladesh and emerged as a major stakeholder of peace in the north eastern region (*Ibid.*, p. 220). However, the July 2016 terror attack in Bangladesh has added a new dimension to India's security concerns. The picture that emerges is that Islamist militant groups in Bangladesh are showing signs of revival (Bashar 2015: 228). In fact, Bangladesh has alerted the Indian security agencies that the mastermind of the Dhaka café terror attack (July 2016) may have fled to India (*The Times of India*, August 2, 2016).

4.2.a.(iii) ***The Problem of Maritime Boundary Demarcation and the New Moore Island Controversy*** India and Bangladesh share their maritime boundary in the Bay of Bengal. There are two disputes—one pertaining to the boundary and second relating to the sovereignty of the New Moore/Talpatty island (Bammi 2010: 135). The issue of demarcating territorial waters led to serious differences between the two countries. Questions of ownership over a new born island known as South Talpatty in Bangladesh and New Moore/ Purbasha in India spotted by a satellite picture in 1975 in the estuary of Hariabhanga River on the border of the two countries has been a source of contention since its discovery. Till now the sovereignty over the island nation remains undecided and recent reports of the press and media suggests that Bangladesh views India with suspicion in its activities over the disputed piece of landmass on the breast of an international water (Dutta 2010: 7-8).

Although negotiations have been going on since 1974, Bangladesh and India were unable to settle the delimitation problem, mainly because of the concave nature of the Bangladesh coast (Rahman 1984: 1308). While Bangladesh, having concave coastlines, delimits its sea border southward from the edge of its land boundary, India stretches its claim southeast wards, covering around thousands of miles in the Bay of Bengal. Due to competing claims of the two countries, delimitation of the sea boundary and determining Bangladesh's Exclusive Economic Zones (EEZ) have remained unresolved (Dutta 2010: 7). It is obvious that the issue has arisen because of the different approaches being adopted by India and Bangladesh. While India has consistently advocated 'equidistance' or 'meridian' principle in delimiting the boundary, Bangladesh has been advocating 'equitable' principle (Bammi 2010: 135). Bangladesh's position is that no rigid principle can be applied in the present case and that India's persistence on equidistance principle ignores the physical features of the coast and hence basic guideline is equity (Rahman 1984: 1308). Moreover, Bangladesh feels that by the equidistance principle, it will be sea-locked between India and Myanmar and will lose out on the vast riches of the Bay of Bengal, as her Exclusive Economic Zones will be narrowed (Bammi 2010: 135-136).

The real crux of the maritime dispute between India and Bangladesh, as pointed out by Marcus Franda, is similar to conflicts over territorial sea limits elsewhere, especially the West German-Netherlands disagreement of 1974-1975 (Franda 1975: 7). Franda also pointed out that this dispute was refused a hearing in the World Court because there were no binding international covenants for the apportionment of the seabed. Instead, the World Court suggested a solution on the basis of equality, a rather platitudinous formulation that India and Bangladesh both accept. Following the series of coups and countercoups in 1975, Bangladesh increased its claims over the seabed. Basing its claim on the principle of 'The Swatch of No Ground,' the state laid claim to a new 7,000 square mile area within a ten-mile belt, which is considered a potential oil-rich area. Following Indian Foreign Minister Narashima Rao's visit to Dacca in August 1980, both countries agreed to meet "with a view to reaching a mutually acceptable solution as early as possible (Hossain 1981: 1123-1124)." Meetings were held in Dacca in December 1980, but with no substantial results.

It is to be noted that the problem of the maritime border demarcation also involves Myanmar. Bangladesh claims a huge continental shelf, since the sea is not considerably deep as seen from its base line. Bangladesh is worried that it might get sea- or zone-locked by both India and Myanmar if both powers insist on resolving the issue based on the principle of equidistance instead of equity. There are tricky issues such as the acceptance of a Bangladeshi baseline, and the fixation of control points with its neighbouring nations from where either of these neighbours would draw the maritime boundary. Linked to it is the dispute over the ownership of an island in the River Hariabhanga, in the south-western part of Bangladesh, bordering India, and adjoining the Bay of Bengal (Alam 2006: 7). The island in dispute is about 24 by 12 kilometers and is situated in the mouth of the river Hariabhanga. The tip of the new island was first noticed in late 1971 by India (Hossain 1981: 1124). In 1975 the formation of the island was picked up by satellite. The Indian BSF erected a number of concrete pillars and put up a board depicting the Indian flag and map on the island in 1978, (*The Bangladesh Times,* April 4, 1980 in Hossain 1981: 1124) and in early March 1980, the West Bengal government hoisted the Indian flag over the island (Hossain 1981: 1124).

The Hariabhanga River, flowing through the Sunderbans, forms the border between India and Bangladesh. Since Purbasha is situated at the mouth of the river, determining the ownership of the island has become more difficult. Apparently, "if the larger of the river's two channels flowed towards the west of the island, it would belong to Bangladesh. If the flow was towards the east it would be India's (*Ibid.*, pp.1124-1125)." Consequently, India claimed the island on the basis that the flow of the Hariabhanga is to the east of the island and the island lies on the natural prolongation of the Indian territory. On the other hand, Bangladesh claims that the river flows to the west of the island, as a result of which it is not possible to distinguish the natural prolongation of India's territory. Bangladesh alleged India of dumping boulders to change the course of the river. It also tried to construct a Light House on the island but withdrew later when India sent its coastguard and deployed BSF on it (Bammi 2010: 138).

The Indian annexation of the island has not only further soured Indo-Bangladesh relations but has also clearly helped in forming an intense anti-Indian public opinion in Bangladesh. For instance, anti-Indian demonstrations were held and the Indian Airlines office was damaged during Indian Foreign Minister Narashima Rao's visit to Dacca in August 1980 (Hossain 1981: 1124). Since then, the island has submerged due to the rise of the sea yet the dispute on the estuary of the River Hariabhanga remains unresolved (Bammi 2010: 138). However, according to an observer "resolving the issue of South Talpatty/New Moore has more to do with the extent of the maritime zone to be potentially acquired in the oil rich delta of the Bay of Bengal than the island itself. As such the island holds the potential to become the core contentious issue between the two nations (Alam 2006: 7)."

A remarkable feat with regard to maritime border has been achieved recently after the visit of the Indian Prime Minister Narendra Modi to Bangladesh in June 2015. With the recent improvement in Indo-Bangladesh ties India has responded positively to resolve the maritime dispute. India's decision to opt for international arbitration to settle her maritime boundary with Bangladesh was a similar gesture of goodwill. It signified a deliberate, a priori relinquishment of its claims on the disputed waters, nearly 80 per cent of which have gone to Bangladesh. Negotiations could never have settled this matter since the India-proposed median line was drawn in a way – taking account of the concave configuration of the coast – that the Bangladeshi waters got confined to a narrow triangle between India and Myanmar (*The Hindu*, May 11, 2015).

The amicable settlement the maritime boundary between India and Bangladesh has opened up vast economic opportunities for both the countries. Recognizing this, the two countries, during Modi's 2015 visit to Bangladesh, agreed to work closely on the development of ocean-based Blue Economy and Maritime Cooperation in the Bay of Bengal and chart out the ways for future cooperation (*Notun Projonmo – Nayi Disha*" June 07, 2015). India's ability to resolve sensitive, sovereignty-related issues of its land and maritime boundaries has provided glimpse towards its neighbourhood policy. India's land and maritime boundary agreements with Bangladesh also exemplifies that intractable issues can be wrapped up between neighbours within an overall relationship of growing trust and friendship (*The Hindu*, May 11, 2015).

4.2.b Fencing of the Border and its Problems

Bangladesh has opposed the idea of India erecting a fence along the border contending that it is an unhealthy gesture on the part of India and that it violates the 1975 border guidelines under which India could only erect a fence 150 yards away from the border. India's plan has led to strong resentment especially in villages that straddle the dividing line and trade in both directions (Pant 2007: 241). However, India contends that the main purpose of the fence is to prevent smuggling, illegal immigration and the use of the open border by insurgents and criminal elements (Karim 2009: 8). Thus, India hardened its position and started fencing its international borders with Bangladesh in 1987. The total length of Indo-Bangladesh border to be fenced is 3286.87 Kms out of which 2735 kms of fencing was completed by March 2011.[32] According to Susheel Kuman, Secretary Border Management under the Indian Union Home Ministry the fencing is to be completed by 2017 (*Indian Express*: June 25, 2016). Even though the entire fence-construction was well within India's territory, the fencing became a controversial bilateral issue, with various officials and non-governmental circles in Bangladesh opposing it; periodic border clashes increased (Datta 2016: 4).

Further, the clashes between the security forces along the border have led to many civilian casualties, thereby creating negative perceptions towards each other. Bangladesh has complained that the overwhelming numerical superiority of Indian security forces along their long common border has spurred the killing of innocent Bangladeshi nationals by India's paramilitary Border Security Force (BSF). According to some estimates, the ratio of Indian to Bangladeshi security forces deployed along the border is 2.5:1. Even when Khaleda Zia was visiting India in March 2006, the border forces on either side were exchanging fire. Such incidents are a regular feature along the border, often resulting in inhumane treatment of each other's forces (*Ibid.*).

India has, however, emphasised on joint border management. During the 2015 Modi's visit, the two countries signed MOUs on Prevention of Smuggling of Fake Currency Notes, and Cooperation between Coast Guards and Prevention of Human Trafficking. During the Modi's visit emphasis was also made on the efficient implementation of the Coordinated Border Management Plan (CBMP) so as to prevent cross border criminal activities, irregular movement, incidents of violence and tragic loss of lives (Pattanaik 2016: 222). It is to be noted that the two countries had signed the CBMP in 2011 and India had assured that it would implement zero killing on the border. However, as BGB Director General Major General Aziz Ahmed points out, "Crime is the cause of illegal trespassing. Border killings will decrease if we can curb the rate of crime in the borders (*Ibid.*)."

Conclusion

The negotiations on the land boundary have run through three main phases; the first phase (1971-1996), the second phase (1996-2015) and the third phase (2015 onwards). In the first phase as mentioned in the preceding chapter, we find enough inferences of soft power. Cooperation is seen both in the water and the boundary issues. In the second phase, as the chapter demonstrates, Bangladesh' Prime Minister Sheikh Hasina, after ascendency to power, adopted various pro-India policies which brought Bangladesh closer to India. Consequently, the cooperation among the two countries began to propel faster. Thus, what can be deduced from this is the fact, that the 'regime compatibility' factor which played a critical role in the resolution of the Farakka issue also played similar roles even in the cooperation on the land boundary is concerned.

The Joint Communiqué of 2010 chartered a new phase of India-Bangladesh bilateral cooperation. This was further strengthened by the then Indian Prime Minister Manmohan Singh's visit to Bangladesh on September 2011. Interestingly many soft power initiatives were initiated to strengthen India-Bangladesh bilateral relations. Chief among them are the $ 1 billion grant to Bangladesh, coupled with India's efforts to address energy needs of Bangladesh (which can earn enough soft power leverage for India), cultural and academic cooperation and so on. However, the most important soft power strategy lies in the initiation of *border haats* which is integral in establishing the *people-to-people* contacts.

The employability of soft power becomes all the more vivid in the third phase (2015 onwards) with the visit of Indian Prime Minister, Narendra Modi to Bangladesh in June 2015. In fact, a critical analysis would reveal that the whole process of the conclusion of LBA, exemplifies the soft power approach. The strategic move to include the West Bengal Chief Minister Mamata Banerjee can be seen from the perspective that India wants to use the Bengali cultural affinity with Bangladesh. Moreover, the inauguration of the Kolkata-Dhaka-Agartala bus and Dhaka-Shillong-Guwahati is a significant move to connect people. Further, India's decision to help Bangladesh to improve its infrastructure and its soft loans all exhibit the ethos of 'Gujaral Doctrine', thereby exemplifying the fact that India is using its soft power to improve its relations with Bangladesh. In fact, it would not be wrong to state that if Gujaral Doctrine played an important part in the conclusion of the 1996 Ganges water Treaty, the 'Modi Doctrine' played a pivotal role in the conclusion of the 2015 LBA. The conclusion of LBA is also an indication of the new trend in India's foreign policy towards its neighbours. It in a way exemplifies India's 'neighbourhood-first' policy.

Though the LBA has addressed the three major issues pertaining to the border, yet it is imperative for India and Bangladesh to understand that a tranquil border will not be achieved without addressing the other border problems. For instance, with regard to the informal trade, especially the cattle smuggling and the question if illegal migration, no clear resolution can be foreseen. These issues are such where soft power has a limited role to play. Nevertheless, soft power can implicitly play a role in creating congenial conditions over which negotiations on contentious issues can foster.

Notes

1. http://indianexpress.com/article/opinion/columns/india-bangladesh-land-boundary-agreement-41-years-in-the-making/
2. These enclaves were a legacy of gambling debts over games of chess indulged between the Rajas of Cooch Bihar and Rangpur in the eighteenth century. Parcels of land owned by each were used as stakes. Following post-partition independence, when these princely states acceded to and merged with India and Pakistan respectively, these parcels of land became effectively converted into enclaves. The tortuous complexity of the enclaves was further compounded by some of them possessing enclaves within enclaves (or exclaves) cited from Tariq A. Karim (2016) "India's Land Boundary Agreement with Bangladesh: Its Importance and Implications."
3. India and Bangladesh Land Boundary Agreement 2015, MEA, p.8 available at https://www.mea.gov.in/Uploads/ Publication Docs/24529_LBA_ MEA_ Booklet_final.pdf 4 http://indiacode.nic.in/coiweb/amend/Constitution%20(119th)%20Bill,%202013.%20SOR.pdf
5. In the eastern border, the Nehru-Noon Agreement of 1958 sought to achieve, among others, three major objectives. First, to resolve differences which impeded demarcation of the boundary in different sectors of the border and the problem of the Union No.12 of Southern Berubari which was a part of India according to the line drawn by Sir Radcliffe but belonged to Pakistan according to his written description. In case of such a conflict written description of the boundary was to prevail. However, the mostly non-Muslim population of the Union opposed the territory going to Pakistan. More than a decade elapsed, but the matter could not be resolved. The South Berubari Union No.12 continued to remain in India as a part of India. The Government of India could not make it over to Pakistan. Nor could the Government of Pakistan take over its possession. In the 1958 Agreement it was agreed to divide the union by two halves, roughly equally, the southern half along with two enclaves going to Pakistan and the northern half remaining with India. Secondly, the Agreement sought to resolve the problems of the enclaves. The Agreement decided to merge the enclaves with the country they fell within. That is, Indian enclaves inside East Pakistan will merge with East

Pakistan and East Pakistan enclaves inside India will merge with India (India would not, however, receive any compensation for the extra area going to Pakistan). Thirdly, the agreement decided to exchange territories as a consequence of the demarcation of the boundary. Territories which were found upon demarcation to be wrongfully held (that is, under adverse possession) were to be transferred to the country they rightfully belonged to. (cited from http://www.asthabharati.org/Dia_Oct%2008/Mosta.htm)

6. http://www.asthabharati.org/Dia_Oct%2008/Mosta.htm
7. Adverse possession is the case of the government or citizens of one country having possession of land beyond the boundaries in another country. In the context of India and Bangladesh, it was found that Indian citizens owned land in Bangladesh, and vice versa.
8. An enclave is a territory, or a part of a territory, that is surrounded from all the three sides by another country.
9. http://www.asthabharati.org/Dia_Oct%2008/Mosta.htm
10. This was the largest arms haul in Bangladesh (10 truckloads of weapons and ammunition, enough to arm an entire brigade), which had taken place on April 2004 in the Chittagong area. Subsequent investigation revealed that the arms were to be supplied to insurgent groups—ULFA and even NSCN-IM—operating in north eastern India. The BNP government had underplayed the issue because some of the top BNP leaders were involved in the case, cited from Sreeradha Datta (2016) "'All-Time High' Relations Herald Greater Regional Integration" in Debate: India-Bangladesh Relations: Scaling Newer Heights 113
11. Smruti S Pattanaik (2016) in "India-Bangladesh Relations: Moving towards Greater Synergy" contends-It needs to be mentioned here that India's role in the liberation war was politicized by vested interests. The two major political parties, the Awami League and the BNP attempted to appropriate history in a manner to glorify the role of only founding father of their respective parties. Moreover, the subsequent military regimes that assumed power highlighted the role of the military and dismissed India's role as 'strategically motivated'.
12. Official website of Ministry of External Affairs, Government of India, Available at http://www.mea.gov.in/pressreleases.htm?dtl/1636/Meeting+of+India Bangladesh+Joint+Boundary+Working+Group
13. India and Bangladesh Land Boundary Agreement, MEA 2015, p.9
14. http://www.mea.gov.in/Portal/ForeignRelation/Bangladesh_Brief.pdf
15. http://www.pharmexcil.org/data/country_files/bangladesh.pdf
16. Annexure V
17. http://zeenews.india.com/exclusive/land-boundary-agreement-completes-unfinished-task-of-partition-expert_1610888.html 121
18. http://www.ndtv.com/india-news/india-bangladesh-sign-historic-land-boundary-agreement-769351
19. http://www.jagranjosh.com/current-affairs/india-bangladesh-signed-land-boundary-agreement-of-1974-1433759676-1 123
20. http://www.mea.gov.in/Uploads/PublicationDocs/24529_LBA_MEA_Booklet_final.pdf

21. In an exclusive interview with Dr. Smruti S Pattanaik, an expert on South Asia, conducted by Kamna Arora, Zee Media discusses PM Modi's visit to Bangladesh in Kamna Arora (June 10, 2015), "Land Boundary Agreement completes unfinished task of partition: Expert" at http://zeenews.india.com/exclusive/land-boundary-agreement-completes-unfinished-task-of-partition-expert_1610888.html
22. http://zeenews.india.com/exclusive/land-boundary-agreement-completes-unfinished-task-of-partition-expert_1610888.html
23. Joint Declaration Between Bangladesh and India during the visit of Prime Minister of India to Bangladesh: "Notun Projonmo – Nayi Disha" (June 07, 2015)
24. http://in.reuters.com/article/2015/06/06/bangladesh-india-land-treaty-idINKBN0OM0IV20150606
25. http://in.reuters.com/article/2015/06/06/bangladesh-india-land-treaty-idINKBN0OM0IV20150606
26. Joint Declaration Between Bangladesh and India during the visit of Prime Minister of India to Bangladesh: "Notun Projonmo – Nayi Disha" (June 07, 2015)
27. http://zeenews.india.com/exclusive/land-boundary-agreement-completes-unfinished-task-of-partition-cxpert_1610888.html
28. http://zeenews.india.com/exclusive/land-boundary-agreement-completes-unfinished-task-of-partition-expert_1610888.html
29. http://zeenews.india.com/exclusive/land-boundary-agreement-completes-unfinished-task-of-partition-expert_1610888.html
30. http://www.jagranjosh.com/current-affairs/india-bangladesh-signed-land-boundary-agreement-of-1974-1433759676-1
31. http://zeenews.india.com/exclusive/land-boundary-agreement-completes-unfinished-task-of-partition-expert_1610888.html
32. http://www.globalsecurity.org/military/world/india/india-bangladesh-fence.htm

Chapter - V

The Issue of Trade and Transit between India and Bangladesh

The chapter will probe into the problems of trade and transit between India and Bangladesh which till date remains a major issue when it comes to the betterment of the relations between the two countries. The chapter is structured into two major sections. The first section will demonstrate the historiography of India-Bangladesh trade relations. The section divides India-Bangladesh trade relations into three phases starting from 1971 till 2015. While doing so, the chapter will demonstrate how trade and economic inducement as a soft power has been used in the past to improve the relations between India and Bangladesh, and how it has become more vivid in the contemporary Indo-Bangladesh relations, the tone of which was set with the June 2015 visit of Indian Prime Minister Modi. As we shall see, issues related to trade has moved into four phases starting from 1971 till present. The first phase (1971-75) deals with India-Bangladesh trade relations under the Indira-Mujib era wherein it is seen that economic inducement and other assistance as soft power assumes importance. It is also seen that trade inducement and agreements also led to the some progress on the water issue when Joint River Commission was formed in 1972.

The second phase (1975-2010) basically deals with the bilateral trade relations in the post-Mujib era. It is clear that trade relations between India and Bangladesh under military regime in Bangladesh suffers a major setback. However, what is clear from this phase is that trade as inducement has often been used to boost their overall relations, including the cooperation on the Farakka issue. The major hallmark of the phase is the signing of the Ganges Water Agreement 1996. Though trade as inducement (soft power) has been only used implicitly, its impact is quite obvious when it comes to interim agreement on the Ganges in 1977. The third phase (2010-2015) starts with a landmark visit of Sheikh Hasina in January 2010 to India wherein a fresh impetus was given to their bilateral economic ties. The joint communiqué of January 2010 also initiated the *border haats* which is a soft power strategy to generate more *people-to-people* contact in the borderland areas. The phase is also significant in a sense that an important step to resolve the Land Boundary issue was initiated. The last phase starting since the Modi's 2015 visit to Bangladesh encrypts a momentous chapter in Indo-Bangladesh trade relations. Apart from the conclusion of the Land Boundary Agreement (LBA) various other agreements which have soft power implications were signed. This phase will demonstrate as to how soft power has become a major tool of diplomacy of India under the Narendra Modi government and how we find plenitude of soft power implications in the negotiations and Agreements reached upon during the June 2015 Modi's visit to Bangladesh.

As we shall see and as the second section will demonstrate, there remain some major challenges with regard to trade that needs attention. The challenges dealt in the section are- the issues of trade deficit, Non-Tariff Barriers (NBTs), informal trade, institutional lacunas, infrastructural deficits and procedural delays and the issue of transit.

5.1 Section-I

Indo-Bangladesh economic relations have been affected by the legacy of history. Bangladesh, after all, was a part of Pakistan for more than two decades when Pakistan had fought two wars with India. History has not ceased casting its long shadow. The mindset and preconceptions inherited from the past linger on, in both countries. Moreover, in the post-independence period, the ebb and flow in political relationships have affected economic relations as well. In fact, in inter-state relationships all over the world, economic and political relations are intertwined. Close or strong economic relationships, including trade and economic cooperation between countries, have often been propelled by the prevailing close political relations or by a desire to strengthen future political relations and vice-versa (Islam 2004: 4069).

Bilateral economic relations between India and Bangladesh has grown since the latter got independence in 1971, albeit at a slow pace. Ups and downs in the political relations between the two countries have had a strong bearing on development of their economic ties (*CUTS International Report* 2014: 4). Though in current times there has been a constant progress in

India's export to Bangladesh, there remain some major challenges in their bilateral economic relations. Indian exports to Bangladesh witnessed a sharp increase from $ 3.7 billion in 2011-12 to $ 6.4 billion in 2014-2015 an increase of more than 70 percent in four years time. Bangladesh currently is India's largest trading partner among SAARC countries (*Annual Reports 2014-15*: 5). Aggregate trade between India and Bangladesh stood at $ 7 billion for the 2014-2015 fiscal year.

However, trade is heavily in favour of India with its exports to Bangladesh at $6.4 billion (Quadir, June 06, 2015).

Table 1: India-Bangladesh Bilateral Trade

Financial Year	*India's Export to Bangladesh (In US $ millions)*	*% change in export*	*India's Import from Bangladesh (In US $ millions)*	*% change in import*	*Total Trade (In US $ millions)*	*Trade Deficit (In US $ millions)*	*% Change*
2007-08	2923.72		257.02		3180.74	2666.7	
2008-09	2497.87	-14.56	313.11	21.82	2810.98	2184.76	-22.05
2009-10	2433.77	-2.56	254.66	-18.66	2688.43	2179.11	-0.25
2010-11	3242.9	33.24	446.75	75.42	3689.65	2796.15	22.06
2011-12	3789.2	16.84	585.73	31.10	4374.93	3203.47	12.71
2012-13	5144.99	35.78	639.33	9.15	5784.32	4505.66	28.90
2013-14	6166.93	19.86	484.34	-24.24	6651.27	5682.59	20.71
2014-15	6451.47	4.61	621.37	28.29	7072.84	5830.1	2.53
2015-16*	3713.92	NA	426.92	NA	4140.84	3287	NA

*(April to November)

Source: Department of Commerce, Government of India

Table 2: Major Items of Export

HS Code	*Export Items*	*2012-13 (in US $ million)*	*2013-14 (in US $ million)*	*Share (%)*
52	Cotton	1506	1577	25.6
10	Cereals	569	924	15.0
87	Vehicles other than Railway or Tramway Rolling Stock, and parts and accessories thereof	374	479	7.8
84	Nuclear reactors, boilers, machinery and mechanical appliances; parts thereof	268	266	4.3
23	Residues and waste from the food industries; prepared animal fodder	190	252	4.1
72	Iron and steel	130	245	4.0
26	Mineral fuels, mineral oils and products of their distillation; bituminous substances; mineral waxes	153	201	3.3

Source: Ministry of Commerce and industry, Government of India

Table 3: Major Items of Imports

HS Code	*Import Items*	*2012-13 (in US $ million)*	*2013-14 (in US $ million)*	*Share (%)*
53	Other vegetable textile fibres; paper yarn and woven fabrics of paper yarn	124	83	17.2
62	Articles of apparel and clothing accessories, not knitted or crocheted	52	79	16.3
8	Edible fruit and nuts; peel or citrus fruit or melons	97	57	11.7
63	Other made up textile articles; worn clothing and worn textile articles; rags	85	48	9.9
25	Salt; sulphur; earths and stone; plastering materials; lime and cement	27	21	4.3

Source: Ministry of Commerce and industry, Government of India

5.1.a India-Bangladesh Trade Relations Before 1971

It is interesting to note that India's economic relation with Bangladesh predates the creation of Bangladesh or when it was known as East Pakistan. Since the partition of India in 1947, India and East Pakistan had huge economic interdependence upon each other. In fact, East Pakistan remained an important trade partner of India during the first few years after the partition (Madaan 1998: 57-58).

Table 4: India's Trade with East Pakistan During 1948-66*
****Data was available only till 1966**

Year	*Export to East Pakistan*	*Imports from East Pakistan*	*Balance of Trade*	*Total Trade*
1948-49	109	257	-148	366
1949-50	77	79	-2	156
1950-51	40	83	-43	123
1951-52	61	162	-101	223
1952-53	32	44	-12	76
1953-54	7	39	-29	49
1954-55	10	39	-29	49
1955-56	8	54	-46	62
1957*	7	23	-16	30
1958*	9	12	-3	21
1959-60	8	16	-8	24
1960-61	11	25	-14	36
1961-62	15	20	-5	35
1962-63	14	21	-7	35
1963-64	10	18	-8	28
1964-65	13	23	-10	36
1965-66	7	10	-3	17

*Calendar years as data were available in terms of calendar years

Source: Davinder K. Madaan (1998), Indo-Bangladesh Economic Relations and SAARC, New Delhi: Deep & Deep Publications, p. 57

It is clear from the Table 4 that in 1948-49, the total trade turnover between India and East Pakistan was US $ 366 million which was an all time record in the history of their. However, an important aspect which is clear from the Table 4 is that during 1948-66, India always had a deficit in its balance of trade with East Pakistan. The main reason of India's trade deficit with East Pakistan during 1948-66 was due to its high imports of raw jute in order to meet the requirements of domestic jute industries which earned major foreign exchange for India (Madaan 1998: 57-59).

5.1.b India-Bangladesh Trade Relations after the Creation of Bangladesh

5.1.b.(i) First Phase (1971-75)

The emergence of Bangladesh as an independent country opened a new era of economic cooperation between India and Bangladesh. On December 6, 1971, India accorded recognition to Bangladesh which was followed by a series of bilateral agreements on defence, foreign relations and trade. India made all out efforts to rehabilitate the war-torn economy of Bangladesh (Madaan 1998: 68-69). Immediately after liberation Bangladesh required consumer goods, especially food which came from India (Kumar 2012: 114). A brief reference to India's economic assistance to Bangladesh during 1972-73 is called for. India gave commodity assistance to the tune over US $ 32 million. Another about $ 12 million of aid was given to Bangladesh to meet its foreign exchange requirements. The Indian Railway Board and the Corps of Engineers of the Indian Army repaired 247 bridges and restored 1, 714 miles of railway tracks. Sappers from the Indian Army and the engineers from the Public Works Department restored river communications and repaired all the major airfields of Bangladesh between 1972 and 1973 (Dixit 1999: 181). Besides India's assistance to Bangladesh to address its food security was of prime importance. In fact, by November 1972, India had supplied 931,000 tons of food to address the food crisis in Bangladesh (*Asian Recorder*, June10-16, 1972 in Nair 2008: 50). What can be deduced from the above inferences is the fact that India was actually using its soft power, in the form of economic inducement and other aids and assistance, in its initial years of its relations with Bangladesh.

Nonetheless, a bilateral agreement between the two countries was signed on March 28, 1972.[1] This was signed in consonance with the Indo-Bangladesh Friendship Treaty. The treaty called for trade between the two countries, which was proposed to be conducted in a three-tier framework (Madaan 1998: 69-70). First, among other things, this Agreement provided for border trade between Bangladesh and neighbouring Indian states of West Bengal, Assam, Meghalaya, Tripura and Mizoram. Free trade in certain commodities was allowed within 16 kilometres of both countries' borders (Hassan 2000: 110). Initiating border trade assumes critical importance and it can be viewed as a soft power strategy to generate *people-to-people* contacts in the borderland areas.

Secondly, the agreement envisaged for a 'Limited Payment Trade' on a large scale for a balancing arrangement under which the countries were to import and export, specified items of the value of Rs. 25 crores ($ 32 million) in each direction, in case of any imbalance with the specified ceiling, an interest free technical credit up to a limit of Rs. 5 crores (over $ 6.5 million) was to be provided in the form of a swing credit from either side, to balance the trade between the two countries at the end of the term. Thirdly, the agreement stated that there would be regular international trade according to economic regulations of the two nations (Madaan 1998: 69-70). With the above agreement between India and Bangladesh, mutual cooperation was extended by both the nations. It is, therefore, clear is that trade and economy as inducement (soft power) was used by India. Such initiatives not only strengthened India-Bangladesh trade relations but also were able to foster cooperation on other areas. Consequently, on June 10, 1972, the two countries decided to cooperate in the areas of atomic energy, space research and higher education (*Ibid.*, p. 70). Soft power seemed to work well and cooperation was also seen on the water issue. On November 24, 1972, the Indo-Bangladesh Joint River Commission was set up for the equitable utilization of the water resources to their mutual gains. Further, on January 5, 1973, a Joint Power Board was set up to ensure effective use of their power and energy resources (*Ibid.*).

The Trade Agreement of 1972 was replaced by another Trade Agreement signed on July 5, 1973 for three years (Hassan 2000: 110). This agreement provided for the Most Favoured Nation (MFN) treatment and a system of Balanced Trade and Payment Arrangement (BTPA).[2] However, trade agreement of 1973 could not achieve the desired level of trade between India and Bangladesh, and showed large imbalance in their trade in the very first year. In fact, 'rupee' trade was found to be a barrier in the bilateral trade of India and Bangladesh. For example, it was beneficial for India to sell coal against foreign exchange. Similarly, Bangladesh was also interested to sell jute against foreign exchange. Therefore, it was decided to abolish 'rupee' payment arrangement. On December 17, 1974, a Protocol to the trade arrangement was signed by India and Bangladesh (Madaan 1998:

71). The new agreement abolished 'rupee' trade from January 1, 1975, and it was decided that the bilateral trade between the two countries would be conducted in free convertible currency (De and Ghosh 2008: 71).

However, prior to December, 1974 Protocol, two significant occurrences which have soft power implications needs mention here. On May 16, 1974, a number of agreements on wide ranging economic and trade co-operation between India and Bangladesh emerged from the five-day high-level discussions between the two countries wherein India agreed to extend three credits amounting to Rs. 41crores ($ 50.6 million) to Bangladesh (Tiwary 2006: 1688). Apart from the economic inducement, efforts were also made to reignite the cultural ties between India and Bangladesh. On September 27, 1974, the two countries signed a Two-Year Protocol for exchange programmes in the fields of culture, education, information and sports. India also offered 100 scholarships and fellowships to Bangladeshi nationals every year for higher studies and research in India. In addition, India agreed to send eminent musicians and dancers to Bangladesh to conduct short-term courses in Bangladesh in classical music and dance. The protocol also provided for exchange of visits by academicians, scientists, educationists, literators, sportsmen, cultural troupes and sports teams. In fact, during Sheikh Mujib period, Indo-Bangladesh co-operation in the trade, science, culture and educational fields were in high spirits (Bindra 1982: 28).

Even at regional/multilateral level trade relations were showing positive signs. On July 30, 1975, Trade agreement known as Bangkok Agreement was signed by five developing countries of Economic and Social Commission for Asia and Pacific (ESCAP), Namely, India, Bangladesh, Sri Lanka, Republic of Korea and Laos, at Bangkok. Under the agreement, India and Bangladesh extended tariff and non-tariff trade preferences to each other (Madaan 1998: 71).

India offered maximum economic assistance to Bangladesh, but could not continue to do so due to its limited resources and ever rising domestic needs. The prevalence of drought in 1972-73 and floods in 1973-74 in Bangladesh economy kept India's influence in Bangladesh at bay as the former could not combat with economic crisis in Bangladesh's economy. Hence, Bangladesh became suspicious about India's ability to meet Bangladesh's requirement. Meanwhile, the Indo-Bangladesh border trade agreement signed in 1972 encouraged smuggling between the two countries and hence in October 1972, border trade was abolished between the two nations by mutual consent (*Ibid.*, p. 73). Such instances undermined India's soft power. India's soft power was also impinged by the disputes regarding the transfer of the Tin Bigha corridor from India to Bangladesh; the Farakka dispute; the question of the Pakistani Prisoners of Wars (POW). Further, the Friendship Treaty of 1972 too began to be criticised. There was a prevailing notion in Bangladesh that India wanted to keep Bangladesh as a client state. Thus, India's motive in Bangladesh's liberation movement was seen from a suspicious perspective. This was further compounded by Mujib's participation in the Islamic Conference at Lahore in 1974, which India saw it as a move towards Islamisation and having pro-Pakistan undercurrents. Further, the controversy over the New Moore/Talpatty Island in the Bay of Bengal also kept India-Bangladesh relations at bay.

5.1.b.(ii) Second Phase (1975-2010)

The assassination of Sheikh Mujibur Rahman on August 15, 1975 in an Army coup provided a major setback to Indo-Bangladesh economic relations. Khondakar Mushtaque, Mujib's Minister of Commerce briefly came to power in Bangladesh. On November 7, 1975, Bangladesh faced another coup, which brought General Zia-ur Rahman in power in Bangladesh. With the coming of a military regime in Bangladesh, the issue of regime compatibility, discussed in the previous chapters, had its impact in Indo-Bangladesh relations. In India, Mrs. Indira Gandhi did not favour military regimes in India's neighbourhood and thus, made little efforts to evolve even a working relationship with General Zia-ur Rahman. Moreover, Zia-ur Rahman followed policies which were completely opposite to Mujib's regime (Pandey 2012: 270).

Nevertheless, on January 12, 1976, India and Bangladesh signed a Trade Protocol which visualized higher volume of trade of coal and newsprint in order to balance the trade (Madaan 1998: 72). Simultaneously, some progress was also made on the Farakka issue. Before the commencement of the 1976 lean season India invited Bangladesh for talks with a view to reach an equitable solution. The talks at the level of experts were held in April and May (1976) and the goodwill delegation which visited Dacca from 18 to 23 June (1976) devoted most of its time to the discussion of this issue (*MEA Annual Report* 1976-77: 9).

On August 14, 1976, India and Bangladesh agreed on Nepal's trade with Bangladesh through Indian territory. On October 5, 1976, Balanced Trade and Payment Arrangement (BTPA) between India and Bangladesh was extended for three years till September 27, 1979, on the request of Bangladesh. The emphasis was given on increasing the volume of their mutual trade (Madaan 1998: 72). In September 1976, India renewed its invitation to Bangladesh for further talks on the Farakka issue which were held in New Delhi from 7 to Sep 10, 1976. During these negotiations, India made far-reaching proposals to reduce its withdrawals at Farakka during the lean season. Further, it offered to undertake joint investigation and study of all possibilities for a long-term solution for augmenting the flow of the Ganga in the lean period (*MEA Annual Report* 1976-77: 9). Consequently, the Trade Agreement between India and Bangladesh and the Indo-Bangladesh Cultural Cooperation Programme which were to expire at the end of September 1976, were extended through exchange of letters. Annual trade talks between the two countries took place in the second week of February 1977 (*Ibid.,* p.10). The spill over of such positive developments was also witnessed in the water issue. India-Bangladesh relations showed some positive signs with the coming of the Desai government in India.

Direct negotiations on the Ganges waters were resumed immediately after the formation of the new Janata Government at New Delhi. An Indian delegation led by Shri Jagjivan Ram, Minister for Defence in the new government, had extended discussions in Dacca in April 1977. These resulted in the arrival of a common understanding in principle on the allocation of waters during the lean season. This was followed by discussions at the official level from 7 to 11 May between the Bangladesh delegation led by Mr. Abbas and the Indian delegation led by the Foreign Secretary, Shri Jagat Mehta. Considerable progress was made in working out the details of a possible solution (*MEA Annual Report* 1976-77: 10). Finally, after several rounds of discussion India and Bangladesh reached to a five year agreement on November 5, 1977.

Trade between India and Bangladesh remained stagnant until October 4, 1980, when the two countries signed another three years trade agreement on and reiterated the 'most favoured nation's treatment' to each other. The agreement was extendable for another three years by mutual consent. Up to September 1980, their mutual trade was governed by BTPA, 1973. It made clear that all payments were to be given in freely convertible currencies. Both the countries also discussed to offer mutually beneficial transportation facilities for trade between them. The protocol on inland water transit and trade between India and Bangladesh was also signed for three years at this occasion. It provided transit facilities for Indian vessels carrying specified goods from Calcutta to Dhubri and Krimgang in Assam. India agreed to give Taka 25 Lakhs (around US $ 0.3 million) as annual conservancy charges for this purpose (*Ibid.*, p. 72). This was followed by a cultural Protocol which was signed between India and Bangladesh On

December 30, 1980, for regular exchange of ideas in science, education and other social activities. Subsequently, during December 1981, first technical cooperation agreement was signed between the two countries (*Ibid.*).

On March 24, 1982, General Ershad captured power in Bangladesh through a bloodless coup from Sattar, who had become President, when Zia-ur Rahman was assassinated on May 30, 1981. Earlier in 1980, the Congress came to power in India under the leadership of Mrs. Gandhi, the old ally of Bangladesh. A summit meet took place between Mrs. Indira Gandhi and Mr. H.M. Ershad in New Delhi on October 7, 1982, which gave fillip to Indo-Bangladesh economic relations. A Joint Economic Commission (JEC) was set up in order to promote mutual trade and to identify the areas of joint ventures and mutual economic cooperation. With the establishment of JEC, private trade was also allowed (*Ibid.*, p. 74). Progress was also witnessed on the water issue. During President H. M. Ershad's visit to India, the two countries agreed to an interim memorandum of understanding (MOU) on the Ganges water issue, which was valid for the next two dry seasons. It was signed on October 7, 1982 by the foreign ministers of Bangladesh and India, A. R. S. Doha and P. V. Narashima Rao, respectively (Hossain 1998: 139). Further, on November 8, 1983, India and Bangladesh renewed a Protocol on inland water transit and trade of 1980 for further three years. In May 1986, India and Bangladesh extended their bilateral trade agreement of 1983 for another three years till October 3, 1989. This was further renewed to October 3, 1992 in 1989 (*Ibid.*, pp. 74-75).

On October 24, 1995, the existing trade agreement was further renewed for three years until October, 1998. The agreement was later amended and formalised in March 2006. This came into force on April 1, 2006 and had its validity till March 2009 (Kumar 2012: 114). This agreement provided for expansion of trade and economic cooperation, making mutually beneficial arrangements for the use of waterways, railways and roadways; the passage of goods through each other's territory; exchange of business and trade delegations and annual consultations to review the working of the agreement (*Ibid.*). However, the agreement does not provide for any bilateral trade concessions. Such tariff concessions are accorded to each other only under the provisions of the South Asian Preferential Trading Arrangement (SAPTA) signed in April 1993, which became effective in December 1995 (De and Ghosh 2008: 71). It is important to note that tariff concessions by India to Bangladesh can generate soft power leverage. As such, India time and again offered tariff concessions through bilateral and multilateral forums. Till date, India has unilaterally extended duty free and quota free access to virtually all, but 26 Bangladeshi products in the Indian market (Karim 2016: 233). However, such preferential arrangements provided by India have not been able to achieve preferred outcomes and have not been able to improve their bilateral economic relations in a significant manner, which is another major concern.

5.1.b.(iii) Third Phase (2010-2015)

After years of disappointment and arguments, a fresh impetus was given to their bilateral economic ties with the visit of Sheikh Hasina in January 2010 to India. In the joint communiqué of this visit both sides agreed to intensify discussions at official and technical levels to provide further impetus to trade and economic exchanges (Kumar 2016: 120). Besides, it was following Prime Minister Sheikh Hasina's visit to India in January 2010 that the Congress-led UPA made a sincere effort to resolve the land boundary issues (*The Daily Star*, May 20, 2015). In fact, during Hasina's 2010 visit to India 51 point MOU was agreed upon, which provided a road map of future cooperation. Both the countries agreed to take steps at the earliest to demarcate the boundary, exchange the enclaves and settle the land that were in 'adverse possession' (Pattanaik 2016: 220).

The joint communiqué of January 2010 also initiated the *border haats* between the two countries. The *haats*, as mentioned earlier, are important in generating *people-to-people* contact and as such is a soft power strategy. The *haats* were aimed to provide the locals a platform to sell locally produced vegetables, fruits, spices, fish, poultry, minor forest produce, produce of local cottage industry, small agricultural household implements, second hand garments, melamine products and processed food items (*Task Force reports* 2011: 47-48). However, an agreement on border *haats* was signed on October 23, 2010. The impact of the visit in turn created a congenial business atmosphere which is evident from the fact that (as per official estimates) exports from Bangladesh to India increased by 56 per cent in the first 10 months of 2010-11. India's export for the same year was $ 3.2 billion against $ 2.4 billion dollar in the previous financial year, thus marking a 33% increase (*Task Force reports* 2011: 48).

The joint communiqué signed between the prime ministers of the two countries in New Delhi in January 2010 included new areas of bilateral cooperation. With a perceptible change in Indo-Bangladesh relations, there are better prospects of Bangladesh developing as a hub for inter and intra-regional trade and transit (*Ibid.*, p. 44). With regard to transit some developments were made. The joint statement made during the 2010 visit of Sheikh Hasina to India. Apart from the decision to allow India to use Bangladeshi sea ports, Namely Chittagong and Mongla, some other areas of cooperation were identified with regard to waterway and rail communication. Among other things, the two countries agreed to include Ashuganj and Silghat as two new ports of call. It is also worth mentioning that India has already started using the transit facility through Bangladesh. For the first time, four consignments of heavy equipments for the Tripura power station went through the Ashuganj port of Bangladesh. India has also given a soft loan of a billion dollars to Bangladesh to build infrastructure to facilitate transit between the two countries (Selim 2012: 104).

Indo-Bangladesh economic ties strengthened further with the visit of the then India's Foreign Minister S. M. Krishna in July 2011, wherein the high commissioners of the two countries signed an agreement for the protection and promotion of investments. This agreement pertained to exchange of instruments of ratification in respect to the Bilateral Investment Promotion and Protection Agreement (BIPPA). Another agreement concerning SOP (Standard Operating Procedure) for entry of trucks from Bhutan into territories of the two countries near the border was also signed during Krishna's visit. BIPPA was received well by the business community in Bangladesh. While it is expected to encourage substantial Indian investment in Bangladesh, it also has the potential of initiating Bangladeshi investments in Northeast India (Habib 2011: 49). This is another soft power strategy which has met with success as, so far, the interaction between the two business communities has been quite encouraging. It has resulted in several joint venture agreements for export-oriented manufacturing activities in Bangladesh (*Task Force reports* 2011: 49).

Apart from it, India also provided a $ 1billion credit line to Bangladesh for a range of projects including railway infrastructure, supply of locomotives and passenger coaches, rehabilitation of Saidpur railway workshop, procurement of buses, and for dredging projects. The agreement also called for the purchase of double-decker buses from India and setting up of a power grid between India and Bangladesh and establishment of state-run standards and testing institute facilities in Bangladesh by India (*Ibid.*). Thus, what is obvious is that after 2010, there are enough soft power references, which India has employed in its relations with Bangladesh. Similarly, when India's commerce and industry minister Anand Sharma visited Bangladesh, a number of important developments took place which has soft power undertones. India offered a tariff-free quota of 10 million pieces of apparel from Bangladesh, making an increase of 25 percent over previous years, while countervailing duties were lifted on all jute exports from Bangladesh (Kumar 2012: 120). Further, in his September 2011 visit to Dhaka, the then Indian Prime Minister, Manmohan Singh, announced duty-free access to 46 textile items from the country. Bangladesh had been pressing to get a duty waiver on 61 products (*The Hindu Business Line*, September 7, 2011). Singh's 2011 visit was also important as a protocol to the 1974 LBA was signed in September 2011. Unfortunately UPA lacked the numerical strength in the Lok Sabha. When it planned to place the Bill in the Parliament, the BJP, then in opposition, stiffly opposed the move (*The Daily Star*, May 20, 2015).

5.1.b.(iv) Fourth Phase (2015 onwards)

After the general elections in India in May 2014 and Narendra Modi ascendency to power in India, Bangladesh' Speaker Dr. Shirin Sharmin Chaudhury, on behalf of Prime Minister Sheikh Hasina, participated in the oath taking ceremony of Prime Minister Narendra Modi in New Delhi. Following this, India's external affairs minister Sushma Swaraj visited Bangladesh from June 25-27, 2014 at the invitation of Foreign Minister of Bangladesh. This visit provided further momentum to the close and friendly relationship between India and Bangladesh. Further, Union Minister of State for Development of North Eastern Region (Independent Charge), External Affairs and Overseas Indian Affairs Gen. (Dr) V. K. Singh (Retd.) accompanied by Chief Minister of Meghalaya Dr Mukul Sangma and Commerce and Industry Minister of Tripura Tapan Chakraborty visited Bangladesh on 24 August 2014 to attend the India-Bangladesh Business Conclave (*MEA Annual Reports*, 2014-15: 2). This was followed by the two Indian Parliamentary delegations, one in September and another in November 2014 visited Bangladesh to attend International Conferences organized by Bangladesh Parliament with Inter-Parliamentary Union (IPU), Geneva and Commonwealth Parliamentary Association and IMF respectively (*MEA Annual Reports*, 2014-15: 5). Similarly the landmark visit of the President of Bangladesh Mr. Mohammad Abdul Hamid to India from 18-23 December 2014, which was the first visit by Bangladesh's ceremonial Head of State after a gap of 42 years, contributed to further strengthening and expanding the close bilateral relations between the two countries (*Ibid.*, p. 2).

Nevertheless, the most significant milestone towards the betterment of Indo-Bangladesh ties was set by the June 2015 visit of India's Prime Minister Narendra Modi to Bangladesh where apart from the historical Land

Boundary Agreement, a plethora of agreements concerning trade and investment were finalised.[3] Interestingly, we can locate plenitude of soft power inferences in it. In this regard, the economic aid of $ 2 billion assumes supreme importance. India took a leap forward and offered Bangladesh a New Line of Credit (LoC) of US$ 2 billion, doubling the previous $ 1billion credit line, offered in 2010 (Datta 2016: 226). It is to be noted that this is the largest single line of credit given by India to any country till date. In the joint declaration at the end of the visit, both the Prime Ministers expressed satisfaction at the utilization of the first line of credit of US$ 800 million, which was enhanced by an additional US$ 62 million and US$ 200 million grant extended by India to Bangladesh (*Notun Projonmo-Nayi Disha*, June 07, 2015). With regard to economic assistance, it is here imperative to mention that the fourth tranche of US $ 25 million out of the US $ 200 million grant committed by the Government of India to Bangladesh in 2012 was paid to the Bangladesh side. With this, India has completed the disbursement of $ 175 million grant assistance to Bangladesh. Steady progress has been achieved in the utilization of the $ 800 million Line of Credit extended to Bangladesh. The 15 ongoing projects are in advanced stages of implementation (*Annual Reports*, 2014-15: 6). Apart from it, in the joint declaration, the two Prime Ministers also welcomed the signing of the MOU to implement the grant assistance of INR 5 crores (about $ 800000) from the India Endowment for Climate Change for installation of 70,000 improved cook stoves in Bangladesh (*Notun Projonmo-Nayi Disha*, June 07, 2015).

That India is actively using soft power is also evident from the fact that during Prime Minister's Modi's visit to Bangladesh, steps were taken to engage Indian private sectors in generating power to help Bangladesh achieve its 2021 target of electricity generation. It is to be remembered that any assistance from India in this regard will improve the India image and as such will earn India soft power. India has agreed to construct the Ramphal power project. Mongla and Bheramara are proposed as sites for Indian Special economic Zones (SEZ) (Pattanaik 2016: 224). It is to be noted that, among other investments, Adani Power Limited and Reliance Power Limited have already signed deals worth over $ 4.5 billion with state-run Bangladesh Power Development Board (BPDB) to develop six units of power plants to produce 4,600 MW of electricity.[4] Consequently as Modi said, "Bangladesh will be able to more than double power imports from India to 1,100 MW from 500 MW at present (Quadir, June 6, 2015)." Noting Bangladesh's interest in importing power in the Bangladesh, Bhutan, India and Nepal (BBIN) framework, India agreed to favourably consider such import subject to grid security, transmission, interconnection and applicable laws, rules and regulations of the respective countries (*Notun Projonmo-Nayi Disha*, June 07, 2015). The two countries established India-Bangladesh Joint Consultative Commission (JCC) at the foreign minister's level to discuss trade and investment, security, connectivity, border management, water, power, shipping, renewable energy, development cooperation, art and culture, people to people exchanges, and human resource development (Pattanaik 2016: 224).

Apart from it, India is also promoting Bangladesh's energy security by encouraging investments in power generation. On the anvil are a 1,320 MW coal-fired plant in Rampal (Upazila of Bagerhat District in Khulna, Bangladesh), and a 130-kilometre long 'Friendship Pipeline' from Siliguri for supply of one million tonnes of diesel annually (*The Hindu*, March 11, 2015). The joint declaration, the two Prime Ministers welcomed the MOU and the Sale-Purchase Agreement signed between Numaligarh Refinery Ltd (NRL) and Bangladesh Petroleum Corporation (BPC) for construction of a pipeline from Siliguri to Parbatipur for supply of High Speed Diesel to Bangladesh (*Notun Projonmo-Nayi Disha*, June 07, 2015). Work on the Bangladesh-India Friendship Power Company, a joint venture thermal power plant that will generate 1320 MW of electricity, is the largest such bilateral joint venture to date, and will become fully operational within next couple of years. The most exciting prospect lies ahead: when the two countries link up their respective north-eastern grids, that could transform into becoming a gateway for India to finally invest in harvesting hydropower up to 60,000-80,000 MW (Bangladesh has expressed desire to obtain 20,000 MW from it) and evacuate the same to India's mainframe national grid via Bangladeshi enablement (Karim 2016: 235).

In addition, India has accorded Bangladesh the status of zero-tariff imports for all but 25 tariff lines. Modi stated, "India will invest more as Bangladesh today offered an exclusive economic zone for India and this investment will help to narrow the gap." Cumulative Indian investments in Bangladesh stood at $ 2.5 billion in 2012-13 (Quadir, June 6, 2015). Keeping in view the growing cooperation between the two countries in the energy sector, the two Prime Ministers, during Modi's June visit to Bangladesh, decided to initiate an annual India-Bangladesh Energy Dialogue to be led jointly by Secretary (Petroleum) of India and Secretary, Power Division of Bangladesh to undertake comprehensive energy sector cooperation including areas of coal, natural gas, LNG, supply of petroleum products in the sub-region, renewable energy, oil and gas pipelines etc. (*Notun Projonmo-Nayi Disha*, June 07, 2015). 155

Similarly, New Delhi took several steps to develop the trade and commercial ties with Bangladesh through institutional arrangement. As part of concessions under the SAARC framework - SAPTA and SAFTA, India has granted Bangladesh duty-free, quota-free access on all items except tobacco and alcohol. Similar concessions have been provided under the Asia Pacific Free Trade Agreement (APTA). During Prime Minister's visit to Bangladesh in June, 2015, further steps have been taken including renewal of the bilateral trade agreement and signing of an MOU on establishment of an Indian Special Economic Zone in Bangladesh. Several instruments for facilitating bilateral trade and economic linkages are in place including the Convention for the Avoidance of Double Taxation and Prevention of Fiscal Evasion (DTAC), Bilateral Investment Protection & Promotion Agreement (BIPPA) and Agreement on Establishment of Joint Economic Commission (JEC). Bilateral mechanisms to discuss trade-related issues are also in place including a Joint Working Group on Trade, Commerce Secretary level talks, Protocol on Inland Water Transit and Trade (PIWTT), etc. Trade & commerce, investment & development cooperation are regularly discussed in high level visits. There are also institutional tie-ups between apex trade bodies from both sides.[5]

During Modi's visit to Bangladesh in June 2015, India and Bangladesh pledged to work closely in furthering relevant regional/sub-regional cooperation processes including SAARC, BIMSTEC and BCIM-EC. India and Bangladesh welcomed the agreement on establishing of the BIMSTEC electricity grid and expressed the hope that the BIMSTEC Free Trade Agreement will be finalized soon. The two countries also expressed confidence that the BCIM-EC Study Group reports would be finalized soon to allow decision making with regard to several projects envisaged under this framework, particularly the Kolkata-to-Kunming Highway Project (*Notun Projonmo-Nayi Disha*, June 07, 2015).

India and Bangladesh are trying to take their relationship beyond bilateral engagement. This was evident from the BBIN (Bangladesh, Bhutan, India and Nepal) countries' decision to go ahead with the Motor Vehicles Agreement for the Regulation of Passenger, Personal and Cargo Vehicular Traffic, which assumes significance in the sub-regional context. This agreement was signed in July 2015 to augment the cooperation that is extant. Bangladesh had earlier expressed its interest in importing electricity from Nepal and Bhutan (Pattanaik 2016: 225). India is a major stakeholder in Bhutan in terms of its investment in the power sector. Similarly, Bangladesh has extended the usage of Chittagong and Mongla to India, Nepal and Bhutan thereby enhancing bilateral synergy through multilateral arrangements. The JWG on Water Management and Power/Hydropower discussed the scope for power trade and inter-grid connectivity between the four countries. All these efforts will augment bilateral relations and revolutionise sub-regional cooperation that has generally been a victim to mistrust and suspicion (*Ibid.*).

The trade between the two countries has further got a fillip by opening of *border haats*. Bangladesh approved opening of two Border *haats* at Srinagar and Kamalasagar in Tripura. Work was in progress at Srinagar (in Feni district) and was inaugurated on 13 January 2015. In principle approval has been given by Bangladesh side for two more Border Haats in Tripura – Palbasti and Kamalpur. 22 *border haats* had been proposed along Meghalaya border in May 2013 of which 4 have been approved by Bangladesh and work is likely to begin soon. The movement of 10,000 MT of rice to Tripura from Kolkata through the Protocol Routes by barges up to Ashuganj and subsequently by road to Agartala was undertaken in two phases of 5000 MT each and was completed in November 2014 (Annual Reports 2014-15: 6). In fact, in the joint declaration issues at the end of the Modi's visit, the two Prime Ministers noted with appreciation the positive experience gained from the functioning of the *Border haats* and stressed the need to open more *border haats* at mutually agreed locations (*Notun Projonmo-Nayi Disha*, June 07, 2015).

Connectivity has been a key aspect of India's neighbourhood policy. Modi during his June 2015 visit to Bangladesh signed two agreements for a Dhaka-Shillong-Guwahati bus service and Kolkata-Dhaka-Agartala bus service. The fact that West Bengal Chief Minister Mamata Banerjee jointly flagged along with Modi and Hasina, has soft power connotations. There is also the Moitree Express that runs between Dhaka and Kolkata through Gede. Both the countries have initiated coastal shipping between Chittagong and Vishakhapatnam. Some more initiatives in this regard will earn enough soft power leverages for both the countries (Pattanaik 2016: 221).

During India's Prime Minister Modi's visit to Bangladesh, India also agreed to consider Bangladesh's proposal to introduce the 2nd Maitree Express between Khulna and Kolkata. In the joint declaration, the two Prime Ministers expressed satisfaction about the ongoing cooperation in the railways sector including the Akhaura-Agartala railway link and revival of the old railway links. They directed the concerned officials of both sides to take measures for ensuring more passenger-friendly customs and immigration facilities for the passengers of Maitree Express. Prime Minister Modi also announced that India will construct a modern International

Passenger Terminal (IPT) at a suitable location in India so as to facilitate customs and immigration requirements of passengers travelling on the Kolkata-Dhaka Maitri Express and other trains that are to connect India and Bangladesh (*Notun Projonmo-Nayi Disha*, June 07, 2015).

Another important achievement of Modi's visit to Bangladesh lies in the signing of the Coastal Shipping Agreement which would open up newer avenues of cooperation in the areas of bilateral & regional trade and connectivity. They also noted with satisfaction the renewal of the Protocol on Inland Water Transit and Trade (PIWTT) with new trade facilitation measures. Both the Prime Ministers agreed on the need for dredging of the India- Bangladesh inland water protocol routes to utilize their full potential. Both the Prime Ministers directed the officials to explore the possibilities of development of entire protocol route with assured Least Available Depth (LAD) with international funding. Prime Minister Modi agreed to provide necessary assistance for enhancing navigability of the routes as envisaged in the Framework Agreement (*Notun Projonmo-Nayi Disha*, June 07, 2015).

As it is evident, India-Bangladesh trade relations has taken a positive turn, especially with the visit of Indian Prime Minister Modi yet there remain some key challenges that can be a hurdle when it comes to the betterment of their bilateral trade relations.

5.2 Section-II

5.2.a Key Challenges in Indo-Bangladesh Trade Relations

In the past, trade has been quite a sensitive issue between India and Bangladesh (Islam 2004: 4070). India and Bangladesh are still characterized by a low level of economic integration, despite their geographical proximity and the fact that their economies are complementary to a large extent and stand to benefit substantially from economic integration. However, compared with their strength, there still exists much potential for developing trade and economic relations between the two countries (De and Bhattacharyay 2007: 2). This has largely been attributed to the trade disputes and its associated problems and the question of transit also have adversely affected India-Bangladesh relations. There are pressing concerns in Bangladesh regarding the large bilateral trade deficit with India and the large volumes of informal imports from India across the land border which avoid Bangladeshi import duties. It is estimated that Bangladesh's bilateral trade deficit with India has been increasing rapidly on average at about 9.5% annually. Political discontentment in Bangladesh tends to stem from the huge trade gap, supported by the fact that India has a lot of non-trade barriers for Bangladeshi exports. Even though exports from Bangladesh are growing at a healthy pace, there is no sign of reducing this trade gap (Dutta 2010: 1). Further, Indian concessions under the South Asian Preferential Trade Agreement (SAPTA) have made little impact and have not resulted in expected gains (Mukharji 2007: 565). Since 2005 bilateral trade has grown at 4-6 percent per annum, Figures vary).

Trade with Bangladesh is important from India's point of view since it is essential for socio-economic development of the North Eastern Region of India. While for Bangladesh, it is important as it will wider the area of cooperation, investment and will help in overall development of the country. It is also contended that the cost of doing trade is high between India and Bangladesh mainly due to lack of trade facilitation. Almost all border crossings lack in modern skilful infrastructure. Other NTBs like regulatory measures and lack of trade services have also resulted in hindering the bilateral trade.[6] Further, there are problems with regard to transit. India and Bangladesh have not been able to come to grant transit facilities. What, however, is interesting is that though both will benefit if they allow transit through each other's territory yet they deny on the basis of political and security concerns. Apart from it, Bangladesh' negative response to the proposed gas pipeline from Myanmar to India via Bangladesh has also impacted Indo-Bangladesh relations (Mukharji 2007: 566). However, the problems related to trade will be enumerated in detail in the following sections.

5.2.a.(i) Trade Deficit

The most primary problem with regard to trade in Indo-Bangladesh relations is the huge trade imbalance between two countries. For long Bangladesh has been asking India to address the growing trade gap between the two countries which has been hovering at around $ 1 billion in favour of India (Datta 2009: 206). From the figures given in table 1, it can be seen that Indo-Bangladesh formal trade in 2012-13 was US$ 5.1 billion and the deficit was US$ 4.5 billion. The total volume of bilateral trade in the financial years 2013-14 was $ 6.6 billion which in 2014-15 was $ 7 billion. While for the 2015-16 (April to November), the total volume of trade stood at $ 4.1 billion. However the trade deficit for the financial years 2013-14, 2014-15, 2015-16 (April to November) are $ 5.6 billion, $ 5.8 billion and $ 3.2 billion respectively. This deficit continues as a major issue of discord and discussion (Rahman 2015: 107).

India-Bangladesh trade relationship is overwhelmingly in favour of India, and the gap has steadily widened as India's exports have increased faster than its imports. While exports rose from $ 3.7 billion in 2011-12 to $ 6.4 billion in 2014-15, an average annual pace of 19.2 per cent, imports from the neighbour went up from $ 5.8 million to $ 6.2 million, witnessing an average annual growth of a mere 11 per cent average annual growth (*CII Report*, June 2015: 6). The major items of India's export to Bangladesh and its import from the same are given in Table 2 and 3 respectively.

However, it is important to understand the reasons behind such a huge trade deficit. First and foremost, India has a clear comparative advantage over Bangladesh. India has a 'revealed comparative advantage' in many goods which is why there is a steady increase of the Indian exports to Bangladesh over the years. Bangladesh, on the other hand, has relatively limited scope for enhancing its exports because it lacks a similar 'revealed comparative advantage' (Sikdar 2006: 2). In other words, there is a structural problem in Bangladesh's economy which does not produce enough goods that can be exported to India because of the lack of a manufacturing base, competition and market conditions (Chakravarty 2016: 213). Consequently, the Bangladeshi products have not been able to find an easy market in India. Further, India has the capability to meet the import requirements (both of products as well as quantity) of Bangladesh. But in most cases, the reverse is not true. Thus, there exists a case of partial complementary or one way complementary between the two countries (Kumar 2012: 114-115). Again, the geo-economics spectrum does not spell a win-win outcome. India's economy is too big for Bangladesh to compete with, which is also true in the case of China. Hence, it is always a lose-win situation for Bangladesh when compared with India. More importantly, as mentioned earlier, Bangladesh's export-base is so narrow and shallow that it constrains greater penetration in the Indian market (Banga 2009: 7).

Dhaka's concern to reduce the trade deficit is genuine. Bangladesh has been asking India to further reduce her 'Negative List' and allow greater imports of ready-made garments and other items. While India is willing to consider any suggestion favourably, Bangladesh should also appreciate that unless it produces items which can attract Indian buyers, it cannot sell more items even if the duty and the negative list is brought down to zero. It is also interesting to note that Bangladesh has trade deficit with USA, China and other developed countries, but its deficit with India gains prominence and more so gets political overtones. However, what is clear is that Bangladesh has to evolve a strategy of high value exports and at competitive prices (Bammi 2010: 139). As such, Bangladesh needs to improve its poor regulatory and business environment to attract adequate foreign investment in manufacturing and service sectors. An improvement in the country's overall business environment will augment its external competitiveness and export penetration into other economies, including India (Bashar 2013: 3).

Huge trade deficit of Bangladesh with India has become not only an economic issue but political issue too (Rashid 2010: 191). Rahman Sobhan observes, "Persistent and growing deficit with India demands attention because of its political as distinct from economic implications." Now this trade imbalance is also heating up the political relations (Karim 2009: 9). The issue of trade-deficit has become a major concern in Bangladesh and has created resentment and fans the perceived fear that Bangladesh is 'dominated' by India in the minds of many Bangladeshis (Rashid 2010: 192). This has led to the generation of general perception in Bangladesh that India wants to restrict its market for Bangladeshi products (Rahman 2015: 107). Coupled with the trade deficit, the problem of NBTs remains a major issue.

5.2.a.(ii) Non-Tariff Barriers (NBTs)

Political discontentment in Bangladesh tends to stem from the huge trade gap, supported by the fact that India has a lot of non trade barriers for Bangladeshi exports. Even though exports from Bangladesh are growing at a healthy pace, there is no sign of reducing this trade gap (Datta 2010: 1). Bangladesh has always raised the issue of tariff and non-tariff barriers from the Indian side as a major irritant, allegedly responsible for an unfavourable balance of trade situation vis-à-vis India (*Task Force Reports* 2011: 48). It is the contention of Bangladesh that it has maintained a more liberal trade regime for a longer period than India. As a result, India enjoys a more liberal access to Bangladesh market than Bangladesh has in the Indian market (Islam 2004: 4070). The unfavourable trade deficit for Bangladesh and a number of tariff and non-tariff barriers to trade on the Indian side has caused significant resentment amongst Bangladeshi's who believe that India has devised numerous trade barriers that deny mutually beneficial trade.[7] This has also led to the generation of general perception in Bangladesh that India wants to restrict its market for Bangladeshi products (Rahman 2015: 107).

The non trade barriers, as pointed out by Bangladesh Commerce Ministry, and cited by the *Daily Star* include (Rahman 2010: 1):

- Laboratory tests in Bangladesh, especially for food products, cosmetics, and leather and textiles products.
- Packaging requirements.

- Inadequate infrastructure facilities such as warehousing, transhipment yard, parking yard and
- Connecting roads at land customs stations also hinder exports from Bangladesh; the land border trade is subject to very serious administrative constraints in Bangladesh. The most important of the Customs posts with comprehensive Customs clearance powers is at Benapole, which borders Petrapole on the Indian side and which is on main roads linking Kolkata with Jessore and Dhaka.

As per the report by Bangladesh Commerce Ministry, trade barriers include (Diganta 2010: 1):

- Imposition of state tax.
- Anti-dumping (AD), which is one of the WTO legitimate measures introduced by India during the 1990s, and
- Countervailing duties.

In fact, the issue of non-tariff barriers is a major issue in the whole of South Asia. As per a report on trade facilitation in South Asia have demonstrated that if various non-tariff barriers and other technical barriers are alleviated from India-Bangladesh bilateral trade, both countries together stand to save a minimum of about 24.36 percent of their current aggregate bilateral trade costs, which is about US$1bn as per 2011 trade figures (*CUTS International, Report*, April 2014: ix). An overwhelming majority of the non-tariff barriers faced by SAARC countries is related to sanitary and phytosanitary measures (SPS) and technical barriers to trade (TBT), which according to an Asian Development Bank study (ADB, 2008), accounts for about 86 percent of all such constraints. Bangladesh also faces a number of SPS and TBT related trade barriers in promoting its export to India (Bashar 2013: 17).

When it comes to India-Bangladesh economic relations it is argued that the lack of clarity and transparency about sanitary & phytosanitary standards of India affects Bangladeshi exports to its market. Bangladesh's export to India is dominated by primary and agricultural products. India requires an approved risk analysis of agricultural imports in biosecurity and sanitary & phytosanitary categories in order to protect the human, animal and plant life. Nearly all livestock, agricultural, and food imports require sanitary & phytosanitary (SPS) certificates and import permits from India's Ministry of Agriculture. It is alleged by Bangladesh that the process of getting these certificates and permits lacks transparency, which in turn affects Bangladesh's exports to India. Bangladesh's products are sent to Indian standards testing laboratories (Bureau of Indian Standards) for certificates on quality, adding another layer of bureaucratic hassle and delay (*Ibid.*).

However, Bangladesh's exports to India have not been constrained by tariff protection. India has been giving Bangladesh extensive tariff preferences under SAPTA (South Asian Preferential Tariff Arrangement, which was a precursor of SAFTA) and many of the tariff barriers applicable to other countries are not imposed on Bangladeshi exporters. This shows that India's trade policy has not been discriminatory towards Bangladesh and that the slow growth of the latter's exports to India is due to other factors such as a low degree of complementarily and weak comparative advantage (Kumar 2012: 115). A report by Confederation of Indian Industry (CII) states that:

India has accorded Bangladesh the status of zero-tariff imports as part of its LDC strategy. However, there is a negative list which has been pruned from 763 items in 2006 to 480 in 2008 and further by 47 items during Sheikh Hasina's visit in 2010. PM Dr. Singh cut another 46 textile items of interest to Bangladesh during his visit in 2011, so that duty-free, quota-free access was granted to all but 25 tariff lines. However, the negative list still continues. Tariff and non-tariff barriers as well as harmonization of standards and mutual recognition agreements are being taken up and India is providing assistance to Bangladesh Standards Testing Institute. However, it is unlikely that the trade balance can be redressed rapidly since the value of Bangladesh's total exports is less than $30 billion and mostly composed of garments and textiles (*CII Report*, June 2015: 6).

The recent June, 2015 Modi visit has made more concessions in this regard. Regarding the issue of tariff and non-tariff barriers both countries have agreed to address the issue of the removal of tariff and non-tariff barriers and port restrictions and facilitate movement of containerised cargo by rail and water. In this context, Bangladesh has welcomed India's initiative to provide duty-free access to SAARC LDCs to the Indian market and reducing the number of items on India's negative list. In January 2008, under the SAFTA provisions the government of India had permitted duty-free entry of Bangladeshi products into India. The negative list had also been reduced from over 700 products to about 400. This includes about 50 items from the 101 items suggested for duty-free access by Bangladesh. The tariff free quota system has been applied where duty-free entry was not possible. Bangladesh was given access to 8 million pieces of readymade garments in 2007 which was raised to 10 million pieces in July 2011 (*Task Force Report* 2011: 48). Currently, India has conceded to Bangladesh duty-free and quota-free entry of Bangladeshi goods as part of India's market access policy towards all countries categorized as Least Developed Countries (LDCs), except items on the negative/banned list (Chakravarty 2016: 213).

5.2.a.(iii) Informal trade

India and Bangladesh share a very long and porous border which gives a natural ground for the rise to informal trade between the two countries. Informal trade carried out through porous land border between India and Bangladesh adds to the trade deficit, dating back to the initial years of Bangladesh's birth (Dutta 2010: 2). There are two important aspects of informal trade-its size and nature. The volumes, in terms of the informal trade between India and Bangladesh are however quite significant (Kumar 2012: 116). A large portion of informal exports take place through West Bengal and the north-eastern region (NER) of India; comprising largely of food items, live animals (mainly cattle) and consumer goods. Similarly, unofficial imports from Bangladesh to India are dominated by a few major products, including synthetic yarn, electronic goods and spices (De and Ghosh 2008: 72).

Studies of informal trade between India and Bangladesh have found a pattern to the flow of formal trade – large volumes of goods are smuggled from India to Bangladesh, but much smaller volumes are smuggled in the other direction. Estimates of informal trade between India and Bangladesh vary a lot and it is difficult to assess the exact size. Taneja (2004), estimates that the magnitude of legal and extra-legal trade between Bangladesh and India are roughly the same (Acharya and Marwaha 2012: 27). The annual value of informal exports to Bangladesh from India in the year 2000 was estimated at between $ 1 billion to $ 1.5 billion (Kumar 2012: 118). A World Bank estimate places illegal trade at three-fourths of regular trade, mostly constituted by Indian exports of consumables (*The Hindu*, May 11, 2015).

The unrecorded trade between the two nations adds to the trade deficit, and the potential loss of customs duties is a major problem for Bangladesh due to the volume of illegal goods flowing into the country.[8] Here it is important to point out that the volume of goods transported to Bangladesh from India is higher than those that come into India from Bangladesh (Islam 2004: 4070). The greater part of this trade is characterised as quasi legal in nature, and is often described as 'informal' rather than illegal, since there is wide participation of local people in the border areas who usually bypass the customs posts or who operate in liaison with the anti-smuggling enforcement agencies. Informal trade of this kind often involves large numbers of local people individually transporting small quantities as head loads or through bicycle rickshaws, also known as *'bootleg'* smuggling (Dutta 2010: 2). Another kind of informal trade, termed *'technical'* smuggling, involves explicit illegal practices such as under invoicing, misclassification and bribery of Customs and other officials. The cause of concern for Bangladesh, thus, is more intense than that of India, since, much larger volumes of goods are smuggled from India to Bangladesh escaping customs duties. Trade deficit is intertwined with other issues like trans-shipment, transit and export of natural gas, one of the natural resource possessed by Bangladesh (*Ibid.*).

A pertinent question to be asked is 'why the magnitude of informal trade is so high between India and Bangladesh?' The informal trade between India and Bangladesh as Pohit and Taneja point out is "encouraged because of the difficulties faced by the traders in the transacting environment. The Indo-Bangladesh trade is characterised by a plethora of regulations, absence of information transparency, the bureaucratic approach of public agents, infrastructure bottlenecks in transportation, communication, and above all, the rent seeking activities of public servants. All these factors translate into additional costs for the traders prompting them to go in for informal trade (Ponit and Taneja 2000: 116-117)."

In addition "the problems faced by the Bangladeshi traders are in the area of licensing, refunds and custom dealings whereas the Indian traders face more problems with banks and transportation (Kumar 2012: 117)." In other words, there is a bourgeoning in informal trade owing to the fact that payment is realised quickly and there is no paperwork or procedural delays. Besides, the transportation costs are also lower (Ponit and Taneja 2000: 116-117). The informal traders engage in illegal trade to avoid the problems they face while transacting through legal channels. Thus it is possible that even in a zero duty regime some informal trade would persist (Kumar 2012: 117). Interestingly, trade policy barriers like tariffs and quantitative restrictions are not factors that lead to informal trade (Ponit and Taneja 2000: 117).

Further, criminal activities like the smuggling of narcotics and contraband substances are also persistent along the border. Women and children are also trafficked on the border. However, the trade in cattle is a little different. Cattle trading are illegal on the Indian side of the border but it becomes perfectly legal the moment the cattle enter Bangladesh. This illegal cattle trade has been the cause of several skirmishes on the border.

At present, it is estimated that around 1.5 million cattle are exported informally to Bangladesh. With the removal of restrictions this trade would increase manifold. Cattle from India are a major source of hides and skins needed for manufacturing export quality finished leather in Bangladesh's slaughterhouses and tanneries (Kumar 2012, 117-118). Besides, Bangladesh is highly dependent on the cattle that come from India for its exports of processed meat to Middle Eastern countries (*CUTS International Report*, April 2014: 24).

Annually, cattle trade is approximated to be worth around US $ 500 million. As the cow is considered holy in Hinduism, it is difficult and politically risky for the government to legalise cow trade. Slaughter of the cow is legally allowed only in two states: West Bengal and Kerala. Therefore, legalising cattle trade is very difficult, especially in an era of coalition governments at the Centre. Also, there is a ban on exporting cattle from India to any other country. In this situation, legalising this trade is an acute problem for the policymakers; any step to control cattle smuggling could also be interpreted as going against Bangladesh and might further vitiate the current relations and atmosphere (*Ibid.*). Thus it is obvious that the informal trade is a major hurdle and a serious concern when it comes to India-Bangladesh trade relations. In fact, the cause of concern for Bangladesh is more intense than that of India, since much larger volumes of goods are smuggled from India to Bangladesh escaping customs duties. Trade deficit is intertwined with other issues like trans-shipment, transit and export of natural gas, one of the natural resource possessed by Bangladesh (Acharya and Marwaha 2012: 27).

5.2.a.(iv) Institutional lacunas

Despite the fact that India and Bangladesh are members of multilateral organizations such as South Asian Association for Regional Cooperation (SAARC) and the Bay of Bengal Initiative for Multi Sectoral Technical and Economic Cooperation (BIMSTEC), yet their economic basis of bilateral ties remains weak and lacks any constructive agenda, making it even more difficult for the two states to move forward on other issues. The Indo-Bangladesh Joint Working Group on Trade Issues was established in 2003 and has held regular meetings ever since. Nonetheless, it has failed to reorient economic ties between the two states in a meaningful way (Pant 2007: 245-246). In other words, such institutional arrangements and various trade agreements and cooperation have not been able to lead to a win-win situation for Bangladesh. This can be attributed to various factors coupled with the fact that India's economy is too big for Bangladesh to compete with. Hence, it is always a lose-win situation for Bangladesh when compared with India (Banga 2009: 9).

Attempts have been also been made to facilitate both way trade through the South Asian Free Trade Agreement (SAFTA), an outcome of the SAARC process, but it has not yielded any meaningful results so far. This as Sreeradha Datta contends, is due to the low coverage of items under SAPTA. Further, India has free trade arrangements with Nepal and Bhutan and has enacted one with Sri Lanka but it is yet to conclude a similar agreement with Bangladesh (Bhattacharya 2004: 5153). In fact, India offered Free Trade Agreement (FTA) to Bangladesh hoping that the FTA would address some of the anomalies in the system. However, the successful Indo-Sri Lanka FTA was not sufficient evidence to induce Bangladesh to sign such a trade agreement (Datta 2009: 206). In fact, a World Bank study revealed that an FTA would benefit Bangladesh more than India. Bangladesh, however, insists on a multilateral framework under the SAFTA (Bhardwaj 2008: 11).

However, it is also important that the intraregional trade between South Asian countries also improves. In fact, the intraregional trade only comprises five percent of the total trade in the region. The performance of South Asia is poor in terms of intra-regional trade. Countries within the SAARC do not have significant trade with one another in spite of their geographical proximity and income levels. For instance, intra-regional trade in ASEAN at present is about 20% per annum, which increased from a mere 5% in the beginning of the 1990s, whereas the same in South Asia is only 4%, and that too has been hovering in the same position for the last decade. At present, the official intra-regional trade in South Asia is about $ 6.25 billion where India alone contributes more than 45% of total intra-regional trade. The rest is equally distributed among Bangladesh, Nepal, Pakistan, and Sri Lanka (De and Bhattacharyay 2007: 7). Stagnation of inter-regional trade between these two countries proves the inefficacy of the partial approach to trade rather than full liberalisation or removing all barriers to two-way trade (Bhattacharya 2004: 5152).

5.2.a.(v) Infrastructural Deficits and Procedural Delays

There exist various issues related to regulations, infrastructure and trade services which hamper trade between the two countries. Gross inefficiency in the existing trade systems and infrastructure of India and Bangladesh, has in turn, encouraged and nurtured informal trade. Because per unit trade cost (including transportation, warehousing, testing and documentation) is rather high, traders adopt the informal mode of trading (*CUTS International Report*, April 2014: x). The trade between the two countries also suffers because of poor infrastructural facilities. The reason behind this under development of infrastructure has often been accorded to the reluctance of Bangladesh to provide trans-shipment facilities to India. This has discouraged both sides from constructing proper road and rail links (Trivedi 2008: 102). However, the three most important areas of infrastructure that need immediate actions are power generation, road connectivity, and management of ports (Bashar 2013: 3).

Further, adherence to regulations has been a persistent issue in bilateral trade. Some of the regulatory bottlenecks in the current trade system are lack of pre-shipment inspection, which is required to ensure the compliance of the traded commodity with due regulation and standards; and discrepancy in the parameters required for testing sanitary and phyto-sanitary measures. Both the countries have set different standards for same products and have adopted different methodology of verifying them (*CUTS International Report*, April 2014: x). Complex cross-border trading procedures in cross-border trade increase the possibility of corruption. For example, at the key border-crossing point between India and Bangladesh, as many as 1,500 trucks queue on both sides of the border with waiting times varying between one and five days to complete documentation requirements. Similarly, goods carried by rail are subjected to inland trans-shipment. As far as maritime transport is concerned, there are no direct sailings. The trans-shipments at the land customs stations impose serious impediments. In fact, they determine the level and the efficiency of international trade between the two countries. The position is further compounded by lack of harmonization of technical standards for rolling stock and infrastructure, both road and rail (De and Bhattacharyay 2007: 35-36).

On the Bangladesh side, it is argued that Bangladeshi exporters often face problems as India refuses to accept certification of Bangladesh Standards and Testing Institute (BSTI) as India accepts BSTI certification on some food items only. In addition Bangladeshi exporters wait for 15-30 days to get clearance certificate from Indian testing labs as such labs are located far away from land ports (*FBCCI Business News,* October – December, 2011:10). Further, lack of warehousing facilities, parking, cold storage and prolonged documentation procedures results in time wastage, hence becomes very costly. Along with that trade services are also not up to the mark at the Land Customs Stations (LCSs) of India and Bangladesh, which if adequate may help in reducing the trade cost. Inadequate banking facilities, absence of fuel stations, unavailability of labour due to labour strikes, harassment of truck driver because of language barrier, etc. are the reason which affects the volume of trade between the two countries (*CUTS International Report*, April 2014: xi). This has been compounded by the irregularity in the administration regimes, disparities in service delivery between the LCSs along the border, difference in working hours and days, non-availability of authorised officials, etc. also delays and affect trade related activities (*Ibid.*).

Moreover, as Basher states, there is a Lack of coordination between central and state government's rules and regulations also affect Bangladesh's export to India. The Directorate General of Foreign Trade (DGFT) of India is not the only authority to impose rules and regulations regarding exports from Bangladesh to India. Even, various state agencies impose different barriers on their own. For example, the state customs departments (tariff agencies) sometimes ban different imports from Bangladesh. The customs authority of West Bengal at Kolkata once banned the import of soap from Bangladesh. DGFT claimed complete ignorance of the matter (Bashar 2013: 18).

With an increased emphasis on administrative reform, governance, and security, the need for an efficient and effective customs administration is felt urgently. Customs is an intrinsic element of any cross-border movement of goods and services, and yields significant influence on the national economy. It is the unique point where the supply chain and routine access to trade intelligence and data meet. Beyond facilitating trade, customs performs other important functions such as revenue collection and protection against dangerous goods. The time taken for clearance of goods has an impact on the competitiveness of countries in the global context (De and Bhattacharyay 2007: 35). Therefore, India and Bangladesh need to minimise trade transaction costs by removing visible and invisible barriers to trade. Countries can tackle transaction costs only through improved and integrated trading infrastructure, which is responsible for faster movement of goods and services across the countries (De and Ghosh 2008: 72-73).

The infrastructural bottleneck was also highlighted by the World Bank which contended that an inter-country railway link between India and Bangladesh would accelerate economic growth between the two countries. Similarly, as Veena Sikri suggests Bangladesh should develop its Mangla port and link it with Haldia port in West Bengal to accelerate trade and reduce trade gap between the two countries (Trivedi 2008: 102).

5.2.f The Issue of Transit

Trade between the two countries has also been constrained by the lack of trans-shipment/transit facilities between Bangladesh and India. Although some policy decisions have been taken in this regard, progress on ground is still awaited. Trans-shipment through Bangladesh is expected to benefit India by cutting the distance between India's northeast and the mainland, thus facilitating the transport of goods. These goods can also be exported through Chittagong port. This will also bring in significant amount of revenue to Bangladesh as port fee (Kumar 2012: 115). Although both the governments agree in principle to give transit access to each other through its roadways and railways, arrangements for such have to be agreed between and there is no concrete agreement as of today (Rashid 2010: 195).

Both India and Bangladesh desire transit facilities through each other's territories for trade. India wants transit facilities to reach its eastern and north-eastern states more expeditiously. Bangladesh desires transit facilities to Nepal and Bhutan to augment its exports. Both sides have reservations about granting these facilities not primarily due to economic considerations. The reservations are based on political considerations and security perceptions (Dixit 2001: 207-208). Transit is a greatly undersold idea in Bangladesh. It has been seen as a concession to India and not as an opportunity for building infrastructure within Bangladesh (Anam 2012: 28). The main reason seems to be Bangladesh's apprehension of India moving its troops and military hardware in disguise of passengers and goods. Anti-India elements have spread this scheme to such an extent that even offers of India to assist Bangladesh in developing her communication infrastructure, either bilaterally or through SAARC or Asian Development Bank have not been viewed favourably (Bammi 2010: 151). In this regard J.N. Dixit recounting his personal experience contends:

> Trade and transit facilities interest both India and Bangladesh and are essential for their economic development. Hurdles to the granting of these facilities are political. Bangladesh's official including political figures, frankly told us that suspicions about India in Bangladesh made it impossible for them to allow transit or trade facilities to India through Bangladesh territory or from port of Chittagong towards north-eastern States of India. Our security and political agencies felt that allowing transit facilities to Bangladesh through our territory to Bhutan and Nepal would only increase the problems that India already faced in terms of illegal migration and security threats (Dixit 1999: 253).

A Bangladeshi observer contends the overall feeling about transit negotiations however is that India is making it a one-sided affair and Bangladesh's interests are not being maintained, especially in sharing with the benefits in transportation cost likely to accrue to the Indian side (Anam 2012: 20). However, another school of thought opines that Bangladesh would reap great financial benefits from the transit and thereby reduce the trade gap that exists between the two countries (Karim 2009: 7).

However, India needs to invest nearly $7 billion to build the necessary infrastructure for transit facilities which, experts say, can be recovered in three to four years (*Task Force Report* 2011: 49-50). In fact, India has undertaken several infrastructural projects in Bangladesh with a view to boost India-Bangladesh trade and economic cooperation. Apart from the construction of the Akhaura-Agartala rail link, India is also engaged in the construction of bridges on the river Feni which will connect Ramgarh (Khagrachhari district, Bangladesh) with Sabroom (South Tripura). The final alignment for the 150 metre-long bridge has already been made by a joint team of engineers of Bangladesh and India. India has also agreed to construct the bridge at a cost of about Rs 13 crore (US $ 2.8 million) to connect Sabroom in South Tripura with the Chittagong Port, which is just 75 kms away. This will provide a major boost to the connectivity between the two sides. India has also agreed to help Bangladesh in upgrading its internal waterways by the dredging of the choked river channels. The Bangladesh government has put the dredging of rivers in fast forward mode and intends to cover 300 rivers by 2025 (*Ibid*., p. 50).

Granting transit facilities is beneficial to both India and Bangladesh. It is believed that if such facilities were granted, trade between India and its own North East could become a major source of revenue gain for Bangladesh (Sengupta 2007: 4). For example, tea from Assam travels 1,400 km to the Kolkata port whereas the distance could be curtailed by 60 per cent if access to Chittagong port was available. Secondly, goods from Agartala travel 1,645 Km to Kolkata, while the direct distance would be 350 km if Bangladesh allows movement through it. Opening up access through Chittagong port could provide an incentive to exploit natural resources in North-East India as well as northern Myanmar, for mutual benefit. Bangladesh could pick up containers from Kolkata and deliver to the North-East in India. This would lead to possibilities of increased investment by India. Promoting investment in telecommunications and Internet Communications Technology sector between the two countries would enhance economic relations further (De 2006: 4). This aspect has also been highlighted by the ADB (Asian Development Bank) Country Director Hua Du, who pointed out that, "Bangladesh can benefit tremendously through opening up of transit and great opportunities for crossing from east to west and giving the land-locked neighbours access to the sea (Choudhury 2009: 3)." In fact, it is estimated that if Bangladesh allows the free movement of Indian goods, it would earn more than US$ 1 billion as a transit fee which could help in reduce the trade imbalance between the two countries (*CII Report*, June 2015: 13).

The future of India-Bangladesh ties and the eastern region of the sub-continent lie in creating a web of connectivity that integrate roads, railways, waterways and coastal shipping for a faster and easier transportation of goods. Connectivity remains the bedrock of a more efficient transportation infrastructure for India's 'Act East Policy' and bringing the north-eastern states into mainstream of the Indian economy (Bhakravarty 2016: 212). However, with the visit of Modi to Bangladesh in June 2015, a game-changer in connectivity is on the horizon. The Bangabandhu multipurpose bridge, over the Padma (Ganges) will provide a much needed link between central and north eastern regions of Bangladesh as well as the south-west, cutting distances drastically. India has contributed funds to this project, including a grant element. The 6.4 kilometre long bridge is expected to be completed in 2018. The existing multipurpose bridge over the river Jamuna (Brahmaputra), also called 'Bangabandhu Bridge', already provides a transport corridor between central and northern Bangladesh. The Dhaka-Kolkata Maitri passenger train uses this bridge. The new bridge over the Padma will provide a new transport corridor, making *inter alia*, the Dhaka-Kolkata journey much shorter. Once the Agartala-Akhaura rail link is established, then passenger and goods trains can run from Agartala via Dhaka to Kolkata. Once the railway is extended from Agartala to Sabroom in south Tripura, it would be possible to connect via Ramgarh to the Bangladeshi rail network and the port city of Chittagong. This will connect Chittagong to the Indian rail network which can then be used for importing goods for the north eastern states (Chakravarty 2016: 212).

However, most recently an important development has taken place with regard to transit. A consignment of 1005 tonnes of steel rods arrived on June 19, 2016 in Tripura from West Bengal through Bangladesh as part of revised 'Inland Water Transit and Trade Protocol' between the two countries.[9] The Kolkata-Ashuganj-Tripura transit facility became operational in June 2016. The transit facility was signed during Prime Minister Narendra Modi's visit to Dhaka in June 2015.[10]

Conclusion

As it is evident from the chapter, the India-Bangladesh trade relations have run through various phases. The first phase (1971-75), clearly exemplifies the employability of soft power. As such, India offered various assistance and economic aids to Bangladesh to reconstruct its economy and to meet with its daily economic needs. The Trade Pact 1972, which was signed in consonance with the Indo-Bangladesh Friendship Treaty is clear testimony of the fact that trade was used to build a partnership with Bangladesh. It is also interesting to note that the *border haats* were also initiated, which of course has a soft power connotations. Consequently, progress was also witnessed on the water issue, in the form of Joint River Commission, which was established to address the water issue. India-Bangladesh trade relations received a major set-back with the assassination of Sheikh Mujibur Rahman. Thus, in second phase (1975-2010) little progress was made as the government fell into the military rule. India-Bangladesh relations received a major boost with the coming Advent of Awami League government in Bangladesh.

With the initiation of the third phase (2010) some progress was witnessed in India-Bangladesh trade relations. Among various initiatives, the initiation of the *border haats* between the two countries in 2010 assumes critical importance. The *haats*, as mentioned earlier, are in fact soft power strategy aimed to generate *people-to-people* contact in the borderland areas. Progress was also made with regard to transit. Bangladesh allowed using Bangladeshi sea ports (Chittagong and Mongla) to India. Besides cooperation on waterway and rail communication were also envisaged. Another soft power strategy is evident in India providing a $ 1billion credit line to Bangladesh for a range of projects in 2011. Further, in his September 2011 visit to Dhaka, the then Indian Prime Minister, Manmohan Singh, announced duty-free access to 46 textile items from the country. Singh's 2011 visit was also laid foundations for the LBA though it failed to get ratified in the Indian Parliament.

The fourth phase (2015 onwards) is marked by the ascendancy of Narendra Modi to power in India. It is imperative to mention that India's foreign policy under Modi has strong soft power undercurrents; the June 2015 visit of Modi to Bangladesh just exemplifies it. From granting $ 2billion loan, to various other assistance; there are replete inferences of soft power. Further, India's aids in helping Bangladesh build its infrastructure, India's effort to engage Indian private investors in energy sector in Bangladesh, establishing new bus services and rail routes, signing of the Coastal Shipping

Agreement, various cultural and academic endeavours and so on, all exemplify the ethos of new trend in India's foreign policy with soft power as its base. It also in a way demonstrates the importance that India accords to its neighbours.

Though the 2015 Modi's visit to Bangladesh has improved their overall bilateral relations, there are still few challenges yet to be addressed. The huge trade deficit that Bangladesh faces has been the most vital problem which needs an immediate attention. Also the various institutional arrangements aimed to improve the business atmosphere between the two countries have proved to be inapt in achieving the desired goals. Coupled with it are the problems of various trade barriers, large volume of informal trade, the issue of Infrastructural deficits and procedural delays and the problem of transit.

Connectivity remains another bone of contention between the two countries. As mentioned earlier granting transit facilities will be beneficial for both India and Bangladesh but this has not been possible till date owing to security and political reasons. It is contended that Bangladesh needs $ 7 billion to develop its infrastructure.

India can employ its soft power by granting soft loans in this regard. Further India's unconditional efforts to develop the infrastructure in Bangladesh will not only add to its soft power but will be beneficial for India economically. Transit till now has not been able to generate enough soft power as trade has. This is primarily because transit is an undersold idea, especially in Bangladesh. Granting transit facility to India is seen as something which is against the sovereignty of the country. In fact, both India and Bangladesh refrain from granting transit facility due to political imperatives and security perceptions. Nevertheless, trade and transit when it comes to soft power has twin dimensions. First, economic inducement and other concessions and aids can be used to make progress on trade and transit. Second, trade and transit itself can be a major tool of soft power in India-Bangladesh relations given the problems pertaining to trade and transit are given due importance and are addressed.

Nevertheless, it is obvious that the crux of the problem in India-Bangladesh relations lies in the negative perception towards each other that has hampered a meaningful and lasting progress towards improving their bilateral economic relations. This is precisely the reason as to why India and Bangladesh have been reticent in providing transit facilities through each other's territory. This also brings into question the nature of diplomacy that the two adopted in the past in their foreign policy decision making. Thus a fresh impetus is needed to improve Indo-Bangladesh economic ties which the soft power offers. Though the implications of soft power can be traced to the initial years what is evident is that a concrete soft power policy implementation is lacking. More initiatives like *border haats*, interactions among the business communities, promoting private investments and so on are required.

Lastly, SAARC has to play a proactive role with regard to removing the various trade barriers and creating a congenial environment for intra regional trade. The issue of non trade barriers is critical as it leads to the creation of general perception in Bangladesh that India wants to restrict its market for Bangladeshi products. Indian concessions under SAPTA and other similar institutional arrangement can supplement India's soft power if it helps in reducing the trade deficit the Bangladesh suffers. Yet it is to be remembered that soft power too has its limits. For instance, soft power may be inapt in dealing with the problems of illegal trade, especially when it comes to formalising cattle trading and but if employed, soft power can definitely create a congenial environment wherein India-Bangladesh economic relations can flourish. An improved business environment can definitely deal with other problems like procedural delays, which in turn also gives room for the flourishing of informal trade.

Notes

1. Trade Agreement between India and Bangladesh March 28, 1972
2. The BPTA system was replaced from January 1, 1975 by payment through freely convertible currencies. This agreement was renewed until September, 1980.
3. http://www.ndtv.com/india-news/india-bangladesh-sign-historic-land-boundary-agreement-769351 153
4. http://www.ndtv.com/india-news/india-bangladesh-sign-historic-land-boundary-agreement-769351 154
5. http://www.mea.gov.in/loksabha.htm?dtl/25529/QNO1461+INDIA+ BANGL-ADESH+BUSINESS+RELATIONS
6. Report prepared by CUTS International (April 2014), India-Bangladesh Trade Potentiality: An Assessment of Trade Facilitation Issues, MS Printer, Jaipur: p. ix
7. http://www.anantaaspencentre.in/pdf/India_Bangladesh_Report.pdf
8. http://www.anantaaspencentre.in/pdf/India_Bangladesh_Report.pdf
9. http://www.newsx.com/world/32874-shipment-arrives-in-tripura-under-new-india-bangladesh-transit-protocol
10. http://currentaffairs.gktoday.in/kolkata-ashuganj-tripura-transit-facility-india-bangladesh-operational-06201633675.html

Chapter - VI

Conclusion

India-Bangladesh relations predate the creation of Bangladesh. Even before the creation of Bangladesh, India had relations with East Pakistan (present Bangladesh). In fact, after the West Pakistan crackdown on East Pakistan, the Mujibnagar government, the Bangladeshi government in exile, got a safe haven in India. Needless to say, Bangladesh was liberated with active moral, financial, and military support of India. After the independence of East Pakistan and the creation of Bangladesh it was thought that their friendship would last forever and that their bilateral dispute would be resolved in an amicable manner. The political realities in both the countries, however, proved to be hindrance in forging a long-term bilateral partnership. Numerous issues cropped up which had detrimental effect to their bilateral ties.

The Indo-Bangladesh friendship treaty 1972, which was envisaged to strengthen Indo-Bangladesh ties, ironically began to be criticised. Article 9 of the Indo-Bangladesh Friendship Treaty came into serious criticism on the ground that the said article could be used by India to subside 'anti-India' elements which aimed at capturing power in Bangladesh. Certain section in Bangladesh feared that India could use the Article to embark military intervention in Bangladesh. Thus, within months after the signing of the treaty, India's intention in Bangladesh Liberation Movement began to be questioned and it began to be viewed as India's ploy to assert its dominance in South Asia. By breaking Pakistan, many in Bangladesh assumed that it would be easier for India to deal with Pakistan. In Bangladesh the treaty was alleged as a ploy to make it as a client state. Subsequently, many other issues came to the fore which Dhaka perceived as against the Bangladesh's national interest. The trade pact 1972 along with the other issues such as the question of the 'Prisoners of War'; Bangladesh allegation that India interfered the day to day administration of Bangladesh also hampered Indo-Bangladesh relations in its initial years. Furthermore, the attitude of many of the Indian advisers was perceived to be arrogant and began to be seen in negative light. The print media of both the countries only accentuated the divide.

However, the most pertinent issues that impinged Indo-Bangladesh Relations in its immediate years was the failure to resolve the three key bilateral issues that of sharing of the Ganges waters and the Farakka issue; the delimitation of sea boundary in the Bay of Bengal and the dispute over land boundary demarcation. Further, Mujib after the Independence of Bangladesh realized that Bangladesh needed recognition from the countries like U.S, China, Pakistan and other Muslim countries. This, as Mujib perceived correctly, would not have been possible if Bangladesh did not distance itself from India. Thus, Mujib sought membership of the Organization of Islamic Countries (OIC) and also travelled to Lahore in 1974 to attend the summit (after which Bangladesh was recognized by Pakistan and its allies). This move of Mujib was not digestible to India who deduced it as Bangladesh shifting from its secularist orientation to being a pro-Islamic country. As a result of all these factors the official level discussions between January 1974 and middle of 1975 remained inconclusive and ended in an impasse. In fact, there was no major interaction between India and Bangladesh between April and August of 1975. It is also pertinent to note that both Sheikh Mujibur Rahman and Mrs. Indira Gandhi were embroiled in domestic crisis at this particular time.

As the subsequent happenings in Indo-Bangladesh relations would demonstrate, two factors would determine their bilateral relations in the subsequent years. One is the Islamisation of Bangladesh politics and the second is the bipolar political spectrum in Bangladesh. After the initial capture by the military, the political power in Bangladesh continues to be dominated by the two political parties, the Bangladesh Nationalist Party (BNP) and the Awami League (AL). With regard to the Islamisation trend in Bangladesh, it is observed that the shift in identity formation played a major role in Bangladesh distancing itself from India. Here it must be noted that Pakistan was created on religious lines. Religion as an identity played a decisive role in the partition of the subcontinent. After the creation of Pakistan, disillusionment among the Bengali masses soon started and this in turn led to the rise of Bengali nationalism which ultimately led to the creation of Bangladesh.

The rise of Bengali nationalism and the values of secularism and democracy brought India and Bangladesh in a closer relation. However, with the independence of Bangladesh, especially in the post Mujib era, there was the advent of Islamic undercurrents. The military regime which captured power in Bangladesh after Mujib gave prominence to Bangladeshi nationalism (which gives salience to Islam) which in turn impinged India-Bangladesh relations. Sreeradha Datta explains the Islamisation trend of Bangladesh in following words-"A number of national, regional and global factors such as changing national identity, dependency upon Islamic nations for external assistance and the Islamic revolution in Iran initiated the process of Islamisation in Bangladesh."

Simultaneously, a major trend was witnessed in Bangladesh's foreign policy. The Awami League government with its emphasis on secularism and democracy became closer to India and began to be termed as 'pro-India' while the non-AL government continued Islamisation process and as such began to termed as 'anti-India', the trend is still strong today. Thus, what is important to note is the fact that the question of 'regime compatibility' became and still is an important yardstick in Indo-Bangladesh bilateral ties. As is well known, given the history of the Bangladesh War of Liberation, the Awami League party in Bangladesh and the Congress party in India have always shared close ties, with the bilateral relations always reflecting this in the last four decades. While typically a non-Congress government in Delhi has not substantially affected these bilateral relations, non-Awami League governments in Dhaka have.

The important question to be asked is this: do we find inferences of soft power in India and Bangladesh relations? The simple answer to this is 'yes'. In fact, we find the employability of soft power since the initial years. One needs to simply recount the help India rendered to the Bangladeshi refugees, supplying them the essential needs, in spite of its weak economy defiantly improved India's image to the world. As mentioned earlier, India also gave refuge to the Mujibnagar government, the Bangladeshi government in exile. Further, India trained the 'Mukti Bahini' personnel and equipped them with the essential warfare items. Finally, Bangladesh was liberated by India's active military assistance along with the support of Mukti Bahini. The military assistance itself has a soft power connotation when seen from Mingjiang Li perspective. Li highlighting the need to broaden the concept of soft power and trying to clarify the 'soft power v/s hard power debate' contends that 'A Soft Use of Power Approach' is a better way to understand the concept of soft power. Thus says Li:

If culture, ideology, and values can be used for coercion, and military and economic strength can be used for attraction and appeal, a better approach to soft power is how the resources of power are used rather than associating sources of power as soft or hard. In essence, soft power lies in the soft use of power to increase a state's attraction, persuasiveness, and appeal (Li 2009: 7). In other words, by seeing India's soft power with the lens of how it uses its capability instead of focusing on the resources of power, we can perhaps have a better understanding of how culture, values, and institutions can be used to better its relations with Bangladesh. As such India's hard power capabilities which it used to liberate Bangladesh also qualify as soft power. Moreover, India had intervened in Bangladesh on humanitarian grounds and the fact that Indian military took barely two weeks to secure Bangladesh's independence definitely improved India's image not only in Bangladesh but at global level at large. Even after the independence we find enough references of soft power which India employed in its historical engagements with Bangladesh.

The book has primarily dealt with the three issues, namely, water, border and trade. As it is evident each of the issues has its own history, the negotiations of which has moved into various phases and having its own logic of categorisation. What is obvious is that the cooperation in all the three spheres during the first phase, starting from 1971, began to move faster than before. After the creation of Bangladesh, it needed consumer goods which came from India. Apart from it, India gave commodity assistance and economic aid to Bangladesh to meet its foreign exchange requirements. Moreover, India also repaired bridges and restored railway tracks in Bangladesh. Indian army once again proved to be a soft power when it along with the Indian Railway Board repaired hundreds of bridges and restored over thousands miles of railway tracks. Sappers from the Indian Army and the engineers from the Public Works Department restored river communications and repaired all the major airfields of Bangladesh between 1972 and 1973 (Dixit 1999:181). Further, India, on Mujib's request agreed to deploy Indian personnel in running its administration in its initial years to subside the anti-Mujib forces. It is also well known that not all even in East Pakistan favoured the partition of Pakistan.

The bilateral trade agreement was signed on March 1972, which was signed in consonance with the India-Bangladesh Friendship treaty. The agreement initiated *border haats* and also envisaged a bilateral trade worth Rs. 25 crores ($ 32 million). Also it is interesting to note that the joint communiqué issued in March 1971 had provisions for cultural cooperation between the two countries. The September 1974 protocol which had its validity for two years envisaged for exchange programmes in fields of culture, education, information and sports. Further, various scholarships and exchange visits were offered under the protocol. Consequently, India and Bangladesh were able to propel the negotiations in the water as well as on the border issues. With regard to water, the Joint River Commission (JRC) was set up for the equitable utilisation of water resources. With regard to border, India agreed to lease the Tin Bigha corridor to Bangladesh. However, the political realities in both the countries hampered the progress on the water and boundary issues. The assassination of the Bangladesh Prime Minister, Sheikh Mujib complicated the matter further. Thus, India-Bangladesh relations in the post-Mujib era got entangled into the political knots thus hampering the progress on the contentious issues. As such, the water and the land boundary issues remained inconclusive in the Mujib era. Some progress was made with regard to trade though the issue of transit remained at the backburner. India's also could not sustain its unilateral economic assistance, due to its weak economy and its limited resources which kept India's influence in Bangladesh at bay. In short, India's soft power was short-lived.

In the post-Mujib era, India-Bangladesh relations became embroiled into the domestic politics, especially in Bangladesh, which pitched the bilateral disputes into conflicts. This has been aptly highlighted by Nye who says that soft power is difficult to wield and sustain. As such the negative propaganda began to flow in its full in both the countries. In fact, it was used especially by the politicians in Bangladesh to achieve their political gain. As such the negative propaganda of India began to continually be entangled into the domestic politics of Bangladesh. Understandably, neither India nor Bangladesh made efforts to use soft power as a concrete tool in foreign policy decision making. Such soft elements in foreign policy were unimaginable at that point of time, though agreements signed between the two countries called for cultural cooperation. Moreover, India did little to improve its deteriorating image.

One of the most important soft power aspects which could have been exploited in the initial years of India-Bangladesh relations is the personality and friendship of Indira and Mujib. The Awami League government with its emphasis on secularism and democracy and its pro-India stance had enough soft power attributes. Similarly, Indira Gandhi's pro-Bangladesh attitude and the help and aid that India provided enhanced India's image at global level and especially in Bangladesh. If only India and Bangladesh had used their cultural affinities, had explored the comradeship between Indira and Mujib, and had shown wisdom to deal with their problems in an amicable manner perhaps India-Bangladesh relations would have been in a better plane.

One of the major issues that impinged India-Bangladesh relations over the years, in the post Mujib era is the sharing of the water resources. Among them the Farakka barrage and the Ganges water dispute stands prominent. Thus, during the second phase of the negotiations in the post Mujib era, it is seen, that focus was made to resolve the Farakka issue. Developments were also witnessed in India-Bangladesh trade relations, with the signing of the trade protocol in 1976. Hence, it can be said, in the second phase starting from 1975, the negotiations on water and trade went parallel. The Farakka dispute in fact was problematic since the days when Bangladesh was part of Pakistan. As such one of the questions which the book engages in is whether soft power has been used in the resolution of Ganges Water dispute between India and Bangladesh? A close observation of the negotiations on the Farakka issue, it is obvious that soft power did play a critical role in the signing of the Ganges Water Treaty 1996. Few important aspects need a careful examination in this regard. One of the main reasons behind the conclusion of the treaty is due to Sheikh Hasina's pro-India policy. Immediately after coming to power Awami League started mending fences with India. In other words, the 'regime compatibility' factor becomes an important driver in Indo-Bangladesh bilateral relations and this again has soft power connotations to it. Bangladesh's pro-India stance pleased India and it generated a pull factor. Consequently, the Farakka Dispute was resolved in the form of Ganges Water Treaty 1996.

Moreover, the AL Government had come to power after a long gap of twenty years and obviously India didn't want to lose an opportunity to improve its relations with Bangladesh (which becomes easier when AL comes to power). Also it is in the Indian interest that AL retains power in Bangladesh. Obviously the solution to the Farakka issue would give AL a better cushion for the next term and also for the LBA issue. What can be deduced from the above inferences is that the issue of 'regime compatibility' holds utmost importance in the bilateral relations between India and Bangladesh. As the negotiations on Farakka have shown, India and Bangladesh tend to reach to negotiations when Awami League is in power in Bangladesh.

The role of soft power becomes all the more evident if we critically analyse the role of West Bengal. West Bengal which is culturally close to

Bangladesh, played a pivotal role in the conclusion of the Agreement. In other words, Bangladesh and India were actually using their cultural affinity or soft power to resolve the major irritant in their bilateral relationship. It is to be remembered that it was on the suggestion of the then Indian External Affairs Minister I.K. Gujral that the Bangladesh Foreign Secretary, when he visited India, met the West Bengal Chief Minister to seek his help and support in finding a permanent solution to the problem of sharing of the Ganges waters. This move proved to be very significant as Jyoti Basu helped in significantly narrowing the differences between the two sides. Moreover, Gujral's 'Gujral Doctrine' with its ethos of 'non-reciprocity' can itself be seen from a soft power perspective and which is definitely seen working in the forging of the Ganges Water Treaty 1996.

The inclusion of west Bengal in negotiations helped in narrowing down the differences between Bangladesh and India. In other words, it is evident as to how soft power can play a critical role in creating a congenial atmosphere. As highlighted in the introductory chapter, soft power helps in building a country's image so that negotiations can take place meaningfully. This applies to the Farakka treaty wherein soft power did play a critical role in the negotiations. The important take away from the chapter, which is also substantiated in the succeeding chapters is that, we can use soft power to create favourable conditions for negotiations to take place. Also important it is to note that, trade as a soft power was constantly used even in the initial years of the Farakka issue, especially till the 1977 interim agreement on the Ganges water. Initiatives to improve their bilateral trade relations can be seen in February 1977, 1982, and 1995. Thus, what is observed here is that, cooperation on one issue were leading to cooperation on the other. Eventually, the Ganges Water Treaty was signed, thus resolving the decades old irritant between the two countries. After the successful resolution of the Ganges/Farakka issue, the focus naturally shifted to the Land Boundary Agreement. Thus, with the initiation of the third phase which roughly starts from 2010, it is seen that the trade and the boundary issues run parallel, with cooperation on one leading to the other. In fact, after the conclusion of the Ganges Water Treaty, some progress was made in the land boundary issue too, when in April 1997, the list of enclaves, along with maps, was jointly reconciled, signed and exchanges between India-Bangladesh.

Nevertheless, what the Farakka issue has shown (which is also substantiated by the chapters on land boundary and trade and transit) is that the domestic politics plays an important role in determining the course of

Indo-Bangladesh relations. The 'India factor' plays a very important role in Bangladesh domestic politics, the spectrum of which revolves around the BNP and the AL. Hence, the domestic politics plays a more detrimental role in Bangladesh than in India. In fact, both India and Bangladesh's approach towards their contentious bilateral disputes have less been premised on technical issues. The propensity of reaching an agreement on their bilateral issues, as the history demonstrates is linked with two critical factors: regime compatibility and the domestic factors. In Bangladesh more often than not, the contentious issues between India and Bangladesh has been politicised for their domestic political ends.

The third phase (roughly starting from 2010) also demonstrates two critical aspects; first, relates to the continuous use of soft power in India-Bangladesh bilateral relations; and secondly, how the issues of land boundary and trade run simultaneously, with developments in one leading to the developments on the other. It was following the visit of Sheikh Hasina to India in January 2010 that Congress-led UPA made efforts to resolve the land boundary issue. In the joint communiqué of January 2010 both the countries agreed to take necessary steps to resolve the Land boundary problems. The communiqué also laid down provision for the extension of bilateral trade, investments and aids. In this regard, it is important to mention that the *border haats* were initiated which definitely has soft power connotations. The 2011 agreement on Bilateral Investment Promotion and Protection Agreement (BIPPA) also symbolised the growing bilateral partnership. Apart from it, India's grant of $ 1 billion credit line to Bangladesh, its offer to of a tariff-free quota of 10 million pieces of apparel from Bangladesh, and so on definitely can be seen from the soft power prism. Such developments also demonstrate how the cooperation on one issue such as Land boundary was leading to various other soft power initiatives in trade.

In the last phase, starting from 2015, the use of soft power as a foreign policy tool becomes all the more evident and prominent. It is interesting to note that there are replete inferences of soft power in the whole process of the conclusion of the LBA. Responding to the question whether soft power was employed on the negotiations on the border and the Land Boundary issue, it is observed that, in the case of LBA, like in the case of Ganges water dispute, West Bengal as a form of soft power played a critical role. The strategic move to include the West Bengal Chief Minister Mamata Banerjee can be seen from the perspective that India wants to use the Bengali cultural affinity with Bangladesh in its bilateral negotiations.

Moreover, the inauguration of the Kolkata-Dhaka-Agartala bus and Dhaka-Shillong-Guwahati along with new train routes, the agreement between Doordarshan (India) and Bangladesh Television (BTV) and the initiation of border *haats* are a significant move to connect people. Further, India's decision to help Bangladesh to improve its infrastructure, its investments in energy, and its soft loans of $ 2 billion (thereby doubling the previous $ 1 billion credit line, offered in 2010, which till now is the largest line of credit India has offered) all exhibit the ethos of 'Gujaral Doctrine', thereby exemplifying the fact that India is using its soft power to improve its relations with Bangladesh. In fact, it would not be wrong to state that if Gujaral Doctrine played an important part in the conclusion of the 1996 Ganges water Treaty, the 'Modi Doctrine' played a pivotal role in the conclusion of the 2015 LBA. It is to be noted that India's current public diplomacy under the Modi Doctrine, exemplifies the ethos of soft power. This, realisation is slowly gaining prominence at the academic circles too.

An important aspect of the LBA 2015, which needs attention, is the domestic politics scenario in both the countries. With regard to the LBA 2015, we witness a dramatic shift wherein in India the BJP was able to build domestic consensus by including the opposition and also overcoming the past reservations of the BJP. Also, a favourable augury is the unanimity among the political parties in India for strengthening bilateral ties with Bangladesh. It is significant that, for the first time, the main opposition party in Bangladesh, the BNP, has welcomed the Land Boundary Agreement, and expressed its appreciation to the Indian Parliament. Nor have there been any serious objection to the slew of agreements signed during Prime Minister Modi's visit. The media in both the countries has also been supportive of the emerging ties between the two countries (Mukharji 2016: 205). Media as such has till date played a negative role. Media can help acquire soft power if it plays a constructive role. Exemplifying Nye's contention it obvious that media has a critical role to play in the information age.

The conclusion of LBA is definitely also an indication of the new trend in India's foreign policy towards its neighbours. It in a way exemplifies India's 'neighbourhood-first' policy. In this regard Smruti Pattanaik contends –"Prime Minister Modi himself has taken keen interest to see that top priority is accorded to India's immediate neighbours to reinvigorate India's historical and socio-cultural ties and to restore the economic and trade linkages that existed before the partition. The invitation to the heads of the governments of the SAARC countries for the swearing-in ceremony in May 2014 provided a glimpse into NDA government's vision for the neighbourhood. In this context, the India-Bangladesh relations hold the promise of a new future (Pattanaik 2016: 219)."

The LBA has put the Bangladesh-India relations on a higher trajectory. The signing of the boundary agreement has no doubt resolved the age old problems pertaining to the border, yet there are other border problems that need to be addressed. As the conclusion of the LBA has shown, long standing disputes can be resolved with prudence and vision. Also important development of Modi's 2015 visit to Bangladesh is India's decision to opt for international arbitration to settle her maritime boundary with Bangladesh; it was a similar gesture of goodwill. It signified a deliberate, a priori relinquishment of its claims on the disputed waters, nearly 80 per cent of which have gone to Bangladesh. India's land and maritime boundary agreements with Bangladesh also show that contentious issues between neighbours can be wrapped up within an overall relationship of growing trust and friendship.

With the conclusion of the LBA, border management appears to be on a scale of improvement, with better coordination between the respective border forces. The LBA has addressed the three major issues pertaining to the border, but a tranquil border will not be achieved without eliminating the smuggling mafias that operate on either side. India is unable to permit export of cattle, for which there is a huge demand in Bangladesh. This, altogether with vested interests in India for the 'export' of cattle, will continue to encourage smugglers. No clear resolution can be foreseen. Related to border management, the question of illegal migration from Bangladesh is a perennial issue, which again has neither clear approach nor resolution (Mukharji 2016: 209).

Another major enquiry of the book is whether trade and transit can be an effective soft power tool when it comes to India and Bangladesh relations? As chapters three and four demonstrates, trade and economic inducements have often been used by India whenever the relationship needs a push. As such it has been observed that improvement in one aspect say trade also leads to some improvement when it comes to issues such as the cooperation on water and/or the land boundary. As far as cooperation on Ganges water is concerned, trade and economic inducement to Bangladesh has often been led to the cooperation on the water issue. This phenomenon is recurring especially till the conclusion of the 1977 treaty on the Ganges. However, after the eventual conclusion of the 1996 Ganges Water Treaty, trade and economic aids has also been used to enhance cooperation on the land boundary issue. This is evident especially since 2010 with the advent of AL to power in Bangladesh. Thus, the 2010 communiqué lays foundations for the enhancement of their bilateral trade relations. This becomes more evident in 2011 and more so during the 2015 visit of Indian Prime Minister Modi to Bangladesh.

As mentioned earlier, India can garner enough soft power leverages by economic inducements and investments. Further, any effort by India to help Bangladesh in boosting its energy sector will earn India soft power. As such during Modi's visit, steps were taken to engage Indian private sectors in generating power in Bangladesh. Consequently Adani Power Limited of India and Reliance Power Limited of India signed deals worth over $ 4.5 billion with state-run Bangladesh Power Development Board (BPDB) to develop six units of power plants to produce 4,600 MW of electricity. However, transit has not been able to generate enough soft power as trade has. This is primarily because transit is an undersold idea, especially in Bangladesh. India and Bangladesh both want transit facilities through each other's territory and more importantly both benefit if they do so. But meaningful progress has not been achieved till now due to political imperatives and security perceptions.

It is to be remembered that trade with Bangladesh is important for India as it is essential for the socio-economic development of the North Eastern Region of India. A better economic environment with Bangladesh will give more impetus to its 'look East/Act East Policy'. On the other hand Bangladesh too cannot develop to its potential if it does not establish friendly relations with India. However, the trajectories of their bilateral relations have not been satisfactory. India and Bangladesh though being neighbouring countries have not been able to come to trading terms as per the potential. Though there has been a constant rise in their bilateral trade, the trade is heavily tilted in favour of India. Several reasons for such an imbalance and policy suggestions have been put forward by various scholars and agencies with minimal impact. Also it is important to note that Bangladesh has trade deficit with China (currently the largest trade partner of Bangladesh) but trade deficit with China does not get politicised or has had a negative impact in their bilateral relations. The trade deficit with India, however, has had a negative impact in their economic relations. This can been further compounded by the fact that Indo-Bangladesh political relations too, which in the past, has been wrought with problems which in turn affects their economic relations. Hence the perceptions remain critical driver in their bilateral relations.

The huge trade deficit that Bangladesh faces has been the most vital problem which needs an immediate attention. Coupled with it are the problems of various trade barriers, large volume of informal trade, the issue of Infrastructural deficits and procedural delays. Also the various institutional arrangements aimed to improve the business atmosphere between the two countries have proved to be inapt in achieving the desired goals. Hence, SAARC has to play a proactive role with regard to removing the various trade barriers and creating a congenial environment for intra regional trade. Connectivity remains another bone of contention between the two countries. It is contended that Bangladesh needs $ 7 billion to build the necessary infrastructure for transit facilities. India can thus, grant soft loans in this regard. India's unconditional efforts to develop the infrastructure in Bangladesh will not only add to its soft power but will be beneficial to India economically too and so for India's northeast region. However, during Modi's 2015 visit to Bangladesh some positive developments were also achieved with regard to transit. Bangladesh's decision to provide access to Chittagong and Mongla port and the recent operation of the Kolkata-Ashuganj-Tripura transit facility in June 2016 show some positive signs for future.

The historiography of India-Bangladesh relations suggests that their bilateral relations have been plagued by neglect, mistrust and suspicion. What is evident is the fact that their bilateral relationship suffers from the negative perceptions that they have for each other. This has more often than not been used by the political gains at the domestic level. As such India-Bangladesh relations get tied in political knots. Viewed in this light, the problem with India and Bangladesh is more psychological rather than physical. A better political environment needs to be generated which in turn is possible if their overall image towards each other improves. Further, traditional diplomacy has been of little help in improving their ties. Hence it becomes imperative to embark strategies to improve counter this neglect, mistrust and suspicion. In other words, a fresh impetus is needed to improve Indo-Bangladesh ties and the 'soft power approach' is a viable option. Though the implications of soft power can be traced to the initial years what is evident is that a concrete soft power policy implementation is lacking.

Soft power approach holds importance with regard to India-Bangladesh relations as India's links with Bangladesh are also cultural and civilizational. With Bangladesh, India shares not only a common history of struggle for freedom and liberation but also enduring feelings of both fraternal as well as familial ties.[1] As such West Bengal will always play a pivotal role when it comes to India-Bangladesh relations. Yet the most important aspect lie in certain policies being made West Bengal centric as it is through West Bengal that India can use the aspects of Bengali nationalism to the utmost. However, as it has been observed, culture though has soft power potentials, India and Bangladesh have not been able to use it to the potential. This is evident from the fact that till date only three agreements on cultural cooperation has been reached coupled with few other academic, scientific and technological engagements. In addition, MOU on Cooperation between Doordarshan and Bangladesh Television was also signed in 2011and 2015 respectively. Such initiatives should be given priority and should be used as a concrete tool of diplomacy. There is also a need for vastly expanded public diplomacy and cultural exchange programmes on both sides. An effective communication strategy is called for.

When it comes to Bangladesh, Bengali culture, literature, movies and music needs to be exploited and we need to find ways and means to make these soft power aspects a concrete foreign policy tool. In this regard Rabindra sangeet can be another source of India's soft power. Academic and literary exchanges need to be more frequent. If these can be put into policy outcomes than probably we can improve the psyche among the people of two countries. For instance, the Indo-Bangladesh food festival, Hilsa festival etc. which is held in Siliguri and Kolkata should be operated at a bigger level involving greater participation from the two countries. In other words, efforts should be made to enhance more people to people contact. For countries that share so much in common, more people-to-people initiatives are needed to counter the negative perceptions that people of either countries have for each other. Apart from the inauguration of bus and train routes and the initiation of border *haats*, interactions among the business communities, artists, academicians and students can be important in creating a friendly atmosphere for improving their bilateral economic relations. India can get soft power leverage by encouraging such initiatives.

In consonance with the 'Gujaral Doctrine', India's public diplomacy under Prime Minister Narendra Modi also termed as 'Modi Doctrine' also qualifies as soft power. India's foreign policy towards its neighbourhood including Bangladesh has changed considerably changed with South Asia now gaining its prominence in the Indian Foreign policy thought. This in turn exemplifies the ethos of both Gujral Doctrine and the Modi Doctrine. In fact, the persona and charisma of Modi for India and Sheikh Hasina for Bangladesh can also be viewed as soft power. The dramatic rise of Narendra Modi as a global leader, his ever growing popularity at the global stage and his charisma defiantly has earned India enough soft power or has raised India's image at the global level. This is evident in India's recent rise at the global stage and India's ability to achieve its national interest. Similarly Sheikh Hasina constant rise at the global level is well known. The Business magazine Fortune named Prime Minister Sheikh Hasina as one of the greatest leaders of the world in March 2016. Hasina has ranked 10th among 50 leaders who "are transforming the world and inspiring others to do the same," the internationally acclaimed magazine said (*The Daily Star*, March 25, 2016). Earlier in 2015 she had been announced as one of the winners of the United Nations' highest environmental accolade, in recognition of Bangladesh's far-reaching initiatives to address climate change.[2] More so, Hasina generates a pull factor for Bangladesh in its bilateral relations with India, especially on the ground being the daughter of Sheikh Mujib. India and Bangladesh need to exploit these soft power assets and should try and address the other impending bilateral issues.

Cricket is another area which has soft power potential. However, cricket as soft power needs another detailed study which the current book has not focused upon. This limitation is basically due to the fact cricket is just a recent phenomenon in Bangladesh. As such cricket and cricket diplomacy have no role to play as far as the current study is concerned. Nevertheless, it is beyond doubt that cricket as soft power, in coming years, will play a critical role in India-Bangladesh relations; for a simple reason that the craze for the game is high in both the countries. Cricket has proved to be a strong soft power resource for India. Thus, Thobbi states— "Call it soft diplomacy or cricket diplomacy, many politicians, national or otherwise; have used Indian cricketers' popularity to weave meaningful relations with the cricket-mad country."[3] On another level, the creation in 2008 of the rich and internationally-popular Indian Premier League (IPL) has reinforced the narrative of India's rise (Blarel 2012: 29-30). In fact, the conclusion of the LBA parallels with the Indian cricket team going to Bangladesh for 'Test' and 'One-Day' series in Bangladesh. On this an observer observes - Both sides will now hope for a successful cricket series featuring one Test and three one-day internationals. For South Asian solidarity, cricket, too, has a big role to play besides politics.[4]

What is evident however, is the fact that India has a plenitude of soft power resources when it comes to bettering its relations with Bangladesh. Perhaps India needs to learn from the Chinese experience in using soft power as a critical tool of regional strategy. While it does possess an edge in the cultural and educational dimensions, it is almost impossible for India to match China in economic assistance at this stage of economic development. It, therefore, has to follow a carefully thought out strategy for optimizing its soft power leverage in the region. Financial limitations must be offset by cultural and educational advantages, with country-specific variations wherever required (Palit & Palit 2011: 25). Equally important it is as Wagner says for India to find ways to transform its soft power capacities into capabilities. Yet the most important aspect lie in certain policies being made West Bengal centric as it is through West Bengal that India can use the aspects of Bengali nationalism to the utmost. Moreover, the most important challenge lies in using the available soft power potentials into policy outcomes. This however will depend on the government recognition and assessment of the role of soft power in Indian diplomacy.

However, it is important to note that, as in the case of other forms of power, even soft power has its limitations. For instance, all forms of soft power may not be deemed fit an all cases and that soft power depends on the country to which it is being applied. In the case of Bangladesh, though Bollywood is India's soft power, it cannot be applicable in India's relation with Bangladesh. At another level, soft power may be inapt in dealing with the problems of illegal migration, terrorism and informal trade. Nevertheless it is beyond doubt that soft power helps in creating a congenial political atmosphere wherein negotiations between countries can foster. The utility of soft power as is the case with 'cultural diplomacy' is that it keeps open negotiating channels with countries where political connections are in jeopardy, and helps to recalibrate relationships.

As India-Bangladesh relations has demonstrated, the conclusion of the 1996 Ganges Water Treaty and the passing of the LBA offer a very good examples. Thus, it is advisable that India continues to employ soft power in its relations with Bangladesh. As mentioned earlier, India's foreign policy under the NDA government exemplifies the ethos of soft power, the conclusion of LBA 2015 and various other agreements are an apt testimony of the fact that India now recognises the utility of soft power and regards it as a concrete tool of diplomacy. Yet two things assume critical importance: first, India should find ways and means to transform its soft power 'capacities' into 'capabilities' and secondly, India's soft power should develop in consonance with its hard power.

Notes

1. Shahnawaz A. Mantoo (2015), "India-Bangladesh Relationship (1975-1990)", *Journal of South Asian Studies*, Vol. 3, No. 3, p. 331

2. http://www.unep.org/newscentre/Default.aspx?Document ID=26844&ArticleID=35426&l=en
3. https://cricket.yahoo.com/news/how-cricket-diplomacy-and-politics-marry-in-india-115315188.html
4. http://www.oneindia.com/sports/cricket/india-bangladesh-cricket-series-must-add-to-pm-modi-s-success-story-1772129.html

Annexure

Annexure - I
List of Agreements/Treaties/Protocols/MOUs between Bangladesh and India (up to 27 July 2015)

1.	Treaty of Friendship, Cooperation and Peace between the People's Republic of Bangladesh and the Republic of India	19 March 1972
2.	Bilateral Trade Agreement	28 March 1972
3.	Agreement between the Government of India and the Government of the People's Republic of Bangladesh for the supply of Crude Oil.	16 May 1972
4.	Protocol on Inland Water Transit and Trade (PIWTT)	11 November 1972
5.	Agreement on Cultural Cooperation	30 December 1972
6.	Agreement between the Republic of India and the People's Republic of Bangladesh on Cooperation in the fields of Peaceful uses of Atomic Energy	27 August 1973
7.	Agreement between the Government of the People's Republic of Bangladesh and the Government of the Republic of India concerning the demarcation of the land boundary between Bangladesh and India and related matters	16 May 1974
8.	Protocol to the agreement between Bangladesh and India concerning the demarcation of the land boundary between Bangladesh and India and related matters	6 September 2011
9.	Exchange of Instruments of Ratification of 1974 Land Boundary Agreement and its 2011 Protocol	6 June 2015
10.	Exchange of letters on Modalities for implementation of 1974 Land Boundary Agreement and its 2011 Protocol	6 June 2015
11.	Protocol between the Government of India and the Government of Bangladesh for a credit of Rs. Sixty million.	16 May 1974
12.	Agreement between the Government of the Republic of India and the Government of the People's Republic of Bangladesh relating to Exchange of Insured Letters and Boxes	27 November 1974
13.	Agreement between the Government of the Republic of India and the Government of the People's Republic of Bangladesh relating to Letter Post	27 November 1974
14.	Agreement between the Government of the Republic of India and the Government of the People's Republic of Bangladesh relating to the Registered Letter Post	25 January 1975
15.	Agreement between the Government of the Republic of India and the Government of the People's Republic of Bangladesh relating to the Exchange of Postal Parcels	23 July 1976

(*Contd...*)

16.	Agreement between the Government of the Republic of India and Government of the People's Republic of Bangladesh on sharing of Ganga Waters at Farakka and on Augmenting its Flows	5 November 1977
17.	Air Services Agreement	5 May 1978
18.	Agreement between the Government of the Republic of India and the Government of the People's Republic of Bangladesh on telecommunication Services	19 May1981
19.	Agreement on Establishment of a Joint Economic Commission (JEC) 1982	7 October
20.	Indo-Bangladesh Memorandum of Understanding on the sharing of Ganga waters at Farakka.	7 October 1982
21.	Agreement between the Government of India and the Government of the People's Republic of Bangladesh on technical and scientific research	17 November 1982
22.	Agreement between the Indian Council of Agricultural Research and Bangladesh Agricultural Research Council on sharing of scientific information and exchange of scientists	15 June 1983
23.	Memorandum of Understanding between India and Bangladesh on the sharingof the waters of common rivers	22 November 1985
24.	Indo-Bangladesh Agreement on the sharing of exceptionally low flows at Farakka for the period 1986-88	22 November 1985
25.	Protocol between the Department of Scientific and Industrial Research of India and the Science and Technology Division of Bangladesh on Scientific and Technical Cooperation	31 July 1991
26.	Convention on Avoidance of Double Taxation and Prevention of Fiscal Evasion	27 August 1991
27.	Agreement between the People's Republic of Bangladesh and the Republic of India on Cultural and Academic Exchange Programme for the years 1993, 1994 and 1995	27 May 1992
28.	Memorandum of Understanding between the State Trading Corporation India Ltd. (STC) and Trading Corporation of Bangladesh (TCB) for expansion of two-way trade between the two countries	12 June 1993
29.	Agreement on Sharing of the Ganges Water at Farakka 1996	12 December
30.	Protocol of Cooperation in Science and Technology between the Government of the People's Republic of Bangladesh and the Government of Republic of India for 1999-2000	10 March 1999
31.	Agreement for the regulation of Motor Vehicle Passenger traffic (Dhaka-Kolkata bus service) and its Protocol	17 June 1999
32.	Credit Agreement between the Government of India and the Government of the People's Republic of Bangladesh for and Indian credit of Rs. 200 Crores.	20 June 1999
33.	MoU between the Government of India and the Government of thePeople Republic of Bangladesh on cooperation in the field of Agriculture	22 January 2000
34.	Agreement for Restoration of rail Traffic between Benapole- Petrapole	4 July 2000
35.	Revised Travel Arrangements 28 January 2013	23 May 2001,
36.	Agreement for the Operation of Passenger Train Service	12 July 2001, 10 December 2008
37.	Agreement for the regulation of Motor Vehicle Passenger traffic (Dhaka-Agartala bus service) and its Protocol	10 July 2001
38.	Agreement on Prevention of trafficking Illegal Drugs and Narcotics	21 October 2006
39.	MoU between Bangladesh Standards and Testing Institute (BSTI) and Bureau of Indian Standards	6 June 2007

(*Contd...*)

40.	MoU on Civilian Air Transport	13 March 2008
41.	Agreement on Reciprocal Promotion and Protection of Investments	9 March 2009
42.	Agreement on Mutual Legal Assistance on Criminal Matters	11 January 2010
43.	Agreement on Transfer of Sentenced Persons	11 January 2010
44.	Agreement on Combating International Terrorism, Organized Crime and Illicit Drug Trafficking	11 January 2010
45.	MOU on Cooperation in Power Sector	11 January 2010
46.	Agreement on 1 billion dollar credit line	07 August 2010
47.	MoU on Border Haat	23 October 2010
48.	Mode of operations of Border Haat	23 October 2010
49.	Standard Operating Procedure (SOP) for movement of cargo vehicles across the Bangladesh-India border	23 October 2010
50.	Standard Operating Procedure (SOP)for movement of Nepalese cargo vehicles across the Bangladesh-India border	23 October 2010
51.	Standard Operating Procedure (SOP) for movement of Bhutanese cargo vehicles across the Bangladesh-India border	07 July 2011
52.	Framework Agreement on Cooperation for Development	06 September 2011
53.	MOU on cooperation in the field on Renewable Energy	06 September 2011
54.	Addendum to the MOU between Bangladesh and India to facilitate Overland Transit Traffic between Bangladesh and Nepal	06 September 2011
55.	MOU on Cooperation in the Field of Fisheries	06 September 2011
56.	MOU on Conservation of the Sundarbans	06 September 2011
57.	Protocol on Conservation of Royal Bengal Tiger of the Sundarbans	06 September 2011
58.	MOU on Cooperation between Doordarshan and Bangladesh Television	06 September 2011
59.	MOU on Cooperation between Dhaka University and Jawharlal Nehru University	06 September 2011
60.	MOU between National Institute of Fashion Technology New Delhi IFTand BGMEA Institute of Fashion Technology Bangladesh	06 September 2011
61.	Extradition Treaty	28 January 2013
62.	MoU between Bangladesh Foreign Service Academy and Foreign Service Institute of India	10 February 2013
63.	MoU on Cooperation in Health and Medical Science	12 February 2013
64.	MoU for the Establishment of the Bangladesh-India Foundation	16 February 2013
65.	MoU to establish rail link between Akhaura (Bangladesh) and Agartala (India)	16 February 2013
66.	Protocol amending the convention for the avoidance of double taxation and the prevention of fiscal evasion with respect to taxes on income	16 February 2013
67.	MoU between the Ministry of Textiles and Jute of Bangladesh and the Ministry of Textiles of India	19 August 2013
68.	MoU for Co-operation in the field of Traditional Systems of Medicine and Homeopathy	9 September 2014
69.	MoU on the Establishment of Nalanda University	20 September 2014
70.	Land Boundary Agreement	6 June 2015
71.	Agreement on Coastal Shipping between Bangladesh and India	6 June 2015
72	Bilateral Trade Agreement (Renewal)	6 June 2015
73.	Bilateral Cooperation Agreement between Bangladesh Standards & Testing Institution (BSTI) and Bureau of Indian Standards (BIS) on Cooperation in the field of Standardization.	6 June 2015
74.	Agreement on Dhaka-Shillong-Guwahati Bus Service and its Protocol	6 June 2015
75.	Agreement on Kolkata-Dhaka-Agartala Bus Service and its Protocol	6 June 2015
	Protocol on Inland Waterways Transit and Trade (PIWTT) [renewal]	6 June 2015

(Contd...)

76.	Memorandum of Understanding between Coast Guards	6 June 2015
77.	Memorandum of Understanding on Prevention of Human Trafficking	6 June 2015
78.	Memorandum of Understanding on Prevention of Smuggling and Circulation of Fake urrency Notes	6 June 2015
79.	Memorandum of Understanding between Bangladesh and India and for Extending a New Line of Credit (LoC) of US$ 2 billion by Government of India to Government of Bangladesh	6 June 2015
80.	Memorandum of Understanding on Blue Economy and Maritime Cooperati on in the Bay of Bengal and the Indian Ocean	6 June 2015
81.	Memorandum of Understanding on Use of Chittagong and Mongla Ports	6 June 2015
82.	Memorandum of Understanding for a Project under IECC (India Endowment for Climate Change) of SAARC	6 June 2015
83.	Memorandum of Understanding on Indian Special Economic Zone in Bangladesh	6 June 2015
84.	Cultural Exchange Programme for the years 2015-17	6 June 2015
85.	Statement of Intent on Bangladesh-India Education Cooperation (adoption)	6 June 2015
86.	Agreement between Bangladesh Submarine Cable Company Limited (BSCCL) and Bharat Sanchar Nigam Limited (BSNL) for leasing of international band -width for internet at Akhaura	6 June 2015
87.	Memorandum of Understanding between University of Dhaka, Bangladesh and Council of Scientific and Industrial Research, India for Joint Research on Oceanography of the Bay of Bengal	6 June 2015
88.	Memorandum of Understanding between University of Rajshahi, Bangladesh and University of Jamia Milia Islamia, India	6 June 2015
89.	Handing over of Consent Letter by Insurance Development and Regulatory Authority (IDRA), Bangladesh to Life Insurance Corporation (LIC), India to start operations in Bangladesh	6 June 2015

Annexure - II

Treaty of Peace and Friendship March 19, 1972

Treaty Of Peace And Friendship Between The Government Of India And The Government Of The People's Republic Of Bangladesh

Dacca

Inspired by common ideals of peace, secularism, democracy, socialism and nationalism,

Having struggled together for the realisation of these ideals and cemented ties of friendship through blood and sacrifices which led to the triumphant emergence of a free, sovereign and independent Bangladesh,

Determined to maintain fraternal and good-neighbourly relations and transform their border into a border of eternal peace and friendship,

Adhering firmly to the basic tenets of non-alignment, peaceful co-existence, mutual cooperation, non-interference in internal affairs and respect for territorial integrity and sovereignty,

Determined to safeguard peace, stability and security and to promote progress of their respective countries through all possible avenues of mutual cooperation,

Determined further to expand and strengthen the existing relations of friendship between them, convinced that the further development of friendship and cooperation meets the national interests of both States as well as the interests of lasting peace in Asia and the world,

Resolved to contribute to strengthening world peace and security and to make efforts to bring about a relaxation of international tension and the final elimination of vestiges of colonialism, racialism and imperialism,

Convinced that in the present-day world international problems can be solved only through cooperation and not through conflict or confrontation,

Reaffirming their determination to follow the aims and principles of the United Nations Charter, the Republic of India, on the one hand, and the People's Republic of Bangladesh, on the other,

Have decided to conclude the present Treaty.

Article 1

The high Contracting Parties, inspired by the ideals for which their respective peoples struggled and made sacrifices together, solemnly declare that there shall be lasting peace and friendship between their two countries and their peoples, each side shall respect the independence, sovereignty and territorial integrity of the other and refrain from interfering in the internal affairs of the other side.

The high Contracting Parties shall further develop and strengthen the relations of friendship, good-neighbourliness and all-round cooperation existing between them, on the basis of the above-mentioned principles as well as the principles of equality and mutual benefit.

Article 2

Being guided by their devotion to the principles of equality of all peoples and states, irrespective of race or creed, the high Contracting Parties condemn colonalism and racialism in all forms and manifestations and are determined to strive for their final and complete elimination.

The high Contracting Parties shall cooperate with other states in achieving these aims and support the just aspirations of people in their struggle against colonialism and racial discrimination and for their national liberation.

Article 3

The high Contracting Parties reaffirm their faith in the policy of non-alignment and peaceful co-existance as important factors for easing tension in the world, maintaining international peace and security, and strengthening national sovereignty and independence.

Article 4

The high Contracting Parties shall maintain regular contacts with each other on major international problems affecting the interests of both States, through meetings and exchanges of views at all levels.

Article 5

The high Contracting Parties shall continue to strengthen and widen their mutually advantageous and all-round cooperation in the economic, scientific and technical fields. The two countries shall develop mutual cooperation in the fields of trade, transport and communications between them on the basis of the principles of equality, mutual benefit and the most-favoured nation principle.

Article 6

The high Contracting Parties further agree to make joint studies and take point action in the fields of flood control, river basin development and the development of hydro-electric power and irrigation.

Article 7

The high Contracting Parties shall promote relations in the fields of art, literature, education, culture, sports and health.

Article 8

In accordance with the ties of friendship existing between the two countries each of the high Contracting Parties solemnly declares that it shall not enter into or participate in any military alliance directed against the other party.

Each of the high Contracting Parties shall refrain from any aggression against the other party and shall not allow the use of its territory for committing any act that may cause military damage to or constitute a threat to the security of the other high contracting party.

Article 9

Each of the high Contracting Parties shall refrain from giving any assistance to any third party taking part in an armed conflict, against the other party. In case either party is attacked or threatened with attack, the high contracting parties shall immediately enter into mutual consultations in order to take appropriate effective measures to eliminate the threat and thus ensure the peace and security of their counties.

Article 10

Each of the high Contracting Parties solemnly declares that it shall not undertake any commitment secret or open, toward one or more States which may be incompatible with the present Treaty.

Article 11

The present Treaty is signed for a term of twenty five years and shall be subject to renewal by mutual agreement of the high Contracting Parties.

The Treaty shall come into force with immediate effect from the date of its signature.

Article 12

Any differences in interpreting any article or articles of the present Treaty that may arise between the high Contracting Parties shall be settled on a bilateral basis by peaceful means in a spirit of mutual respect and understanding.

DONE in Dacca on the nineteenth day of **Sd/- SHEIKH MUJIBUR RAHMAN**

March nineteen hundred and seventy two. **Prime Minister For the People's Sd/- (Smt) INDIRA GANDHI Prime Republic of Bangladesh Minister For the Republic of India**

Annexure - III

Agreement1 Between The Government Of The People's Republic Of Bangladesh And The Government Of The Republic Of India On Sharing Of The Ganges Waters At Farakka And On Augmenting Its Flows

The Government of the People's Republic of Bangladesh and the Government of the Republic of India,

Determined to promote and strengthen their relations of friendship and good neighbourliness,

Inspired by the common desire of promoting the well-being of their peoples,

Being desirous of sharing by mutual agreement the waters of the international rivers flowing through the territories of the two countries and of making the optimum utilisation of the water resources of their region by joint efforts,

Recognising that the need of making an interim arrangement for sharing of the Ganges waters at Farakka in a spirit of mutual accommodation and the need for a solution of the long-term problem of augmenting the flows of the Ganges are in the mutual interests of the peoples of the two countries,

Being desirous of finding a fair solution of the question before them, without affecting the rights and entitlements of either country other than those covered by this Agreement, or establishing any general principles of law or precedent, Have agreed as follows:

A. Arrangement For Sharing Of The Waters Of The Ganges At Farakka

Article I.

The quantum of waters agreed to be released by India to Bangladesh will be at Farakka.

Article II.

(i) The sharing between Bangladesh and India of the Ganges waters at Farakka from the 1st January to the 31st May every year will be with reference to the quantum shown in column 2 of the Schedule annexed hereto which is based on 75 percent availability calculated from the recorded flows of the Ganges at Farakka from 1948 to 1973.

(ii) India shall release to Bangladesh waters by 10-day periods in quantum shown in column 4 of the Schedule:

-provided that if the actual availability at Farakka of the Ganges waters during a 10-day period is higher or lower than the quantum shown in column 2 of the Schedule it shall be shared in the proportion applicable to that period;

-provided further that if during a particular 10-day period, the Ganges flows at Farakka come down to such a level that the share of Bangladesh is lower than 80 percent of the value shown in column 4, the release of waters to Bangladesh during that 10-day period shall not fall below 80 percent of the value shown in column 4.

Article III.

The waters released to Bangladesh at Farakka under article I shall not be reduced below Farakka except for reasonable uses of waters, not exceeding 200 cusecs, by India between Farakka and the point on the Ganges where both its banks are in Bangladesh.

Article IV.

A Committee consisting of the representatives nominated by the two Governments (hereinafter called the Joint Committee) shall be constituted. The Joint Committee shall set up suitable teams at Farakka and Hardinge Bridge to observe and record at Farakka the daily flows below Farakka Barrage and in the Feeder Canal, as well as at Hardinge Bridge.

Article V.

The Joint Committee shall decide its own procedure and method of functioning.

Article VI.

The Joint Committee shall submit to the two Governments all data collected by it and shall also submit a yearly report to both the Governments.

Article VII.

The Joint Committee shall be responsible for implementing the arrangements contained in this part of the Agreement and examining any difficulty arising out of the implementation of the above arrangements and of the operation of Farakka Barrage. Any difference or dispute arising in this regard, if not resolved by the Joint Committee, shall be referred to a panel of an equal number of Bangladeshi and Indian experts nominated by the two Governments. If the difference or dispute still remains unresolved, it shall be referred to the two Governments which shall meet urgently at the appropriate level to resolve it by mutual discussion and failing that by such other arrangements as they may mutually agree upon.

B. Long-term Arrangements

Article VIII.

The two Governments recognise the need to cooperate with each other in finding a solution to the long-term problem of augmenting the flows of the Ganges during the dry season.

Article IX.

The Indo-Bangladesh Joint Rivers Commission established by the two Governments in 1972 shall carry out investigation and study of schemes relating to the augmentation of the dry season flows of the Ganges, proposed or to be proposed by either Government with a view to finding a solution which is economical and feasible. It shall submit its recommendations to the two Governments within a period of three years.

Article X.

The two Governments shall consider and agree upon a scheme or schemes, taking into account the recommendations of the Joint Rivers Commission, and take necessary measures to implement it or them as speedily as possible.

Article XI.

Any difficulty, difference or dispute arising from or with regard to this part of the Agreement, if not resolved by the Joint Rivers Commission, shall be referred to the two Governments which shall meet urgently at the appropriate level to resolve it by mutual discussion.

C. Review And Duration

Article XII.

The provisions of this Agreement will be implemented by both Parties in good faith. During the period for which the Agreement continues to be in force in accordance with article XV of the Agreement, the quantum of waters agreed to be released to Bangladesh at Farakka in accordance with this Agreement shall not be reduced.

Article XIII.

The Agreement will be reviewed by the two Governments at the expiry of three years from the date of coming into force of this Agreement. Further reviews shall take place six months before the expiry of this Agreement or as may be agreed upon between the two Governments.

Article XIV.

The review or reviews referred to in article XIII shall entail consideration of the working, impact, implementation and progress of the arrangements contained in parts A and B of this Agreement.

Article XV.

This Agreement shall enter into force upon signature and shall remain in force for a period of 5 years from the date of its coming into force. It may be extended further for a specified period by mutual agreement in the light of the review or reviews referred to in article XIII.

In Witness Whereof the undersigned, being duly authorised thereto by the respective Governments, have signed this Agreement.

Done in duplicate at Dacca on the 5th November 1977, in the Bengali, Hindi and English languages. In the event of any conflict between the texts, the English text shall prevail.

Rear Admiral

MUSHARRAF HUSAIN KHAN

SURJIT SINGH BARNALA

Chief of Naval Staff and Member,

President's Council of Advisers in

charge of the Ministry of Communications,

Flood Control, Water Resources and Power,

Government of the People's Republic of Bangladesh

SURJIT SINGH BARNALA

Minister for Agriculture and Irrigation

Government of the Republic of India

Annexure - IV

Treaty Between The Government Of The People's Republic Of Bangladesh And The Government Of The Republic Of India On Sharing Of The Ganga/Ganges Waters At Farakka

The Government Of The People's Republic Of Bangladesh And The Government Of The Republic Of India,

Determined to promote and strengthen their relations of friendship and good neighbourliness,

Inspired by the common desire of promoting the well-being of their peoples,

Being desirous of sharing by mutual agreement the waters of the international rivers flowing through the territories of the two countries and of making the optimum utilisation of the water resources of their region in the fields of flood management, irrigation, river basin development and generation of hydro-power for the mutual benefit of the peoples of the two countries,

Recognising that the need for making an arrangement for sharing of the Ganga/Ganges waters at Farakka in a spirit of mutual accommodation and the need for a solution to the long-term problem of augmenting the flows of the Ganga/Ganges are in the mutual interests of the peoples of the two countries,

Being desirous of finding a fair and just solution without affecting the rights and entitlements of either country other than those covered by this Treaty, or establishing any general principles of law or precedent,

Have Agreed As Follows:

Ariticale – I

The quantum of waters agreed to be released by India to Bangladesh will be at Farakka.

Ariticale – II

(i) The sharing between India and Bangladesh of the Ganga/Ganges waters at Farakka by ten day periods from the 1st January to the 31st May every year will be with reference to the formula at Annexure I and an indicative schedule giving the implications of the sharing arrangement under Annexure I is at Annexure II.

(ii) The Indicative schedule at Annexure-II, as referred to in sub-para (i) above, is based on 40 years (1949-1988) 10-day period average availability of water at Farakka. Every effort would be made by the upper riparian to protect flows of water at Farakka as in the 40-years average availability as mentioned above.

(iii) In the event flow at Farakka falls below 50,000 cusecs in any 10-day period, the two Governments will enter into immediate consultations to make adjustments on an emergency basis, in accordance with the principles of equity, fair play and no harm to either party.

Ariticale – III

The waters released to Bangladesh at Farakka under Article I shall not be reduced below Farakka except for reasonable uses of waters, not exceeding 200 cusecs, by India between Farakka and the point on the Ganga/ Ganges where both its banks are in Bangladesh.

Ariticale – IV

A Committee consisting of representatives nominated by the two Governments in equal numbers (hereinafter called the Joint Committee) shall be constituted following the signing of this Treaty. The Joint Committee shall set up suitable teams at Farakka and Hardinge Bridge to observe and record at Farakka the daily flows below Farakka Barrage, in the Feeder Canal, and at the Navigation Lock, as well as at the Hardinge Bridge.

Ariticale – V

The Joint Committee shall decide its own procedure and method of functioning.

Ariticale – VI

The Joint Committee shall submit to the two Governments all data collected by it and shall also submit a yearly report to both the Governments. Following submission of the reports the two Governments will meet at appropriate levels to decide upon such further actions as may be needed.

Ariticale – VII

The Joint Committee shall be responsible for implementing the arrangements contained in this Treaty and examining any difficulty arising out of the implementation of the above arrangements and of the operation of Farakka Barrage. Any difference or dispute arising in this regard, if not resolved by the Joint Committee, shall be referred to the Indo- Bangladesh Joint Rivers Commission. If the difference or dispute still remains unresolved, it shall be referred to the two Governments which shall meet urgently at the appropriate level to resolve it by mutual discussion.

Ariticale – VIII

The two Governments recognise the need to cooperate with each other in finding a solution to the long-term problem of augmenting the flows of the Ganga/Ganges during the dry season.

Ariticale – IX

Guided by the principles of equity, fairness and no harm to either party, both the

Governments agree to conclude water sharing Treaties/Agreements with regard to other common rivers.

Ariticale – X

The sharing arrangement under this Treaty shall be reviewed by the two Governments at five years interval or earlier, as required by either party and needed adjustments, based on principles of equity, fairness, and no harm to either party made thereto, if necessary. It would be open to either party to seek the first review after two years to assess the impact and working of the sharing arrangement as contained in this Treaty.

Ariticale – XI

For the period of this Treaty, in the absence of mutual agreement on adjustments following reviews as mentioned in Article X, India shall release downstream of Farakka Barrage, water at a rate not less than 90% (ninety percent) of Bangladesh's share according to the formula referred to in Article II, until such time as mutually agreed flows are decided upon.

Ariticale – XII

This Treaty shall enter into force upon signature and shall remain in force for a period of thirty years and it shall be renewable on the basis of mutual consent. IN WITNESS WHEREOF the undersigned, being duly authorised thereto by the respective Governments, have signed this Treaty.

DONE at New Delhi on 12th December, 1996 in Hindi, Bangla and English languages. In the event of any conflict between the texts, the English text shall prevail.

Signed Signed

(SHEIKH HASINA)	(H.D.DEVE GOWDA)
PRIME MINISTER	PRIME MINISTER
PEOPLE'S REPUBLIC OF BANGLADESH	REPUBLIC OF INDIA

Annexure V

Press Release

Text of Exchange of Letters on Modalities for Implementation of Inc Bangladesh Land Boundary Agreement 1974 and Protocol of 2011 tc Land Boundary Agreement

विदेश मंत्रालय, नई दिल्ली-11
MINISTRY OF EXTERNAL AFFAIRS
NEW DELHI-110011
Phone: 2301 2318 Fax: [illegible]
E-mail: [illegible]

विदेश सचिव
FOREIGN SECRETARY

No. 9596/FS/2015

June 6, 2015

Excellency,

In pursuance of the exchange of Instruments of Ratification between our two governments on June 6, 2015 to bring into effect the Agreement between the Government of the Republic of India and the Government of the People's Republic of Bangladesh concerning the Demarcation of the Land Boundary between India and Bangladesh and Related Matters, 1974 and the 2011 Protocol to the said Agreement, I have the honour to propose the following subsequent steps to implement the said Agreement and Protocol.

I. Enclaves

(i) India and Bangladesh agree that the Indian enclaves in Bangladesh and Bangladesh enclaves in India exchanged pursuant to the 1974 Agreement and 2011 Protocol shall stand transferred to the other with effect from the midnight of July 31, 2015. This shall be referred to as the 'Appointed Day";

(ii) Prior to the Appointed Day, representatives of the two Governments shall conduct a joint visit to the enclaves for the following purposes

a. Informing the residents of the enclaves of the provisions contained in the 1974 Agreement and the 2011 Protocol including their rights relating to nationality and citizenship

b. Identifying the residents who wish to continue to retain the nationality they hold prior to the actual transfer of territory. This right is available only to those residents who are included in the joint headcount of the population of the enclave finalised and exchanged by the two governments in July 2011 and to the children born to such residents from July 2011 till date;

c. Collection of data, including photographs, required for issue of entry passes or any other document to facilitate the travel and entry of an enclave resident choosing to retain his original nationality;

(iii) The entry, stay and secure functioning of the representatives in the joint visit, and setting up of camps shall be facilitated by both Governments;

(iv) Both Governments shall facilitate orderly, safe and secure passage to residents of enclaves along with their personal belongings and moveable property to the mainland of India or Bangladesh, as the case may be, including through provision of travel documents;

(v) The travel of the residents who exercise the option of moving from an enclave to the mainland of India or Bangladesh, as the case may be, will be arranged by the respective Governments through cooperation as mutually agreed, and will take place by November 30, 2015. Entry/exit points would be Haldibari, Burimari and Banglabandha on the India-Bangladesh border.

(vi) Both Governments shall ensure the safe custody and integrity of land records, where available, and other immovable properties of residents of enclaves till the date of actual transfer when the said enclaves shall vest in the sovereign jurisdiction of the other State and the records shall be exchanged through the relevant designated District Administrations of the two Governments latest by November 30, 2015.

II. Adverse Possessions

(vii) As regards the Adverse Possessions covered under the 2011 Protocol, India and Bangladesh shall print, sign at the plenipotentiary level and exchange the interim strip maps prepared as provided in Article 3 of the 2011 Protocol to complete the transfer of territorial jurisdiction on the Appointed Day. The ground demarcation of the boundary as per the Interim strip maps will be completed by the respective Survey Departments of the two Governments by June 30, 2016.

III. Undemarcated Boundary

(viii) India and Bangladesh shall print, sign at plenipotentiary level and exchange the interim strip maps of the undemarcated sectors prepared as provided in Article 2 of the 2011 Protocol by the Appointed Day. The ground demarcation of the boundary based on these Interim strip maps will be completed by June 30, 2016.

IV. Ownership and Transfer of Immovable Properties

(ix) The enclave residents exercising the option of moving from an enclave to the mainland of India or Bangladesh, as the case may be, shall inform the relevant district administrations prior to the Appointed Day details of the records and specifications of immovable property held by them. The respective district administrations shall put these records in the public domain prior to their moving so as to avoid misuse or usurpation of such property and to enable sale by the owner of the property. The two Governments shall facilitate remittance of sales proceeds of above mentioned immovable properties as appropriate.

2. The existing mechanism of India-Bangladesh Joint Boundary Working Group (JBWG) will finalize all further details in this regard. The same mechanism will be used to address any issue that may arise after the transfer for the next five years till June 2020. Issues pertaining to modalities to facilitate sale of immovable properties referred to in paragraph 1(ix) above and remittance of such sales proceeds will be addressed by the JBWG at an early date.

3. Excellency, I have the honour further to propose that this letter and your Excellency's reply thereto, confirming that the above sets out correctly the understanding between us shall constitute an Agreement between our two Governments.

(Dr. S. Jaishankar)

H.E. Mr. Md. Shahidul Haque
Foreign Secretary
Government of the People's
Republic of Bangladesh
Dhaka

The Letter from the Bangladesh Foreign Secretary:

GOVERNMENT OF THE
PEOPLE'S REPUBLIC OF BANGLADESH
DHAKA

পররাষ্ট্র সচিব
Foreign Secretary

June 6, 2015

Excellency,

In pursuance of the exchange of Instruments of Ratification between our two governments on June 6, 2015 to bring into effect the Agreement between the Government of the People's Republic of Bangladesh and the Government of the Republic of India concerning the Demarcation of the Land Boundary between India and Bangladesh and Related Matters, 1974 and the 2011 Protocol to the said Agreement, and your letter of June 6, 2015, I have the honor to confirm that the following correctly sets out the subsequent steps to implement the said Agreement and Protocol:

I. Enclaves

(i) Bangladesh and India agree that the Bangladeshi enclaves in India and Indian enclaves in Bangladesh exchanged pursuant to the 1974 Agreement and 2011 Protocol shall stand transferred to the other with effect from the midnight of July 31, 2015. This shall be referred to as the "Appointed Day";

(ii) Prior to the Appointed Day, representatives of the two Governments shall conduct a joint visit to the enclaves for the following purposes:

a. Informing the residents of the enclaves of the provisions contained in the 1974 Agreement and the 2011 Protocol, including their rights relating to nationality and citizenship;

b. Identifying the residents who wish to continue to retain the nationality they hold prior to the actual transfer of territory. This right is available only to those residents who are included in the joint headcount of the population of the enclave finalised and exchanged by the two governments in July 2011 and to the children born to such residents from July 2011 till date;

c. Collection of data, including photographs, required for issue of entry passes or any other document to facilitate the travel and entry of an enclave resident choosing to retain his original nationality.

(iii) The entry, stay and secure functioning of the representatives in the joint visit and setting up of camps shall be facilitated by both Governments;

(iv) Both Governments shall facilitate orderly, safe and secure passage to residents of enclaves along with their personal belongings and movoable property to

3/3

the mainland of Bangladesh or India, as the case may be, including through provision of travel documents;

(v) The travel of the residents who exercise the option of moving from an enclave to the mainland of Bangladesh or India, as the case may be, will be arranged by the respective Governments through cooperation as mutually agreed, and will take place by November 30, 2015. Entry/exit points would be Haldibari, Burimari and Banglabandha on the Bangladesh-India border.

(vi) Both Governments shall ensure the safe custody and integrity of land records, where available, and other immovable properties of residents of enclaves till the date of actual transfer when the said enclaves shall vest in the sovereign jurisdiction of the other State and the records shall be exchanged through the relevant designated District Administrations of the two Governments latest by November 30, 2015.

II. Adverse Possessions

(vii) As regards the Adverse Possessions covered under the 2011 Protocol, Bangladesh and India shall print, sign at the plenipotentiary level and exchange the interim strip maps prepared as provided in Article 3 of the 2011 Protocol to complete the transfer of territorial jurisdiction on the Appointed Day. The ground demarcation of the boundary as per the Interim strip maps will be completed by the respective Survey Departments of the two Governments by June 30, 2016.

III. Undemarcated Boundary

(viii) Bangladesh and India shall print, sign at plenipotentiary level and exchange the interim strip maps of the undemarcated sectors prepared as provided in Article 2 of the 2011 Protocol by the Appointed Day. The ground demarcation of the boundary based on these Interim strip maps will be completed by June 30, 2016.

IV. Ownership and Transfer of Immovable Properties

(ix) The enclave residents exercising the option of moving from an enclave to the mainland of Bangladesh or India, as the case may be, shall inform the relevant district administrations prior to the Appointed Day details of the records and specifications of immovable property held by them. The respective district administrations shall put these records in the public domain prior to their moving so as to avoid misuse or usurpation of such property and to enable sale by the owner of the property. The two Governments shall facilitate remittance of sales proceeds of above mentioned immovable properties as appropriate.

2/3

2 The existing mechanism of Bangladesh-India Joint Boundary Working Group (JBWG) will finalize all further details in this regard. The same mechanism will be used to address any issue that may arise after the transfer for the next five years till June 2020. Issues pertaining to modalities to facilitate sale of immovable properties referred to in paragraph 1(ix) above and remittance of such sales proceeds will be addressed by the JBWG at an early date.

3. Excellency, I have the honour to confirm that the above understanding between us on the modalities for implementation of the 1974 Land Boundary Agreement and its 2011 Protocol shall constitute an Agreement between our two Governments.

4. Please accept, Excellency, the assurances of my highest consideration

(Md. Shahidul Haque)

H.E. Dr. S. Jaishankar
Foreign Secretary
Ministry of External Affairs
Government of the Republic of India
New Delhi

References

Primary Sources

Treaties and Agreements

Agreement between the Government of the People's Republic of Bangladesh and the Government of the Republic of India on sharing of the Ganges waters at Farakka and on augmenting its flows (November 5, 1977)

Treaty Between the government of the Republic of India and the government of the People's Republic of Bangladesh on Sharing of the Ganga/Ganges Waters at Farakka (December 12, 1996)

Treaty of Peace and Friendship between the Government of India and the Government of the People's Republic Of Bangladesh (March 19, 1972)

"*Notun Projonmo – Nayi Disha*", (June 07, 2015), Joint Declaration between Bangladesh and India during the visit of Prime Minister of India to Bangladesh

Reports

CUTS International Report (2014), "*India-Bangladesh Trade Potentiality: An Assessment of Trade Facilitation Issues*", Jaipur: MS Printer.

Government of India, *Annual Report* (2014-15), Ministry of external Affairs, New Delhi

Government of Pakistan (1956), *Report of the Electoral Reforms Commission* Government of Pakistan (1972), *Joint Declaration of the Prime Ministers of India and Bangladesh*, Ministry of Foreign Affairs

Government of India, *Annual Report* (1976-77), Ministry of external Affairs, New Delhi

Foreign Affairs Record, (February 1972), Vol. XVIII No. 2

Foreign Affairs record, (July 1973), Vol. XIX, No. 7

IDSA Task Force Report (September 2011), "*India-Bangladesh Relations: Towards Convergence*", New Delhi. 218

News Paper Articles

"Bangladesh Alerts India about Dhaka Cafe Attack Mastermind" (2 August, 2016),

Bangladesh Garment Makers Welcome Duty Waiver" (September 7, 2011), *The Hindu*

"Bangladesh vows not to allow terrorists to use its land," (December 6, 2009),' *Daily News and Analysis,*

"Delhi tip-off' helped foil coup" (January 21, 2012), *The Telegraph*

"Farakka at UN: Unfortunate and Regrettable", (August 27, 1976); *Amrit Bazar Patrika*

"Hasina 10th greatest world leader" (25 March, 2016), *The Daily star*

"Teesta Failure Unfortunate", (September 8, 2011), *The Daily Star*

"Two Laskar Men Held Inside Indian Border", (November 23, 2009), *The Daily Star*

"Ulfa Chief Handed Over to India," (December 4, 2009), *Deccan Chronicle,*

Habib, Haroon. (August 2, 2011), "Entente across the border," *The Hindu*

Haque, M. I. (2011), "What Happened to Teesta Waters", *The Daily Star*

Hariharan, R. (2012), "A tale of two interventions", *The Hindu*

Hasan, Mahmood (2015), "Land Boundary Agreement and Bangladesh-India relations", *The Daily Star*

Indo-Bangladesh Joint Statement of August (August 19, 1980), *The Bangladesh Joint Times*

Jayant Prasad (May 11, 2015), "Breakthrough in India-Bangladesh Ties", *The Hindu*

Kirby, Alex (June 2, 2000), "Dawn of a Thirsty Century", *BBC News*

Mahmood Hasan (May 11, 2015), "Land Boundary Agreement and Bangladesh-India relations" *The Daily Star*

Mohan, C Raja (June 5, 2015), "South Asia's Berlin Wall," *Indian Express*, 2015

Mohan, C. R. (2003), "Indian Diaspora and 'Soft Power'," *The Hindu*

Parsi, G. (2011), "The Tale of Two Rivers", *The Hindu,* 219

Prasad, Jayant (May 11, 2015), "India-Bangladesh Land Boundary Agreement: Breakthrough in Ties", *The Hindu*,

Quadir, Serajul (June 06, 2015), "India, Bangladesh sign historic land boundary agreement", *The Daily Star*

Rahman, Sajjadur (January 11, 2010), "Analysts urge India to erase trade barriers to Bangladesh", *The Daily Star.*

Times of India

Secondary Sources

Books

Ali, S.M. (1973), *After the Dark Night: Problems of Sheikh Mujibur Rahman*, New Delhi: Thompson Press.

Bammi, Y.M. (2010), *India Bangladesh Relations: The Way Ahead*, New Delhi: Vijay Books India.

Bhattachargee, G. P. (1973), *Renaissance and Freedom Movement in Bangladesh*, Calcutta: Miverva Associates.

Bindra, S.S. (1982), *Indo-Bangladesh Relations*, New Delhi: Deep & Deep Publications.

Carlsnaes, Risse and Simmons (eds.) (2013), *Handbook of International Relations*, Sage Publications

Carr, E. H. (1946), *The Twenty Years' Crisis, 1919-1939: An introduction to the Study of International Relations*, New York: Harper and Row.

Crow, Ben and D. Wilson (1995), *Sharing the Ganges: The Politics and Technology of River Development*, New Delhi: Sage Publication.

Dixit, J. N. (1999), *Liberation and Beyond: Indo-Bangladesh Relations*, Delhi: Konark Publishers.

—. (2001), *India's Foreign Policy and its Neighbours*, New Delhi: Gyan Publishing House.

Dubey, M. (2013), *India's Foreign Policy: Coping with the Changing World*, Noida: Saurabh Printers.

Dutt, V.P. (2008), *India's Foreign Policy in a Changing World*, New Delhi: Vikash Publishing House.

Hasan, S. (1991), *Environmental concerns in South Asia*, London: Adelphi Papers.

Jahan, R. (1972), *Pakistan: Failure in National Integration*, New York: Columbia University Press.

Jowett, G. and Victoria J. O'Donnell (1986), *Propaganda and Persuasion,* Beverly Hills, CA: Sage Publications.

Kushner, B. (2006), *The Thought War*, Honolulu: University of Hawai' Press

Madaan, Davinder K. (1998), *Indo-Bangladesh Economic Relations and SAARC*, New Delhi: Deep & Deep Publications.

Mason, E. S. et al (1971), *Conflict in East Pakistan: Background and Prospects*, London: Bangladesh Action Committee.

Morgenthau, H. J. (1948), *Politics among Nations: The Struggle for Power and Peace,* New York: Alfred A. Knopf.

—(1954), *Politics Among Nations: The Struggle for Power and Peace*, 3rd ed. Chicago: University of Chicago Press.

Nair, P. S. (2008), *Indo-Bangladesh Relations*, New Delhi: A.P.H. Publishing House.

Nordlinger, E. A. (1972), *Conflict Regulation in Divided Societies*, Cambridge Mass: Harvard University Press

Nye, Joseph S. (2002), *The Paradox of American Power: Why the World' Only Superpower Can't Go It Alone*, Oxford University Press.

—(2004), *Soft Power: The Means to Success in World Politics,* U.S: Public Affairs.

—(2004), *Power in the Global Information Age: From Realism to Globalization,* London: Routledge

—(2008), *The Powers to Lead*, Oxford University Press.

—(2011), *The future of Power,* New York: public Affairs. 221

Pattanaik, Smruti S. (ed.) (2012), *Four Decades of India-Bangladesh Relations: Historical Imperatives and Future Directions*, IDSA, New Delhi: Gyan Publishing House.

Paul, T.V. and Baldev Raj N. (2003), *India in the World Order: Searching for Major Power Status,* Cambridge: Cambridge University Press.

R. Ahmed (ed.) (2001) *Understanding Bengali Muslims,* New Delhi: Oxford University Press.

Vishal Chandra (ed.) (2015) *India and South Asia: Exploring Regional Perceptions*, New Delhi: Pentagon Press.

Rashid, H. U. (2002), *Indo-Bangladesh Relations: An Insider's view*, New Delhi: Har-Anand Publications.

Rashid, H. U. (2010), *Bangladesh-India Relations: Living With a Big Neighbour*, Dhaka: A.H. Development Publishing House.

Sayeed, K. B. (1967), *The Political System of Pakistan,* Boston: Houghton Mifflin.

Singh, Anita I. (1987), *The Origins of the Partition of India 1936-1947*, New Delhi: Oriente Moderno.

Sisson, R. et al (1990), *War and Secession: Pakistan, India, and the Creation of Bangladesh*, University of California Press.

Smruti Pattanaik (ed.) (2003), *Four Decades of India-Bangladesh Relations: Historical Imperatives and Future Directions*, Gyan Publishing House.

Strange, S. (1996): *The Retreat of the State: The Diffusion of Power in the World Economy*, Cambridge Studies in International Relations.

Tharoor, S. (2007), *The Elephant, the Tiger and the Cellphone*, UK: Penguin.

Trivedi, R. (2008), *India's Relations with her Neighbours*, Delhi: ISHA Books.

Umar, B. (2006), *The Emergence of Bangladesh: Rise of Bengali Nationalism (1958-1971)*, Vol. 2, Karachi: Oxford University Press.

Verghese, B.G. (2007), *Waters of hope: From vision to reality in Himalaya–Ganges development cooperation*. New Delhi: India Research Press. 222

Waltz, K. (1979): *Theory of International Politics*, Massachusetts: Addison-Wesley.

Articles

Acharya, Loknath and Ashima M. (2012), "India–Bangladesh Economic Relations", *Federation of Indian Chambers of Commerce and Industry*

Ahmad, M. (1971), "Failure of Nation-Building in Pakistan?" *Pakistan Forum*, Vol. 2(3).

Ahmed, F. (1971), "Why Pakistan's Unity Was Jeopardized?", *Pakistan Forum*, Vol. 2(3).

Anam, Mahfuz (2012), "Bangladesh: A fine bilateral balance" in *Neighbourhood Views of India,* Gateway House Research Paper No. 7.

Banerjee, Sumanta (2001), "Indo-Bangladesh Border: Radcliffe's Ghost", *Economic and Political Weekly*, Vol. 36 (18).

Barnett, M. and Raymond D. (2005), "Power in International Politics", *International Organization* Vol. (59)

Bashar, Iftekharul (2015), "Islamist Militancy on the Rise in Bangladesh", *East Asia Forum*

Basher, Md. Abul (2013), "Indo-Bangla Trade: Composition, Trends and Way Forward", *Commonwealth Secretariat.*

Bhardwaj, Sandeep (2008), "India-Bangladesh Relations: Are the carrots working?" *Institute of Peace and Conflict Studies*, New Delhi

Bhardwaj, Sanjay (2003), "Bangladesh Foreign Policy vis-a-vis India", *Strategic Analysis,* Vol. 27 (2)

Bhattacharya, Joyeeta (2015), "Indo-Bangladesh Border Management the Challenge of Cattle Smuggling," *Meghalaya Times*

Bhattacharya, Swapan K. (2004), "Does Bangladesh Benefit from Preferential Trade with India? A Gravity Analysis", *Economic and Political Weekly*, Vol. 39 (48)

Blarel, N. (2012), "India's Soft Power: From Potential to Reality?" London: *London School of Economics* 223

Callard, K. (1971), "Failure of Nation-Building in Pakistan?" *Pakistan Forum*, Vol. 2(3).

Chakma, B. (2012), "Bangladesh-India Relations: Sheikh Hasina's India-positive Policy Approach", Singapore: *S. Rajaratnam School of International Studies,* vol. No. 252

Chakravarty, Pinak R. (2016), "Bangladesh-India Ties: Pragmatic Transformation" in Debate: India-Bangladesh Relations: Scaling Newer Heights.

Choudhury, G. W. (1972), "Bangladesh: Why It Happened", *International Affairs (Royal Institute of International Affairs* Vol. 48(2).

Chowdhury, K. (1997), "Of History, Nationalism and Poetry", *India International Centre Quarterly*, Vol. 24(2/3).

Colombi, S. B. and Robert W. Bradnock (2003), "Geopolitics, Water and Development in South Asia: Cooperative Development in the Ganges-Brahmaputra Delta, *The Geographical Journal*, Vol. 169(1).

Crow, B. (1997), "Bridge Over Troubled Waters? Conflict and Cooperation over the Waters of South Asia" in Sony Devabhaktuni (ed.) *Regional Cooperation in South Asia: Prospects and Problems,* The Henry L. Stimson Center.

Cull, Nicholas J. (2008), "Public Diplomacy: Taxonomies and Histories", *The Annals of the American Academy of Political and Social Science*, Vol. 616.

Datta, Sreeradha (2016), "India-Bangladesh Land Boundary Agreement: Follow-up Concerns Need a Fair Approach", *ISAS Working Paper*.

Datta, V. N. (2002), "Iqbal, Jinnah and India's Partition: An Intimate Relationship", *Economic and Political Weekly*, Vol. 37(50).

De, Prabir and B. Ghosh (2008), "Reassessing Transaction Costs of Trade at the India-Bangladesh Border", *Economic and Political Weekly*, Vol. 43 (29)

De, Prabir and B. N. Bhattacharyay (2007), "Prospects of India–Bangladesh Economic Cooperation: Implications for South Asian Regional Cooperation", *ADBI*, Discussion Paper No. 78.

Dutta, Piyali (2010), "India-Bangladesh Relations: Issues, Problems and Recent Developments", *IPCS Special Report*, Vol. No. 97. 224

Franda, Marcus F. (1975), Indo-Bangladesh Relations, *American Universities Field Staff Reports*, Vol. 19.

Godbole, Madhav (2001), "Management of India's International Borders: Some Challenges Ahead", *Economic and Political Weekly*, Vol. 36(48).

Grix, J. & Donna Lee (2013), "Soft Power, Sports Mega-Events and Emerging States: The Lure of the Politics of Attraction", *Global Society*, Vol. 27(4).

Hassan, M. Kabir (2000), "Trade Relations with SAARC Countries and Trade Policies of Bangladesh" *Journal of Economic Cooperation*, Vol. 21(3)

Raju, V. (2016), "India-Bangladesh Border – Issues and challenges", *IJARIIE,* Vol-2 Issue-3.

Hossain, Ishtiaq (1981), "Bangladesh-India Relations: Issues and Problems", *Asian Survey*, Vol. 21(11).

—(1998), "Bangladesh-India Relations: The Ganges Water-Sharing Treaty and Beyond", *Asian Affairs*, Vol. 25(3).

Hossain, S. (2012), "Cooperation on the Water Issue: Bangladesh Perspectives" in Smruti Pattanaik (ed.) *Four Decades of India-Bangladesh Relations: Historical Imperatives and Future Directions*, Gyan Publishing House.

Islam, Nurul (1981), "Islam and National Identity: The Case of Pakistan and Bangladesh" *International Journal of Middle East Studies*, Vol. 13(1).

—(2004), "Indo-Bangladesh Economic Relations: Some Thoughts", *Economic and Political Weekly*, Vol. 39(36).

Iyer, R. R. (1999), "Conflict-Resolution: Three River Treaties", *Economic and Political Weekly*, Vol. 34(24).

Jackson, R. (1975), "South Asia Crisis: India, Pakistan and Bangladesh, London: Chatto and Windus" in Rounaq Jahan (ed.) (2005), *Bangladesh Politics: Problems and Issues*, Dhaka: The University Press Limited.

Jamwal, N. S. (2004), "Border Management: Dilemma of Guarding the India-Bangladesh Border", *Strategic Analysis,* Vol. 28(1). 225

Joy, K. J. and S. Paranjape (2007), "Understanding Water Conflicts in South Asia", *Contemporary Perspectives*, Vol. 1(2)

Kabir, M. H. and Sufia Khanom (2008), "India's River Linking Project: Possible Implications for Bangladesh", *BIISS Journal*, Vol. 29 (2).

Kabir, Mahfuz (2012), "Bangladesh-India Trade and Investment: Bangladesh Perspectives", in Smruti Pattanaik (ed.) (2012) *Four Decades of India-Bangladesh Relations: Historical Imperatives and Future Directions*, New Delhi: Gyan Publishing House.

Karim, M. Aminul (2009), "Bangladesh-India Relations: Some Recent Trends", *ISAS* Working Paper, Vol. No. 96.

Karim, T. A. (1998), "The Bangladesh–India treaty on sharing of the Ganges waters: Genesis and significance", *BIISS Journal*, 19(2).

Khan, M. Shamsur R. (2009), "Towards Better India-Bangladesh relations", New Delhi: *Institute for Defence Studies & Analysis.*

Khan, Z. R. (1985), "Islam and Bengali Nationalism" *Asian Survey*, Vol. 25(8)

Khosla, I.P. (2005), "Bangladesh–India Relations", *South Asian Journal*, Vol. No. 4(3).

Klare, Michael T. (2001), "The New Geography of Conflict", *Foreign Affairs*

Kumar, Anand (2012), "India-Bangladesh Trade: Problems and Prospects", in Smruti Pattanaik (ed.) (2012) *Four Decades of India-Bangladesh Relations: Historical Imperatives and Future Directions*, New Delhi: Gyan Publishing House.

Lee, G. (2004), "A Theory of Soft Power and Korea's Soft Power Strategy", Graduate School of International Studies, Seoul National University

Li, M. (2009), "Soft power: Nurture Not Nature" in Mingjiang Li (ed.) (2009) *Soft Power: China's Emerging Strategy in International Politics,* Lexington Books United Kingdom.

Majlis, Duad (1978), "Letter from Dacca", *Far Eastern Economic Review.*

Malone, David M. (2011), "Soft Power in Indian Foreign Policy", *Economic & Political Weekly*, Vol. xlvi(36). 226

Mantoo, S. A. (2015), "India-Bangladesh Relationship (1975-1990)", *Journal of South Asian Studies*, Vol. 3(3).

Mattern, J. Bially (2007), "Why 'soft power' isn't so soft: Representational force and attraction in world politics" in Berenskoetter and Williams (eds.) (2007) *Power in World Politics*, Routledge.

Morgenthau, H.J. (1946), "Scientific Man versus Power Politics", Chicago: University of Chicago Press.

Mukharji, Deb (2007), "Distant Neighbours: India and Bangladesh" in *Indian Foreign Policy: Challenges and Opportunities*, New Delhi: Foreign Service Institute.

— (2016), "Indo-Bangladesh Relations: A Clear Paradigm Shift" in Debate: India-Bangladesh Relations: Scaling Newer Heights.

Mukherjee, R. (2014), "The False Promise of India's Soft Power", *Geopolitics, History, and International Relations,* Volume No. 6(1)

Nye, Joseph S. (1990), "Soft power" *Foreign Policy*, Vol. 80

Oldenburg, P. (1985), "A Place Insufficiently Imagined: Language, Belief, and the Pakistan Crisis of 1971", *The Journal of Asian Studies*, Vol. 44(4).

Palit, P. S. & Amitendu Palit (2011), "Strategic Influence of Soft Power: Inferences for India from Chinese Engagement of South and Southeast Asia", ICRIER Policy Series, Vol. No.3.

Pandey, P. (2012), "Revisiting the Politics of the Ganges Water Dispute between India and Bangladesh", *India Quarterly*, Vol. No. 68(3)

Pant, Harsh V. (2007), "India and Bangladesh: Will the Twain Ever Meet?" *Asian Survey*, Vol. 47(2).

Pattanaik, Smruti S. (2012), "Transcending India-Bangladesh Relations: Framing Mutual Security Parametres" in Smruti S. Pattanaik (ed.) (2012) *Four Decades of India-Bangladesh Relations: Historical Imperatives and Future Directions*, New Delhi: Gyan Publishing House.

— (2016), "India-Bangladesh Relations: Moving towards Greater Synergy" 227

Paul, T. V. (2005), "Causes of the India–Pakistan enduring rivalry" in T.V. Paul (ed.) *The India–Pakistan Conflict: An Enduring Rivalry,* Cambridge: Cambridge University Press.

Paul, T.V. (2014), "Indian Soft Power in a Globalizing World", *Current History*

Pohit, Sanjib and Nisha T. (2000), "India's Informal Trade with Bangladesh and Nepal: A Qualitative Assessment" *Indian Council for Research on International Economic Relations,* Working Paper No. 58.

Purushothaman, U. (2010), "Shifting Perceptions of Power: Soft Power and India's Foreign Policy", *Journal of Peace Studies*, Vol. 17 (2&3).

Qureshi, S. M. M. (1972/1973), "Pakastani Nationalism Reconsidered" *Pacific Affairs*, Vol. 45(4)

Rahman, M. Habibur (1984), "Delimitation of Maritime Boundaries: A Survey of Problems in the Bangladesh Case", *Asian Survey*, Vol. 24(12).

Rahman, T. (2002), "Language, Power and Ideology", *Economic and Political Weekly*, Vol. 37 (44/45)

Ray, A. (2012), "India, Bangladesh: Water Disputes and Teesta River Diplomacy", *Global Voices*

Riaz, A. (2007), "God Willing: The Politics and Ideology of Islamism in Bangladesh," *Comparative Studies of South Asia, Africa, and Middle East* Vol. 23(1/2), pp. 310–320.

Schuman, H. (1972), "A Note on the Rapid Rise of Mass Bengali Nationalism in East Pakistan", *American Journal of Sociology*, Vol. 78(2)

Selim, Ishtiaque (2012), "Bangladesh-India Connectivity: A focus on Transit" in Smruti Pattanaik (ed.) (2012) *Four Decades of India-Bangladesh Relations: Historical Imperatives and Future Directions*, New Delhi: Gyan Publishing House.

Sengupta, Jayshree (2007), "Time to Boost India-Bangladesh Trade and Economic Relations", *ORF* Issue Brief 10

Sengupta, R. (2007), "Why India Is Concerned about Bangladesh?" *Asian Survey*, Vol. 47(2).

Signitzer, B. H. and Timothy Coombs (1992), "Public Relations and Public Diplomacy: Conceptual Convergences" *Public Relations Review* Vol. 18(2). 228

Sikdar, Chandrima (2006), "Prospects of Bilateral Trade between India and Bangladesh", *Foreign Trade Review*, Vol. 41(1).

Singh, R. S. N. (2005), "Bangladesh under Seize", *Indian Defence Review.*

Sobhan, F. (2008), "India-Bangladesh Relations: Past, Present and Future", *ORF Discourse*, Volume 3, Issue No 3.

Spate, O. H. K. (Jan., 1948), "The Partition of India and the Prospects of Pakistan", *Geographical Review*, Vol. 38 (1)

Sreeradha, D. (2002), "Indo-Bangladesh Relations: An Overview of Limitation and Constraints", *Strategic Analysis*, Vol. 96.

Swain, A. (1996), "Displacing the Conflict: Environmental Destruction in Bangladesh and Ethnic Conflict in India", *Journal of Peace Research*, Vol. 33 (2).

Tharoor, S. (2008), "India as a Soft Power", *India International Centre Quarterly*, Vol. 35 (1).

Tiwary, R. (2006), "Conflicts over International Waters", *Economic and Political Weekly*, Vol. 41 (17)

Uddin, Salah and Shoaib C. (2009), "Transit, Asian Highway and other issues on table for Bangladeshi Government", *American Chronicle*,

Wagner, C. (2005), "From Hard Power to Soft Power? Ideas, Interaction, Institutions, and Images in India's South Asia Policy", *South Asia Institute,* Department of Political Science, University of Heidelberg Working Paper No. 26

— (2010), "India's Soft Power: Prospects and Limitations", *India Quarterly*, Vol. 66(4).

Wilson, Ernest J. (2008), "Hard Power, Soft Power, Smart Power" *Annals of the American Academy of Political and Social Science*, Vol. 616

Wright, Denis (2007), "Bangladesh and the BJP," *South Asia: Journal of South Asian Studies,* vol. 25 (3)

Zafar, S.A. (1993), "Indo-Bangladesh Relations: Problems and Prospects" *Pakistan Horizon*, Vol. 46(¾). 229

Internet sources

"India and Bangladesh exchange drafts of Teesta Water-sharing Agreements", [Online: web] http://articles.timesofindia.indiatimes.com/2010-03-21/india/28145156_1_teesta-waters-ramesh-chandra-sen-tapaimukh-dam-project

"How cricket diplomacy and politics marry in India," (September 08, 2014) [Online: web] https://cricket.yahoo.com/news/how-cricket-diplomacy-and-politics-marry-in-india115315188.html

"Land Boundary Agreement completes unfinished task of partition: Expert" (June 10, 2015), [Online: web] http://zeenews.india.com/exclusive/land-boundary-agreement-completes-unfinished-task-of-partition-expert_1610888.html

"Bangladesh - Liberation War", [Online: web] http://www.globalsecurity.org/military/world/war/liberation-war.htm

Ealhi, K. M. and M. Tajuddin Sikder, "Mega Dams in the Himalayas: An Assessment of Environmental Degradation and Global Warming" [Online: web] http://www.benjapan.org/iceab10/1.pdf.

"India, Bangladesh Sign Historic Land Boundary Agreement," (June 07, 2015), [Online: web] http://www.ndtv.com/india-news/india-bangladesh-sign-historic-land-boundary-agreement-769351

"India, Bangladesh signed Land Boundary Agreement of 1974," (8 June, 2015) [Online: web] http://www.jagranjosh.com/current-affairs/india-bangladesh-signed-land-boundary-agreement-of-1974-1433759676-1

Jha, Ram K. and Saurabh Kumar (2015), "A Boost for India-Bangladesh Relations", *The Diplomat* [Online: web] http://thediplomat.com/2015/05/a-boost-for-india-bangladesh-relations/

"India, Bangladesh: Water Disputes and River Diplomacy", (June 8, 2012) [Online: web] http://isnblog.ethz.ch/global-voices/india-bangladesh-water-disputes-and-river-diplomacy

"Water Conflict an Cooperation between Bangladesh and India", [Online: web] http://www.scribd.com/doc/13264275/Ganges-Water-Conflict 230

"Awami League's Victory in Bangladesh and Relations with India" (January 5, 2009) [Online: web] http://www.ipcs.org/article/india-the-world/awami-leagues-victory-in-bangladesh-and-relations-with-india-2771.html

"Rajya Sabha passes amended Indo-Bangladesh Land Boundary Agreement Bill," (May 11, 2015) [Online: web] http://zeenews.india.com/news/india/rajya-sabha-passes-amended-indo-bangladesh-land-boundary-agreement-bill_1593234.html

Rashid, H. U. (2009), "Awami League's Victory in Bangladesh and Relations with India" [Online: web] http://www.ipcs.org/article/india-the-world/awami-leagues-victory-in-bangladesh-and-relations-with-india-2771.html

Wolf, A. T. and Joshua T. Newton (not dated), "Case Study of Transboundary Dispute Resolution: The Ganges River controversy", [Online: web] http://www.transboundarywaters.orst.edu/research/case_studies/Ganges_New.htm

Zakzaman (2006), "India's Water War Against Bangladesh and its Impact on Bangladesh", [Online: web] www.bdsdf.org/forum.

"41 years in the making," (May 12, 2015) [Online: web] http://indianexpress.com/article/opinion/columns/india-bangladesh-land-boundary-agreement-41-years-in-the-making/

"India launches Maitreee Radio to strengthen communication with Bangladesh," (August 23, 2016) [Online: web] http://theindianawaaz.com/india-launches-moitreee-radio-to-strengthen-communication-with-bangladesh/

"Policy on Sharing River Water between India and Bangladesh," (May 02, 2015) [Online: web] http://udayindia.in/2015/05/02/policy-on-sharing-river-water-between-india-and-bangladesh/

"Efforts Underway to Resolve Teesta Isue with Bangladesh: Indian Envoy Pankaj Saran," (September 14, 2015) [Online: web] http://www.ndtv.com/india-news/efforts-underway-to-resolve-teesta-isue-with-bangladesh-indian-envoy-pankaj-saran-1217511

"India-Bangladesh cricket series must add to PM Modi's success in Dhaka," (June 09, 2015) [Online: web] http://www.oneindia.com/sports/cricket/india-bangladesh-cricket-series-must-add-to-pm-modi-s-success-story-1772129.html

"Bangladesh-India joint declaration," (June 07, 2015) [Online: web] http://www.thedailystar.net/online/bangladesh-india-joint-declaration-93490 231

"India-Bangladesh: 21st Century Battle for Water Sharing," [Online: web] http://www.sos-arsenic.net/english/groundwater/waterbattle.html

"India-Bangladesh Water Dispute," [Online: web] http://www1.american.edu/ted/ice/indobang.htm

"How crucial is soft power to the successful conduct of diplomacy," (March 13, 2011) [Online: web] http://thenewdiplomats.blogspot.in/2011/03/how-crucial-is-soft-power-to-successful.html

"Tipaimukh a plea for rational and scientific discussion," (March 06, 2016) [Online: web] http://lookeast.in/tipaimukh-a-plea-for-rational-and-scientific-discussion/

"India-Bangladesh Relations (2010)," [Online: web] http://www.pharmexcil.org/data/country_files/bangladesh.pdf

"Kolkata-Ashuganj-Tripura transit facility between India, Bangladesh becomes operational," (June 16, 2016) [Online: web] http://currentaffairs.gktoday.in/kolkata-ashuganj-tripura-transit-facility-india-bangladesh-operational-06201633675.html

"Shipment arrives in Tripura under new India-Bangladesh transit protocol," (June 19, 2016) [online: web]

http://www.newsx.com/world/32874-shipment-arrives-in-tripura-under-new-india-bangladesh-transit-protocol

"Hasina 10th greatest world leader" (March 25, 2016), [online: web]

http://www.thedailystar.net/frontpage/hasina-10th-greatest-world-leader-1199284

"A tale of two interventions," (July 28, 2012), [online: web]

http://www.thehindu.com/opinion/lead/a-tale-of-two-interventions/article3693348.ece

Index

E

F

G

H

I